Politics Is a Joke!

Politics Is a Joke!
How TV Comedians Are Remaking Political Life

S. Robert Lichter
George Mason University

Jody C Baumgartner
East Carolina University

Jonathan S. Morris
East Carolina University

With the assistance of
Daniel Amundson

WESTVIEW
PRESS

A Member of the Perseus Books Group

Westview Press was founded in 1975 in Boulder, Colorado, by notable publisher and intellectual Fred Praeger. Westview Press continues to publish scholarly titles and high-quality undergraduate- and graduate-level textbooks in core social science disciplines. With books developed, written, and edited with the needs of serious nonfiction readers, professors, and students in mind, Westview Press honors its long history of publishing books that matter.

Westview Press books are available at special discounts for bulk purchases in the United States by corporations, institutions, and other organizations. For more information, please contact the Special Markets Department at the Perseus Books Group, 2300 Chestnut Street, Suite 200, Philadelphia, PA 19103, or call (800) 810-4145, ext. 5000, or e-mail special.markets@perseusbooks.com.

Designed by Jack Lenzo

Library of Congress Cataloging-in-Publication Data
Lichter, S. Robert.
   Politics is a joke! : how TV comedians are remaking political life / S. Robert Lichter, George Mason University, Jody C Baumgartner, East Carolina University, Jonathan S. Morris, East Carolina University.
      pages cm
   Includes bibliographical references and index.
   ISBN 978-0-8133-4717-2 (pbk.) -- ISBN 978-0-8133-4718-9 (e-book) 1. Television in politics--United States. 2. Television talk shows--Political aspects--United States. 3. United States--Politics and government--1993-2001--Humor. 4. Television comedies--United States--Influence. 5. Political satire, American--History and criticism. I. Baumgartner, Jody C., 1958- II. Morris, Jonathan S. III. Title.
   HE8700.76.U6L52 2014
   973.9302'07--dc23
                            2014003779

10 9 8 7 6 5 4 3 2 1

Everything is changing. People are taking their comedians seriously and the politicians as a joke.

—Will Rogers

Contents

List of Tables and Figures

List of Boxes

Preface

It may seem hard to believe today, but once upon a time there was almost no political humor on television. Until the 1980s, the broadcast networks were the only game in town, and their prime time sitcoms rarely ventured into the realm of politics. The main action took place after prime time on NBC. In the 1970s, *Saturday Night Live* featured some political comedy, and *SNL* cast member Chevy Chase became famous for portraying then-president Gerald Ford as a klutz who tripped over his own feet and many other objects. On weekdays in the same time slot, talk show host Johnny Carson's *Tonight Show* monologues included some one-liners that skewered politicians, unlike follow-up act in the 1980s David Letterman, who mostly steered clear of political material on *Late Night*.

Then Lee Atwater, the campaign manager for 1988 Republican presidential candidate George H. W. Bush, mentioned that he paid close attention to the political jokes in Carson's monologues as a barometer of how the candidates were playing in the "real" America outside Washington, DC. That comment in turn brought the content of late night talk shows to the attention of the Center for Media and Public Affairs (CMPA), a research center that conducts studies of the news and entertainment media, of which I am director.

Up until then, the CMPA had concentrated on analyzing the content of political journalism—news coverage of presidential elections, controversial policy issues, political scandals, and the like. Its forays into entertainment media consisted mainly of counting instances of sex and violence on television, along with a study of social themes in TV entertainment, which became the basis of my book *Prime Time:*

How TV Portrays American Culture (Regnery Publishing, 1993). In those days before the rise of "infotainment," few people in politics or journalism cared about anything TV talk show hosts said or did. Even if they discussed politics, their comments were assumed to be too frivolous to take seriously.

More or less as a lark, the CMPA started tracking the political jokes featured in the Carson and Letterman monologues. This tracking process proved popular with the student coders, who enjoyed tracking the utterances of Carson and Letterman a lot more than those of Rather, Brokaw, and Jennings (the network evening news anchors at the time). The data produced from the tracking of the monologues proved even more popular with journalists, who rewarded the CMPA's efforts by providing its work with a heavy dose of publicity. It was probably the first time most journalists had ever thought about late night in a political context. And if it was news to them, that made it news for their readers as well. So, in a small and inadvertent way, the CMPA may have contributed to the rise of infotainment, or at least to the rise in attention paid to infotainment by serious journalists.

It didn't hurt that, at the 1988 Republican nominating convention, George Bush gave comedians a gift that kept on giving by choosing Indiana Senator Dan Quayle as his running mate. If you know who Dan Quayle is, you don't need any further explanation. If you don't, you're in for a treat as you encounter the wealth of Quayle jokes recounted in this book. The gale of jokes blew so hard that it almost swept Quayle off the public stage altogether. And by almost being laughed off the ticket, he personified the rising influence of political humor on the real world of politics.

In light of the positive response to the CMPA's initial studies, it continued to track the monologues throughout the campaign season and periodically thereafter until the early 1990s, when it began continuous tracking with the same kind of detailed analysis used for its studies of news content—cataloguing not only whom each joke was about but also what it was about (an extensive list broken out into topics and subtopics). Of course, it wasn't just the technical aspects of the work that created an audience for it; it was the fun of learning who were the most-joked-about politicians or candidates or public figures, as well as the simple enjoyment of the jokes themselves. Over the years, as a new generation of late night talk show hosts provided more and more material, the CMPA's reports became a marker and a measure of a new force in American politics.

Meanwhile, back in academia, scholars had taken notice of this phenomenon, and studies began appearing that examined the effects of late night jokes on audiences. Among these researchers were Jody Baumgartner and Jonathan Morris, whose interest in the subject came about almost accidentally. Soon after they started teaching at East Carolina University in the fall of 2003, they began casting about for ideas that might make for fruitful collaborative research. The following spring, during a six-hour drive home from a conference, Morris suggested combining his interest in media effects with Baumgartner's in presidential campaigns by conducting an experiment. His idea was to expose students to short video clips from *The Daily Show with Jon Stewart* to determine what effect, if any, viewership of the program had on presidential candidate evaluations.

The resulting publication explored the program's multiple effects on viewers' attitudes toward candidates as well as the electoral process as a whole. However, the substance of the findings was almost secondary to the publication's reception. The authors were completely unprepared for the attention this research received from national and local media outlets. After reading a number of stories focused on the article and granting numerous interviews, the obvious occurred to them: perhaps they had stumbled upon a research agenda. Since that time Baumgartner and Morris have, individually and together, written a number of articles examining the effects of viewing political humor as well as edited a book titled *Laughing Matters: Humor and American Politics in the Media Age* (Routledge, 2007). They both consider themselves fortunate to have a research agenda that provides interesting and important questions. It doesn't hurt that keeping up with the political humor landscape is as fun for scholars as it is for students and journalists.

A few years ago, in preparing for another project, Baumgartner and Morris contacted me at the CMPA about the possibility of sharing their data. While that particular project never got off the ground, a relationship was forged that led to their collaboration on this book. In 2011, we jointly raised the possibility of writing this book together with Westview Press editor Toby Wahl, who responded enthusiastically and set the project in motion. In 2012, Ada Fung became our editor and expertly shepherded the project to fruition. We owe a great deal to Toby and Ada; without their tireless efforts, this material would still be limited to journal articles and press releases. Others at Westview Press we'd like to thank include our project editor, Carolyn Sobczak, and our copyeditor, Christine Arden. In addition, we would like to acknowledge the peer reviewers who took the time to share their comments on our manuscript at various stages of development, including Linda Beail (Point Loma Nazarene University), Stephanie Dyer (Sonoma State University), Michael Fitzgerald (University of Tennessee), Terri Jett (Butler University), Dave Kaszuba (Susquehanna University), Janet McMullen (University of North Alabama), Dannagal Young (University of Delaware), and others who wished to remain anonymous.

Our greatest debt, however, is to CMPA research director Dan Amundson, who has directed the CMPA's political humor project ever since its inception a quarter of a century ago. Dan applied his encyclopedic knowledge of the material to working it into a data set that became the basis for this book. Without Dan's expertise and hard work, there would not only be no book, there would be nothing for us to write a book about. We salute his efforts on our behalf, as well as those of the many students who worked under Dan's direction to code more than a hundred thousand jokes over the past quarter century. We hope readers will enjoy this material as much as we have.

S. Robert Lichter

Chapter 1

Introduction: Politics Is a Funny Business

Does late night political humor matter? Is it simply entertaining, or is it something more? Most contemporary political humorists publicly claim that their humor has no importance beyond its comedic value. Jon Stewart, for example, regularly downplays his iconoclastic status by reminding viewers and journalists that he is "just a comedian."[1] He once famously told the hosts of CNN's *Crossfire* in 2004 that *The Daily Show with Jon Stewart* could not be taken seriously because "the show that leads into [it] is puppets making crank phone calls."

Regardless of the political significance, many people find the humor of late night talk shows entertaining—as evidenced, in part, by the popularity of David Letterman and Jay Leno. (Letterman has been hosting a late night talk show since 1982; and Jay Leno, from 1992 through 2014.) A recent report suggested that a third of the adult population watched either *The Tonight Show with Jay Leno* or *The Late Show with David Letterman* at least some of the time,[2] while approximately one-quarter sometimes watched *The Daily Show* or *The Colbert Report*.[3] Late night television and the hosts of these programs also garner their share of entertainment awards. Jon Stewart, for example, appeared on the cover of *Newsweek* magazine in 2004 and was listed among *Time* magazine's "Top 100 most influential people in the world" in 2005.[4]

But beyond its value as entertainment, many people take late night comedy seriously. In fact, throughout the ages political humorists and satirists have been perceived as agents of societal and political change. In certain ancient societies, satire was associated with magic, and because of this the satirist was accorded great respect.[5] The idea that humor and humorists have political power is perhaps best illustrated by the almost legendary role that Thomas Nast's newspaper cartoons played in exposing the corruption of "Boss" Tweed and Tammany Hall, a political machine that dominated New York City politics in the mid-nineteenth century. Nast illustrated and published so many cartoons about Tammany Hall that Tweed was said to have reacted by ordering his aides to "stop them damn pictures."[6]

A more contemporary example of the power of political humor involves the publication of cartoons depicting the prophet Muhammad in a Danish newspaper in September 2005. Many Muslims were insulted by the cartoons, and violence and rioting erupted as a consequence. The protests surrounding this controversy resulted in over two hundred deaths worldwide.[7] Even some humorists seem to think they may be important social and political actors. After the 2008 Republican presidential nominee John McCain canceled a planned appearance on *The Late Show with David Letterman* during the fall campaign, a clearly offended Letterman reminded viewers of something he had said—tongue in cheek, to be sure—for years: "The road to the White House runs through me."

Many see late night political comedy as a legitimate alternative news source. In their view, including these programs in a balanced news-viewing repertoire may promote better citizenship.[8] This is particularly the case with the programming on Comedy Central. Some see *The Daily Show with Jon Stewart* as a new and distinctive form of journalism, partly because Jon Stewart eschews a strictly objective approach.[9] Others argue that Stewart and Stephen Colbert (the host of *The Colbert Report*) help inform and educate us simply by virtue of the fact that they show us the absurdities of the system—and, by extension, how absurd we ourselves have become for accepting these absurdities.[10] In fact, several studies have indicated that the amount of news coverage in *The Daily Show* and *The Colbert Report* is comparable to that of traditional news broadcasts.[11] Furthermore, data from the

2012 election campaign show that almost one-third (31 percent) of the public reported learning about the campaign or the candidates from late night comedy shows such as *The Tonight Show with Jay Leno, Saturday Night Live,* or *The Daily Show.*[12]

A number of journalists agree that late night comedy should be viewed as legitimate "news." This, again, is especially true with respect to *The Daily Show* and *The Colbert Report. NBC Nightly News* anchor Brian Williams once confessed that his editorial team often talks "about what *The Daily Show* did the night before."[13] In another interview Williams referred to Stewart as "a separate branch of government . . . an essential part of modern media and society" and went on to suggest that if it came to a choice between watching traditional news and *The Daily Show,* "by all means watch *The Daily Show.*"[14]

TV news commentator Bill Moyers once speculated that Stewart may be practicing a "new form of journalism,"[15] and Leslie Moonves, president and chief executive officer of CBS, went so far as to suggest—albeit half-jokingly—that he would consider Stewart a viable replacement for Katie Couric as anchor of the *CBS Evening News.*[16] A 2007 survey report suggested that Stewart was the fourth-most-trusted journalist in America, behind Tom Brokaw, Dan Rather, and Anderson Cooper.[17]

Others—mostly scholars—see late night humor as a necessary and valid form of social and political commentary or expression. *The Daily Show,* for example, has been widely praised for its "dissident humor."[18] While some consider the humor of *Saturday Night Live* and broadcast network late night talk shows like *Leno* or *Letterman* to be fundamentally apolitical, political satirists like Stewart, Colbert, Bill Maher, and the like can serve as watchdogs on government and politicians.[19]

These programs are also credited with serving as legitimate forms of political activism (contrary to the protestations of their hosts) as well as antidotes to the cynicism engendered by the political system.[20] In addition, such shows can be the basis of legitimate academic research. A case in point is the collection of essays edited by scholar Jason Holt in which he relates the philosophy of *The Daily Show* to classical philosophy.[21]

In short, there is no question that humor (late night or otherwise) is an enduring and entertaining mode of presenting political ideas. Beyond this, as we discuss in Chapter 2, humor can help shape people's understanding of the political world. Research has demonstrated that viewing political humor has an effect on people's attitudes toward the targets of the humor as well as the political system in general.

Indeed, the power of late night political humor extends far beyond the realm of its effects on individuals. Late night political humor can act as a grand echo chamber, helping to spread negative messages about politicians and other aspects of political life.[22] Collectively the comedy of late night talk shows constitutes a constant barrage of critical commentary about politics and politicians. Preexisting negative images, beliefs, perceptions, truths, and half-truths about the political realm are picked up and propagated even further by late night comics, who in turn likely help to strengthen these impressions.

This negative effect results from virtually all types of late night political comedy: the simpler stand-up comedy of Leno and Letterman, the more sophisticated political satire of Stewart and Colbert, and the sketch comedy of *Saturday Night Live*. It is even possible that such messages decrease trust in—and increase cynicism toward—politicians, government, and the political system.

In the first five chapters of this book, we review the content of late night political humor—the jokes themselves. As we examine this body of work by late night comics in some depth, it is apparent that the overall message being sent is overwhelmingly negative. And as we show in Chapter 6, this negativity seems to mirror the predominantly negative news coverage of individual politicians, suggesting that negative news about politicians and late night political humor tend to move in concert, one reinforcing the other. This is the "echo chamber" effect at work.

Mandy Grunwald, media adviser to Bill Clinton in 1992 and to Hillary Clinton in 2000, acknowledged that once the late night comedians "are making jokes about you, you have a serious problem. Whatever take they have on you is likely to stick much more solidly than what is in the political ads in papers like the *Washington Post*."[23] In this sense, as noted earlier, late night comics actually serve (along with the traditional news media) as watchdogs of sorts. Chris Lehane, Al Gore's campaign press secretary in 2000, saw these late night shows as a political weathervane: "If [a story] makes it onto *Leno* or *Letterman,* it means something."[24] Many accounts suggest that *Saturday Night Live*'s spoof on the first presidential debate in 2000 was at least partly responsible for Gore's decision to change the way he presented himself to the public.[25]

Politicians not only understand this effect, they have developed ways of coping with it. As we discuss in Chapter 7, presidential candidates, who are skewered by late night comedians on a nightly basis, now regularly appear on these same programs as a way to improve their image and perhaps reach potential voters who are more familiar with the late night talk shows than with the evening newscasts. During the 2008 presidential campaign, for example, Jay Leno featured twenty-two such candidate appearances on his program, and Jon Stewart had twenty-one.[26] In total there were over a hundred such visits to late night programs by various candidates. Of course, these visits are made at least in part to deflect, preempt, or otherwise deflate the power of the hosts' nightly barrage of negative messages.

In order to provide some context for our examination of late night televised political humor, we turn next to a brief history of political humor. While it might be tempting to believe that political humor is a product of the modern age, nothing could be further from the truth. Following this, we introduce the unique data utilized in our exposition of televised late night political humor. The chapter concludes with a short discussion of the plan of the book, previewing the remaining chapters.

A BRIEF HISTORY OF POLITICAL HUMOR

Political humor seems to be an inherent part of the human condition that has persisted throughout history.[27] While a full historical analysis of political humor is beyond the scope of this chapter, it is not difficult to find prominent and well-known examples throughout the ages. For example, the unpopular father-in-law of the Egyptian leader

Tutankhamen was the subject of an unflattering caricature drawn by an unknown artist in approximately 1360 BC.[28] Satirical drawings of other Egyptian leaders, including Cleopatra, have also been found. Indian cartoonists poked fun at inept rulers and the Hindu god Krishna.[29] Many pre-Islamic Arab tribes had a poet who, prior to a battle, composed humorous verses about the enemy.

Vases and wall paintings from ancient Greece often represented their Olympian gods in profane parodies.[30] The comedies of Greek playwright Aristophanes frequently targeted Athenian leaders and other notables. In his play *The Clouds,* Aristophanes even lampooned Socrates.[31] During the Roman Empire, political satire targeted at military commanders and various fringe religions could be found represented on walls.[32] The Roman poet Horace is credited by some scholars with developing satire as a literary form in its own right.[33]

In the modern era, many literary authors poked fun at politics through their works. Dante's *Divine Comedy* displayed his views on any number of subjects, including politics—in fact, he placed many political leaders directly in Hell.[34] Shakespeare poked fun at Elizabethan politics in *Richard II.*[35] In the 1700s, Jonathan Swift published a number of satirical works, including the well-known "Modest Proposal" (formally, "A Modest Proposal for Preventing the Children of poor People in Ireland, from being a Burden to their Parents or Country; and for making them beneficial to the Publick") in 1729.

In this work, Swift suggests, tongue in cheek, that Irish parents should eat their children as a way of preventing them from becoming a burden both to their parents and to society. In one passage he claims to have been "assured by a very knowing American of my acquaintance in London, that a young healthy child, well nursed, is, at a year old, a most delicious, nourishing, and wholesome food." In reality, Swift was ridiculing the British government's policies toward Ireland. Swift's best-known work, *Gulliver's Travels* (1726), was a popular symbolic tale poking fun at the pettiness of politics, from the perspective of his close association with many Tory government leaders.

Voltaire's *Candide,* published in 1759 and perhaps the most widely read of his many works, is a tale that satirizes governments, politics, and social institutions. Candide, the protagonist, is a rather simple fellow who optimistically believes, like some philosophers of the time, that "they lived, and died, in the best of all possible worlds."[36] However, a succession of hardships and misfortunes eventually causes Candide to change his worldview.

Even a brief discussion of political humor must include the popularity of political cartoons in the nineteenth century. Although caricatures of political leaders had become popular in Great Britain, France, and the Netherlands during the 1600s, the editorial cartoon as we know it today did not emerge as a form of political humor until the next century, with the cartoons of William Hogarth in Great Britain.[37] Editorial cartoons in America date to the mid-eighteenth century as well. Benjamin Franklin's famous "JOIN, or DIE" cartoon, published in the *Pennsylvania Gazette* on May 9, 1754, shows a snake cut into pieces, symbolizing the need for the colonies to stand together.[38]

Franklin also published satirical articles in the *New England Courant, Poor Richard's Almanac,* and other venues. For example, his "Rules by Which a Great Empire May Be Reduced to a Small One," penned in 1773, targeted what he perceived to be the arrogant and ignorant policies of Great Britain in the colonies. Colonial governors targeted by satire and parody included Francis Nicholson, Alexander Spotswood, and Robert Dinwiddie in Virginia; Samuel Shute, Jonathan Belcher, and William Shirley in Massachusetts; William Cosby in New York; James Oglethorpe in Georgia; and William Keith in Pennsylvania.[39]

In the nineteenth century, the rise of the editorial cartoon was facilitated by increased literacy rates and the growth of the print media.[40] The work of Thomas Nast in particular is the stuff of legend, and rightly so. Nast not only institutionalized the popular representations of Santa Claus and Uncle Sam but also created the Republican elephant and the Democratic donkey.[41]

Notable late-nineteenth- and early-twentieth-century political satirists included Mark Twain and Will Rogers, though both wore other hats besides that of humorous political commentators.[42] Generations of schoolchildren have grown up reading classic political satire from the early part of the twentieth century, such as George Orwell's *Animal Farm* and Aldous Huxley's *Brave New World*. In recent decades political humor in the United States has come from a wide range of sources, such as newspaper columnist Art Buchwald; stand-up comedians Lenny Bruce, Mort Sahl, and Dick Gregory; Garry Trudeau, creator of the Doonesbury cartoons; the satirical newspaper *The Onion*; and movies like *Dr. Strangelove or: How I Learned to Stop Worrying and Love the Bomb, Wag the Dog,* and *Dave*.

Of course, the United States has no monopoly on political humor. Indeed, political humor is not even unique to democracies. Numerous essays, for example, examine political jokes and the role of political humor in Nazi Germany, the Soviet Union and Communist-controlled Eastern Europe, Cuba, China, and other nondemocratic regimes.[43] Interestingly, many political jokes seem to appear in more than one country, with the name or names of the appropriate authoritarian dictator, party, or bureaucracy substituted in the transfer.

A FEW WORDS ABOUT OUR ANALYSIS

In this book we use the term *political humor* (or *political comedy*) to refer to any form of communication that alludes to something political and is intended to make people laugh. For our purposes, this communication will typically be a joke or message that is delivered verbally but may derive some of its ability to make an audience laugh from non-verbal cues like movement, facial expressions, or physical imitation. It may also make use of humorous pictures, videos, or music.

We make no distinction as to exactly how "political" the humorous bit must be in order to be classified as political humor (or, for that matter, how humorous an intended joke is—clunkers qualify just as much as side-splitters). However, most of the political humor contained in the current late night television environment is what we might consider "mainstream," meaning that it is not extremely partisan or ideological. Again, for our purposes it is enough that the joke references people who are engaged in politics, political institutions such as government and parties, or issues of a political nature.

Three major types of late night televised political humor are included in our discussion. The first is the straightforward joke, typically a one-liner, that is standard fare for stand-up comics like Leno and Letterman. The second is the more complex political satire of Stewart and Colbert. Finally, we include in our discussion the sketch comedy of *Saturday Night Live,* although *SNL* sketches are not part of the data analysis portion of this book.

In the context of classical rhetoric, these three types of humor should be treated as separate categories in terms of their contemporary functions and historical genres of political speech. Moreover, while all political humor has the objective of making people laugh, a commentary by Jon Stewart is often motivated by a desire to make them think (or reflect) as well, something that can rarely be said of a one-liner by Jay Leno.

However, in this book all these variants of political humor are treated equally. Our rationale for this approach is straightforward. First, with respect to all three types, the primary intent is to make people laugh. Second, in almost all cases the political humor is overwhelmingly negative in tone; that is, the negativity of political humor does not vary according to type. Third, this negativity is an essential characteristic of political humor, beyond its objective to amuse. It is the negativity of their message that is helping late night television comics remake American political life. They criticize with a smile, but also with a bite.

Our analysis makes use of a unique data set constructed by George Mason University's Center for Media and Public Affairs (CMPA). The Center is a nonpartisan research and educational organization that employs content analysis to study news coverage and entertainment media. Content analysis is a method for producing an objective and systematic description of communicated materials. To be scientific, such analysis requires explicit rules and procedures that minimize a researcher's subjective predispositions. Categories, criteria, decision rules, and so on are rigorously defined and applied consistently to all material. Because it is systematic, content analysis is more reliable than impressionistic generalizations, which are subject to individual preferences and prejudices.

The CMPA has been tracking the content of late night political humor, as well as that of the broadcast network evening news shows, for nearly a quarter of a century. Trained observers have tabulated every joke in the monologues of the most popular late night talk show hosts and comedians. In particular, the CMPA has focused on jokes about US political figures at every level of government, government institutions at every level, and foreign governments and leaders (including royalty). These include jokes about the families of any political or public figure. Beyond this, jokes about social institutions, such as churches/religious groups, businesses, the military, and schools, have been included if (1) the institutions were engaged in political activities or public policy debates; (2) the institutions were involved in some sort of scandalous or criminal behavior; or (3) the jokes addressed a general social or economic problem that stirs political controversy (race relations, gay rights issues, global warming, the declining economy, rising gas/energy prices, inflation, etc.).

Jokes were coded only during the opening monologue or opening section of the shows, and the coding stopped when the first guest appeared. The sole exception to this rule was for David Letterman's "Top Ten" lists, which have occurred at various points in *The Late Show* over the years. For coding purposes each punch line was its own unit of analysis. Each joke was separately coded with a topic, a subtopic, and a target. Initially the jokes were transcribed by CMPA coders. After they became available in the latter 1990s, CMPA pulled jokes from the closed captioning transcripts of these shows. As such, there may be some variation in wording between the transcribed jokes that are coded (and appear in this book) and what the comedian actually said word for word. However, we feel that these variations are fairly minor and don't affect the gist of the joke. In addition, it is important to note that the coding was based on viewing the shows, not reading the transcripts.

Topics were coded based on a list of approximately three hundred items (a number that has grown over the years to match changing events). The objective was to identify the central issue or institution that was discussed in the joke. Subtopics were chosen from a list that now includes over six hundred items. (This list, too, has expanded over the years to represent new controversies and issues.) Subtopics were selected to narrow the focus of the topical category.

The target of the joke was coded based on the person, group, or institution that the joke was making fun of. We did not code people who are mentioned in the joke but are not the butt of the joke. In most cases, targets were clearly identified by name in the joke, but targets could also be identified and coded based on references to situations that were specific to them. Our coding system did allow us to code more than one target per joke for the relatively small number of jokes in which this occurred. We also conducted reliability tests to ensure that all coders agreed at least 80 percent of the time on the targets and topics of jokes.

It is this collection of late night joke data that we use to examine systematically how late night comics have treated public officials, candidates for political office, and other politically related targets since 1988. Table 1.1 shows the number of jokes included in the database, by program, from 1992 through 2011.

The database contains a total of 102,435 jokes. Some are from programs that were either short-lived (e.g., *The Jon Stewart Show*, 1993–1995) or have only fairly recently been included in the database (e.g., *Late Night with Jimmy Fallon*, *The Tonight Show with Conan O'Brien*, 2009–2010). Bill Maher's *Politically Incorrect* is included only in its broadcast network version (it ran on ABC from 1997 to 2002). Most of Comedy Central's *The Daily Show with Jon Stewart* and *The Colbert Report* are included as well. However, the bulk of the jokes (76 percent) come from *The Tonight Show* (including material from hosts Johnny Carson, Jay Leno, and Conan O'Brien), *The Late Show with David Letterman*, and *Late Night with Conan O'Brien*.

The frequency of late night political jokes throughout the year seems aligned with the schedule of the government in Washington, which also matches up well with the hosts' vacation schedules. The months of July, August, and December have noticeably fewer jokes (an average of about 7 percent per month of the total jokes in the database) than other months. September has the most jokes, partly due to the

Table 1.1 Number of Political Jokes, by Late Night Program (1992–2011)

	Tonight Show*	Letterman	Late Night (O'Brien)	Jon Stewart Show	Arsenio Hall	Politically Incorrect	Daily Show	Colbert Report	Jimmy Fallon	Total Jokes (by Year)
1992	1,975	1,117	—	—	653	—	—	—	—	3,745
1993	1,535	883	109	—	176	—	—	—	—	2,703
1994	1,739	1,218	300	90	51	—	—	—	—	3,398
1995	1,546	1,156	281	—	—	—	—	—	—	2,983
1996	2,244	2,055	504	—	—	—	—	—	—	4,803
1997	1,386	1,023	398	—	—	188	—	—	—	2,995
1998	2,165	1,949	492	—	—	654	—	—	—	5,260
1999	2,467	1,102	302	—	—	654	—	—	—	4,525
2000	2,454	1,406	634	—	—	451	—	—	—	4,945
2001	1,957	1,007	363	—	—	100	—	—	—	3,427
2002	1,941	848	312	—	—	—	—	—	—	3,101
2003	1,321	837	305	—	—	—	215	—	—	2,678
2004	2,227	1,480	515	—	—	—	1,024	—	—	5,246
2005	1,397	709	374	—	—	—	738	—	—	3,218
2006	2,561	1,915	512	—	—	—	1,447	—	—	6,435
2007	1,809	1,206	519	—	—	—	1,373	308	—	5,215
2008	3,812	3,187	1,242	—	—	—	2,641	2,376	—	13,258
2009	1,845	3,206	283	—	—	—	2,261	1,830	913	10,994
2010	1,991	2,412	—	—	—	—	2,357	1,949	853	9,612
2011	1,791	1,434	—	—	—	—	—	—	669	3,894
Total	40,869	30,150	7,445	90	880	2,047	12,056	6,463	2,435	102,435
Avg. per Year	2,002	1,528	438	90	114	409	1,507	1,616	812	5,122
Percentage Total Jokes	39.9%	29.4%	7.3%	0.1%	0.9%	2.0%	11.8%	6.3%	2.4%	

* Includes jokes by Johnny Carson as host in 1992 (365) and 1993 (151) as well as jokes by host Conan O'Brien in 2009 and 2010 (706).

fact that every four years a presidential campaign kicks into high gear during that month. The next highest number of jokes occurs during January, when presidents are inaugurated and congressional sessions begin (and when the Monica Lewinsky scandal broke in 1997).

In sum, this data set provides an empirical basis for drawing generalizations about the nature of late night political humor.

PLAN OF THE BOOK

The remainder of this book is organized as follows: In Chapter 2 we provide an overview of the evolution of political humor on late night television, from *The Tonight Show* and its competitors to *Saturday Night Live* to Comedy Central's political humor programming.

We then situate late night political humor in the world of soft news, noting that political humor has become a major source of political information. We also examine what recent research has uncovered about the effects of late night political humor on political knowledge, attitudes, and participation. In short, this chapter partly explains why political humor matters: more people are getting more "news" and information from late night comics, and this in turn affects public attitudes and opinions and the behavior of political actors.

Chapters 3 through 5 constitute the heart of our analysis, drawing on the CMPA data set that has allowed us to track the content of late night political humor from 1992 to the present. Chapter 3 focuses on the highest-profile targets in American politics: sitting presidents, vice presidents, and candidates for these offices. From Dan Quayle and George Bush to Bill and Hillary Clinton to Barack Obama and Sarah Palin, we examine the slings and arrows of outrageous fortune that our most powerful politicians have suffered at the hands of late night comedians.

In Chapters 4 and 5 the focus shifts from *who's* funny to *what's* funny in late night comedy. We catalogue the types of events and traits that bring out the best (or worst) in the comedians and their joke writers. In Chapter 4 we examine scandals involving sex, money, and influence-peddling, which are the greatest sources of inspiration to late night comedians. In Chapter 5 we consider character flaws, intellectual deficits, and personal traits involving appearance, such as attractiveness, weight, and dexterity, that become associated with particular politicians. We also look at topical areas that are the backdrop for many jokes, such as the economy and the "war on terror."

In Chapter 6 we examine how late night humor interacts with the news in shaping the public images of political leaders. Our data analyses of late night jokes are matched up with the findings from content analyses of political news that the CMPA has conducted during presidential campaigns from 1992 to 2008. We compare the two data sets with respect to subject matter, tone, and partisan direction. We then see how these trends are correlated with aggregate public opinion data on public perceptions of presidential candidates.

Late night comedians are also talk show hosts. Ever since Bill Clinton appeared on *The Arsenio Hall Show* in 1992, politicians have trolled for votes by making nice to their tormentors in person. During the 2008 election season, the various presidential candidates appeared more than a hundred times on late night shows, and in 2009 Barack Obama made the first late night presidential appearance by going on *The Tonight Show with Jay Leno*. Chapter 7 explores the role of late night talk shows as stopovers on the road to the White House.

In Chapter 8, the final chapter, we attempt to make some sense of our findings. Does this study help us better understand how political humor operates in the current media climate? Do the observations from our examination of political humor help predict the various public image successes and failures of individual politicians? Are there any inherent biases in the targets of late night political humor? If so, what are they, where do they come from, and what effect do they have? Finally, what does the future hold for the increasingly close connection between comedy and politics?

One last introductory note: as this book entered production, Jay Leno ended his twenty-two-year run hosting *The Tonight Show*. Taking over the show was Jimmy Fallon, who had hosted NBC's

Late Night with Jimmy Fallon since 2009. Unfortunately we were not able to incorporate this development into the text beyond this brief acknowledgment.

NOTES

1. Howard Kurtz, "The Campaign of a Comedian: Jon Stewart's Fake Journalism Enjoys Real Political Impact," *Washington Post,* October 23, 2004, p. A1.

2. Pew Research Center for the People, April 2008, retrieved May 14, 2013, from the iPOLL Databank, The Roper Center for Public Opinion Research, University of Connecticut, http://www.ropercenter.uconn.edu/data_access/ipoll/ipoll.html.

3. Pew Research Center for the People, May 2012, retrieved May 14, 2013, from the iPOLL Databank, The Roper Center for Public Opinion Research, University of Connecticut, http://www.ropercenter.uconn.edu/data_access/ipoll/ipoll.html.

4. Jody C Baumgartner and Jonathan S. Morris, "Stoned Slackers or Super-Citizens? 'Daily Show' Viewing and Political Engagement of Young Adults," in *The Stewart/Colbert Effect: Essays on the Real Impacts of Fake News,* ed. Amarnath Amarasingam (Jefferson, NC: McFarland & Co., 2011).

5. Robert C. Elliott, *The Power of Satire: Magic, Ritual, Art* (Princeton, NJ: Princeton University Press, 1960).

6. Albert Bigelow Paine, *Th. Nast: His Period and His Pictures* (New York: Harper, 1904).

7. Ilan Danjoux, "Reconsidering the Decline of the Editorial Cartoon," *PS: Political Science and Politics* 40 (2007): 245–248.

8. Dannagal Goldthwaite Young, "*The Daily Show* as the New Journalism: In Their Own Words," in *Laughing Matters: Humor and American Politics in the Media Age,* eds. Jody C Baumgartner and Jonathan S. Morris (New York: Routledge, 2008), 241–259; Dannagal Goldthwaite Young and Sarah E. Esralew, "Jon Stewart as Heretic? Surely You Jest: Political Participation and Discussion Among Viewers of Late-Night Comedy Programming," in *The Stewart/Colbert Effect: Essays on the Real Impacts of Fake News,* ed. Amarnath Amarasingam (Jefferson, NC: McFarland & Co., 2011), 99–115; Bruce A. Williams and Michael X. Delli Carpini, "Real Ethical Concerns and Fake News: *The Daily Show* and the Challenge of the New Media Environment," in *The Stewart/Colbert Effect: Essays on the Real Impacts of Fake News,* ed. Amarnath Amarasingam (Jefferson, NC: McFarland & Co., 2011), 181–192.

9. Geoffrey Baym, "'The Daily Show': Discursive Integration and the Reinvention of Political Journalism," *Political Communication* 22 (2005): 259–276; Geoffrey Baym, "Serious Comedy: Exploring the Boundaries of Political Discourse,"

in *Laughing Matters: Humor and American Politics in the Media Age,* eds. Jonathan S. Morris and Jody C Baumgartner (New York: Routledge, 2008), 21–38.

10. Geoffrey Baym, "Stephen Colbert's Parody of the Postmodern," in *Satire TV: Politics and Comedy in the Post-Network Era,* eds. Jonathan Gray, Jeffrey P. Jones, and Ethan Thompson (New York: New York University Press, 2009), 124–144.

11. Paul R. Brewer and Emily Marquardt, "Mock News and Democracy: Analyzing *The Daily Show," Atlantic Journal of Communication* 15 (2007): 249–267; Julia Fox, Glory Colon, and Volcan Sahin, "No Joke: A Comparison of Substance in *The Daily Show with Jon Stewart* and Broadcast Network Television Coverage of the 2004 Presidential Election Campaign," *Journal of Broadcasting and Electronic Media* 51 (2007): 213–227; Mark K. McBeth and Randy S. Clemons, "Is Fake News the Real News? The Significance of Stewart and Colbert for Democratic Discourse, Politics, and Policy," in *The Stewart/Colbert Effect: Essays on the Real Impacts of Fake News,* ed. Amarnath Amarasingam (Jefferson, NC: McFarland & Co., 2011), 79–98.

12. Pew Research Center, "Internet Gains Most as Campaign News Sources but Cable TV Still Leads," October 25, 2012, http://www.journalism.org/2012/10/25 /social-media-doubles-remains-limited/.

13. Kathy A. McDonald, "Mainstream Media Remains in on Joke," *Daily Variety,* January 22, 2009, pp. A4–A5.

14. Baumgartner and Morris, "Stoned Slackers or Super-Citizens?," p. 65.

15. James Trier, "The Daily Show with Jon Stewart," *Journal of Adolescent & Adult Literacy* 51, no. 5 (2008): 424.

16. Toni Fitzgerald, "Seriously, Jon Stewart as Anchorman," *Media Life,* April 3, 2009, http://www.medialifemagazine.com/artman2/publish/Dayparts_update _51/Seriously_Jon_Stewart_as_anchorman.asp.

17. Baumgartner and Morris, "Stoned Slackers or Super-Citizens?"

18. Jamie Warner, "Political Culture Jamming: The Dissident Humor of *The Daily Show with Jon Stewart," Popular Communication* 5, no. 1 (2007): 17.

19. Jeffrey P. Jones, "With All Due Respect: Satirizing Presidents from *Saturday Night Live* to *Li'l Bush,"* in *Satire TV: Politics and Comedy in the Post-Network Era,* eds. Jonathan Gray, Jeffrey P. Jones, and Ethan Thompson (New York: New York University Press, 2009), 37–63; Russell L. Peterson, *Strange Bedfellows: How Late-Night Comedy Turns Democracy into a Joke* (New Brunswick, NJ: Rutgers University Press, 2008).

20. Joanne Morreale, "Jon Stewart and *The Daily Show:* I Thought You Were Going to Be Funny!," in *Satire TV: Politics and Comedy in the Post-Network Era,* eds. Jonathan Gray, Jeffrey P. Jones, and Ethan Thompson (New York: New York University Press, 2009), 104–123; Richard Van Heertum, "Irony and the News: Speaking Cool to American Youth," in *The Stewart/Colbert Effect: Essays on the*

Real Impacts of Fake News, ed. Amarnath Amarasingam (Jefferson, NC: Mc-Farland & Co., 2011), 117–135; Julia R. Fox, "Wise Fools: Jon Stewart and Stephen Colbert as Modern-Day Jesters in the American Court," in *The Stewart/Colbert Effect: Essays on the Real Impacts of Fake News,* ed. Amarnath Amarasingam (Jefferson, NC: McFarland & Co., 2011), 138–148; Amber Day, *Satire and Dissent: Interventions in Contemporary Political Debate* (Bloomington: Indiana University Press, 2011).

21. Jason Holt, ed., *The Daily Show and Philosophy: Moments of Zen in the Art of Fake News* (Malden, MA: Wiley-Blackwell, 2007).

22. Kathleen Hall Jamieson and Joseph N. Cappella, *Echo Chamber: Rush Limbaugh and the Conservative Media Establishment* (New York: Oxford University Press, 2010).

23. Howard Kurtz, "Trial of the Century Now Joke of the Day," *Washington Post,* January 26, 1999, p. A1.

24. Martha Sella, "The Stiff Guy vs. the Dumb Guy," *New York Times,* September 24, 2000, http://nytimes.com/2000/09/24/magazine/the-stiff-guy-vs-the-dumb-guy.html?src=pm&pagewanted=1.

25. Ben Voth, "'*Saturday Night Live* and Presidential Elections," in *Laughing Matters: Humor and American Politics in the Media Age,* eds. Jonathan S. Morris and Jody C Baumgartner (New York: Routledge, 2008).

26. Associated Press, "Politicians Found Late-Night an Asset in 2008," December 29, 2008, http://www.cmpa.com/news/12_29_2008.pdf.

27. Gregor Benton, "The Origins of the Political Joke," in *Humor in Society: Resistance and Control,* eds. Chris Powell and George E. C. Paton (New York: St. Martin's, 1998).

28. Danjoux, "Reconsidering the Decline of the Editorial Cartoon."

29. Paul Martin Lester, *Visual Communication: Images with Messages,* 4th ed. (Belmont, CA: Thomson Wadsworth, 2005).

30. Ibid.

31. Gilbert Highet, *The Anatomy of Satire* (Princeton, NJ: Princeton University Press, 1962); Michael J. Vickers, *Pericles on Stage: Political Comedy in Aristophanes' Early Plays* (Austin: University of Texas Press, 1997).

32. Danjoux, "Reconsidering the Decline of the Editorial Cartoon."

33. Highet, *The Anatomy of Satire.*

34. Joan Ferrante, *The Political Vision of the Divine Comedy* (Princeton, NJ: Princeton University Press, 1993).

35. Jessica Bloustein, "Political Punch Lines," *Newsweek* (Web Exclusive), September 11, 2008, http://www.newsweek.com/id/158301.

36. Highet, *The Anatomy of Satire.*

37. Lester, *Visual Communication.*

38. Ibid.

39. Alison Gilbert Olson, "Political Humor, Deference, and the American Revolution," *Early American Studies* 3 (2005): 363–382.

40. Edward J. Lordan, *Politics, Ink: How Cartoonists Skewer America's Politicians, from King George III to George Dubya* (Lanham, MD: Rowman & Littlefield, 2005).

41. Paine, *Th. Nast.*

42. Arthur P. Dudden, "The Record of Political Humor," *American Quarterly* 37, no. 1 (1985): 50–70.

43. Benton, "The Origins of the Political Joke"; Christie Davies, "Humour and Protest: Jokes Under Communism," *International Review of Social History* 52 (2007): 291–305; Alexander Rose, "When Politics Is a Laughing Matter," *Policy Review* (2001): 59–71; Hans Speier, "Wit and Politics: An Essay on Laughter and Power," *American Journal of Sociology* 103 (1998): 1352–1401; Mary Beth Stein, "The Politics of Humor: The Berlin Wall in Jokes and Graffiti," *Western Folklore* 48 (1989): 85–108.

Chapter 2

The Rise of Late Night Comedy

How powerful have television's late night talk show hosts become? If you believe David Letterman, they are America's new kingmakers. On September 24, 2008, Letterman proclaimed on his program: "The road to the White House runs through me." As noted in the previous chapter, Letterman made this statement after Republican presidential candidate John McCain canceled his scheduled appearance on the show that evening. Of course, Letterman was exaggerating his importance in the presidential selection process. Nonetheless, his claim was rooted in a new political reality: doing well in the late night talk show campaign can help a presidential candidate, while doing poorly (as McCain learned) can be a nightmare.

How did we get to this place? How did late night talk show hosts replace newspaper editorial boards in vetting candidates for voters in modern presidential campaigns, as a 2008 Center for Media and Public Affairs report concludes?[1] In this chapter we trace the evolution of political humor on late night television from the original *Tonight Show* to its current iteration and its late night talk show competitors, as well as to *Saturday Night Live* and late night programming on Comedy Central. We then situate political humor in the world of entertainment-based political news, showing how late night jokes have become a major source of political information. Finally, we summarize the effects of late night political humor on the political knowledge, attitudes, and participation of its viewers.

LATE NIGHT TALK (AND OTHER POLITICAL COMEDY): A BRIEF HISTORY

In the early days of television, TV programs were similar in many respects to radio programs. The reason for this was simple: TV was a new medium whose unique possibilities had yet to be explored. Thus, the talk show was an early staple on television. In 1954, the National Broadcasting Company (NBC) began airing *Tonight!* from 11:15 p.m. (when the late news ended) to 1:00 a.m. The program's first host was a former radio and television variety show host named Steve Allen. From the start, it featured interviews and discussions with guests. In fact, on occasion the entire program was devoted to a discussion with just one guest.[2]

In 1957, Allen left the program and turned over the reins to Jack Paar, another former radio announcer and most recently host of the rival Columbia Broadcasting System's (CBS) morning show. Paar was more of a conversationalist than the humorist Allen. However, Paar's relations with network management were sometimes strained, and he left the program in 1962.

The Heyday of Late Night: Johnny Carson Takes Over

Paar's successor, Johnny Carson, institutionalized—and for many years monopolized—late night talk.[3] Like Allen and Paar, Carson had a background in local radio and television. He had previously hosted a short-lived variety show on CBS and a long-running game show (*Who Do You Trust?*) on the American Broadcasting Company (ABC) network. So he was somewhat familiar to the national television audience, which was part of what the NBC executives liked about him.

Originally reluctant to leave his successful game show, Carson eventually settled on what was then a hefty sum of $100,000 per year to host *The Tonight Show*. Included in the agreement was the idea that the show would be tailored to fit Carson's personality and style. The format that was settled on is by now easily recognizable:

> A fifteen-minute monologue followed by guests from the entertain-
> ment world . . . sketches and skits . . . adventures among the audi-
> ence . . . guests with books or ideas to discuss . . . and musical acts.[4]

The new format was an instant success, with the average viewership roughly doubling Paar's audience levels.[5]

Part of Carson's commercial success and staying power during the 1960s could probably be attributed to *The Tonight Show*'s tendency to steer clear of social or political controversy.[6] Carson's guest list was mostly filled with entertainers. However, this is not to say that Carson completely avoided politics—he told many a political joke during his monologues. For example, "Democracy means that anyone can grow up to be president, and anyone who doesn't grow up can be vice president." During the Watergate crisis, Carson quipped, "Did you know Richard Nixon is the only president whose formal portrait was painted by a police sketch artist?"

Carson assessed a proposed presidential race "dream ticket" of actor-turned-politician Ronald Reagan and accident-prone Gerald Ford in 1980 by commenting: "That would have been a great ticket, Reagan and Ford—an actor and a stuntman." Carson also once asked the audience, "You get the feeling that Dan Quayle's golf bag doesn't have a full set of irons?"—referring to President George H. W. Bush's vice president, an ardent golfer who gained notoriety by misspelling *potato* at an elementary school spelling bee.[7]

But the jokes Carson told were never risky or cutting-edge. Instead, they were more a reflection or barometer of the public mood. For example, although he made a number of jokes about the Watergate scandal, he stopped short when Judge Sirica ordered President Nixon to release audiotapes of recorded Oval Office conversations, at which point the scandal morphed into a national crisis.[8]

Carson's *Tonight Show* held a virtual monopoly over the late night talk landscape until the start of what TV talk historian Bernard Timberg calls "the first late-night talk-show wars."[9] Beginning in 1967, both ABC and CBS tried to compete with NBC for the late night talk market share. Some of their hosts were more political than others. For example, ABC's Dick Cavett was known for his in-depth interviews and willingness to engage in controversial issues. On one episode Cavett paired Vietnam War swift boat commander and anti-war activist John Kerry with John O'Neill, another swift boat veteran, whom President Nixon had convinced to engage Kerry on the issue.[10] The debate between the two, like many of the debates on Cavett's program, is now part of television lore.[11] Cavett's late night program on ABC aired from 1969 to 1974.

On CBS, veteran talk show host Merv Griffin also engaged controversial guests. He was chastised by network executives for booking anti–Vietnam War activists such as Abbie Hoffman, who appeared on the show in 1970 wearing a shirt that resembled an American flag. (Flags were being burned by protesters at the time, and using the flag as an article of clothing was seen by many Vietnam War supporters as disrespectful and possibly even treasonous.) Griffin's approach created enough controversy that the network canceled *The Merv Griffin Show* in 1972.

Another player in the late night talk wars was the British-born journalist David Frost, previously known for his work on a popular satirical BBC TV series called *That Was the Week That Was.* Like Cavett, Frost was known for his more serious and in-depth approach to interviews, as opposed to being simply an entertainer. His syndicated late night program, *The David Frost Show,* ran from 1969 through 1972. But he is best known for conducting a televised series of interviews with ex-president Richard Nixon in 1977 that probed Nixon's role in the Watergate scandal.[12]

In spite of the new competition, Carson reigned supreme on late night talk through the late 1970s and most of the 1980s. That said, a few challengers of note emerged during the 1980s. Among them was Arsenio Hall, who hosted the syndicated late night *Arsenio Hall Show,* which began in 1989.[13] As the first African American late night talk host, Hall highlighted black culture in a way that had not previously been done in the genre. In addition, his was the first late night talk show to host a presidential candidate. In June 1992, in an effort to increase his visibility and popularity among young and minority voters, Democratic presidential candidate Bill Clinton appeared on Hall's program wearing dark sunglasses and playing "Heartbreak Hotel" on the saxophone.[14] Although the program remained popular to the end, in 1994 CBS forced it off the network's affiliate stations in order to make room for *The Late Show with David Letterman*.[15]

Late Night from the 1980s to Today: Transition and Expansion

By the mid-1980s, speculation had begun over who would succeed Carson on *The Tonight Show*. Among the contenders was David Letterman, then the host of *Late Night with David Letterman,* which followed *The Tonight Show* and had become a late night staple since debuting in 1982. Another contender was Jay Leno, a frequent *Tonight Show* guest host who had been making the comedy rounds in Los Angeles.[16]

By the time Carson announced that he would retire in 1992, the choice of his successor had been narrowed down by network executives to either Letterman or Leno. Letterman had been dreaming of the opportunity since he first appeared on the program. However, he had a history of being prickly with network executives, and the NBC brass were not convinced that his sometimes offbeat humor would translate well to the more mainstream 11:30 p.m. time slot. Leno was more of a traditional stand-up comic in the Carson mold, who excelled at delivering a series of well-crafted one-liners. In the end, as we know, NBC went with Leno, while a disappointed Letterman signed a lucrative contract with CBS to directly compete with *The Tonight Show. The Late Show with David Letterman* debuted in August 1993.[17]

With the appearance of Letterman on the scene, the days of NBC's dominance in the late night talk show world finally ended. Throughout the 1990s, Leno and Letterman jockeyed with each other for ratings. While Leno ultimately prevailed in the ratings war, this was at least partly a result of structural differences between the NBC and CBS affiliates on which the programs aired. Leno and Letterman together were the face of mainstream late night talk in the 1990s, and though the field is more crowded now, they remained very much part of the picture up to Leno's retirement in 2014. Both hosts continued the tradition of targeting presidents, other politicians, policy issues, and political institutions like Congress and the political parties. Recent gems from Jay Leno include:

Earlier this week the Senate voted 97-to-0 for tougher regulations. For example, when corporations buy a senator, they must now get a receipt.

How much do you think Senators make? They now make $154,700 a year. But they say it will stimulate the economy because eventually that money will trickle down to the liquor stores, the hookers, the brothels . . . then it will get back in the community.

Today is the anniversary of the Watergate break-in. That's the day the Republicans tried to steal the Democrats' plans. That's also the last time the Democrats had any plans worth stealing. It's also the last time a Republican president had a plan and actually carried it out.

Leno's hosting gig on *The Tonight Show* was interrupted from June 2009 through February 2010, as a result of a complicated set of circumstances. When Letterman left NBC's *Late Night with David Letterman* (the 12:30 program that followed *The Tonight Show*) in 1993, he was replaced with Conan O'Brien. Eleven years later, in an attempt both to avoid another succession controversy like the one that occurred when Carson retired and to entice O'Brien to sign another contract, NBC offered to give O'Brien *The Tonight Show* in 2009. The idea was that after fifteen years Leno, who would be sixty, could step aside gracefully. At the time this idea seemed reasonable.

As the time for retirement grew near, however, Leno began questioning the wisdom of the move, noting that *The Tonight Show* was still winning the ratings war. Therefore, as a way to satisfy both hosts, NBC gave Leno a nightly program at 10:00 p.m. (*The Jay Leno Show*) and O'Brien took over *The Tonight Show*. Unfortunately, ratings for both shows were mediocre, affiliate stations complained, and the experiment soon ended. Although NBC tried to keep both men happy by offering O'Brien a 12:05 a.m. slot following a shortened *Tonight Show*, O'Brien refused. Instead he found a new home at 11:00 p.m. on the Turner Broadcasting System (TBS) cable network.[18]

Since the 1990s, the late night talk universe has expanded dramatically. There are now multiple offerings on different channels and at later times. As mentioned above, TBS now offers *Conan* at 11:00 p.m., and for a brief time it was followed by George Lopez's show, *Lopez Tonight,* at midnight. In January 2003, ABC entered the late night talk show fray with *Jimmy Kimmel Live!,* and in 2013 the show moved to an 11:35 time slot. As of publication, Jimmy Fallon had taken over the hosting job at *The Tonight Show* on NBC, which is followed by *Late Night with Seth Meyers* (at 12:35 a.m.) and *Last Call with Carson Daly* (at 1:35 a.m.). Letterman is followed by *The Late Late Show with Craig Ferguson* on CBS. On April 3, 2014, Letterman announced his intention to retire in 2015. Stephen Colbert was announced as his replacement.

Thus far we have been dealing almost exclusively with late night talk shows on the major broadcast networks. In particular, we have focused on a number of programs that have largely followed the format and structure of the original *Tonight Show.* Each show begins with a humorous monologue, which is typically followed by another comedy routine of some sort, such as a sketch. Subsequently, the host interviews one or more guests, and the segment concludes with a musical or comedy performance.

In terms of structure, many of these shows have a co-host and a "house" band, the performances are filmed in front of a live studio audience, and the host sits behind a desk for most of the show. A final similarity that is especially relevant for our purposes is that most hosts spend at least some time focusing on the political happenings of the day, although these shows could by no means be considered predominantly political in nature. Politics is given roughly equal treatment with celebrity activities, popular culture, science and health trends, and other news topics that catch the attention of the host and writers.

Beyond Broadcast Late Night Talk: Comedy Central and *Saturday Night Live*

Several other late night programs that deviate from the *Tonight Show* formula are noteworthy primarily because they present a blend of humor and politics that is more heavily skewed toward the latter. In particular, the cable network Comedy Central airs two programs that have become highly popular, especially among young people. *The Daily Show with Jon Stewart* and *The Colbert Report* deal not just in political humor but in political satire, which is a much rarer commodity on television. Moreover, neither resembles traditional talk shows in format or substance.

The Daily Show, which airs for thirty minutes starting at 11:00 p.m. on Monday through Thursday, began in 1996. It was originally hosted by former sports anchor Craig Kilborn and focused heavily on providing humorous perspectives on the entertainment world. When Stewart took over in 1999, he shifted the focus of the program from popular culture to politics and the media. The show bills itself as a "fake news" program. Under his stewardship, ratings have increased dramatically and the show has received numerous Emmy and other entertainment awards. It is now critically acclaimed as one of the most incisive political shows on television.

Stewart himself is considered by many to be a modern-day Mark Twain or Will Rogers. During his October 2004 appearance on CNN's *Crossfire* (a program built around dueling opinions between liberals and conservatives), Stewart criticized the program as illustrating what's wrong with television journalism. Below is an exchange between Stewart and *Crossfire* co-host Tucker Carlson:

> **Stewart:** In many ways, it's funny. And I made a special effort to come on the show today, because I have privately, amongst my friends and also in occasional newspapers and television shows, mentioned this show [*Crossfire*] as being bad. . . . And I wanted to—I felt that wasn't fair and I should come here and tell you that I don't—it's not so much that it's bad, as it's hurting America. So I wanted to come here today and say . . . Stop, stop, stop, stop, stop hurting America. . . . What you do is partisan hackery. . . . You have a responsibility to the public discourse, and you fail miserably.
>
> **Tucker Carlson:** Wait. I thought you were going to be funny. Come on. Be funny.
>
> **Stewart:** No. No. I'm not going to be your monkey.

Stewart's criticism of *Crossfire* went viral on the Internet and sparked a controversy that ended with the network canceling the show in January 2005, as CNN's incoming president agreed with Stewart's criticisms. Years later, Stewart also appeared to get the best of CNBC host Jim Kramer regarding the latter's questionable financial advice in a series of public exchanges in 2009.[19]

Because his program is structured differently from late night talk shows, Stewart has more time to develop the treatment and critiques of his targets. And because he is not writing for a broader broadcast network audience, his humor can be more biting. For example, in September 2009, Congressman Joe Wilson from California yelled "You lie" at President Obama during an address to a joint session of Congress on health care. In the week following the incident, late night talk show hosts produced numerous one-liners poking fun at Wilson's perceived boorish behavior. However, Stewart used reactions from the House leadership, as well as rank-and-file members, to draw attention to the fact that similar incidents have been exploited by both Republicans and Democrats to score political points (see Box 2.1).

The Colbert Report satirizes talk shows hosted by conservative commentators such as Fox News's *O'Reilly Factor,* with Stephen Colbert assuming the persona of a blustery, ideologically driven host. The show is a spin-off of *The Daily Show,* where Colbert began as a correspondent. In 2005, he was given his own thirty-minute program following *The Daily Show.* The political satire of *The Colbert Report* is easily as sophisticated as that of *The Daily Show,* but it is also a parody. In the context of Colbert's character as a right-wing talk show host, his apparent defense of conservative politicians and policies is actually intended as criticism.[20]

Colbert has taken his act as a right-wing pundit beyond his thirty-minute television show and into the real world, rarely breaking out of character. In 2006, he was the featured speaker at the White House Correspondents dinner, where he roasted President George W. Bush while seemingly praising him.[21] In October 2007, he announced he was running for president as both a Republican and a Democrat. He went so far as to file as a Democrat in the South Carolina primary. (His application was rejected by the party.)[22]

BOX 2.1

Excerpts from Jon Stewart's "Jackass Carousel," September 16, 2009

Jon Stewart: . . . Remember Joe Wilson, Republican, South Carolina, has truth Tourette's? Six days ago he shouted, "You lie!" at President Obama. [It] Caused a bit of a stir. He called the White House, apologized, they accepted his apology. Everyone, even the Speaker of the House, put the incident into perspective.

[Clip] **Nancy Pelosi (Speaker of the House):** As far as I'm concerned, the episode was unfortunate. Mr. Wilson has apologized. It's time for us to talk about healthcare, not Mr. Wilson.

Stewart: Damn straight, Speaker. Time to deal with our nation's hurt bodies, not our hurt feelings. Time to move on. Cut to two days later.

[Clip] **News commentator:** The House Speaker has told Joe Wilson that he must publicly apologize to Congress from the House floor.

[. . .]

Stewart: House Republicans were quick to remind us all that Congress had bigger fish to fry.

[Clip] **Rep. Cathy McMorris Rodgers (R-WA):** Mr. Speaker, how much longer does this go on? What are we really accomplishing here today? The President accepted Mr. Wilson's apology. Let's stop wasting time. Let's focus on tackling the challenges that face our country.

Stewart: Hear ye hear ye. Representative Cathy McMorris Rodgers all business. At least Republicans weren't wasting time demanding meaningless apologies.

[Clip, from earlier in the year] **Rep. Thaddeus McCotter (R-MI):** Mr. Speaker, tonight I've introduced H. Res 680 calling upon President Obama to retract and apologize for his remarks regarding the conduct of Cambridge, Massachusetts police sergeant James M. Crowley, Jr.

Stewart: Yes, these apologies keep going around and around. It appears our Congress is trapped on a Jackass Carousel. One party demands an apology, the other party declares it a waste of time. Time better spent demanding their own equally pointless apology, which, in a beautiful pot of doo, the first party then declares a waste of time. For example, Rahm Emanuel obviously thought Obama issuing an apology to that policeman was a distraction and a waste of time. A waste of time certainly, that's not how he spent his time in Congress.

(continues)

BOX 2.1 CONTINUED

[Clip] **Rahm Emanuel (White House Chief of Staff):** We have to endure
the words of a hate monger like Ann Coulter. In her new book, *The God-
dess of the Right,* she slanders the 9/11 widows. She should apologize
to all of us who have lost our fellow citizens on 9/11.

Stewart: . . . But of course, if there is to be an actual Jackass Carousel,
the circle must be completed. So let us call back to our opening jackass, Joe Wilson, discussing the resolution to disapprove of his "You
lie" outburst.

[Clip] **Rep. Joe Wilson (R-SC):** It is clear to the American people that
there are far more important issues facing this nation than what we are
addressing right now.

Stewart: Issues such as?

[Clip] **Wilson:** Mr. Speaker, 33 years ago today John Kerry appeared before the Senate to talk about Vietnam. John Kerry accused American
soldiers of rape, torture, murder, and even offered up comparisons of
Genghis Khan. John Kerry owes them an apology.

Stewart: Jackass!

In 2010, Colbert appeared before a House subcommittee on immigration to speak to the idea that Americans were not willing to take
agricultural jobs.[23] That same year he legally formed a super-PAC called
"Americans for a Better Tomorrow, Tomorrow," which he used to highlight changes in campaign finance laws that had emerged as a result
of the Supreme Court's decision regarding *Citizens United v. Federal
Election Commission* in 2010.[24] Although it was clearly intended as a
vehicle for satirizing the campaign process, his super-PAC raised over
$1 million and aired several spoof advertisements, including one for
candidate "Rick Parry" (a deliberate misspelling of 2012 GOP presidential candidate Rick Perry) in the summer of 2011 in Iowa.[25]

This book is focused primarily on late night talk shows on the
broadcast television networks as well as the two above-mentioned
Comedy Central shows. These programs have accounted for a substantial majority of the political humor that most television viewers
experience. However, a few other programs have proven sufficiently
popular to deserve mention.

In 1993, Comedy Central debuted *Politically Incorrect*, a thirty-minute show hosted by Bill Maher. The program featured Maher, whose background is in stand-up comedy, and four guests, typically a mix of politicians, activists, journalists, and entertainers. All appeared onstage together and discussed and debated the news of the day. Although the show drew few viewers at the start, its popularity increased over the next few years. In January 1997, ABC picked up the program to follow its popular news show *Nightline*.

Despite its good ratings, the network canceled the show in 2002, partly because of a controversial remark Maher made in the aftermath of the 9/11 attacks, in which he implied that the American military was more cowardly than the terrorists for firing missiles from a long distance rather than personally piloting planes into buildings.[26] In a slightly modified form and retitled *Real Time with Bill Maher,* the show moved to Home Box Office (HBO), where it now runs for one hour weekly.

Another program that must be mentioned in any discussion of late night comedy is *Saturday Night Live* (*SNL*). Unlike the programs discussed above, *SNL* is not a talk show but a weekly variety and sketch comedy show. The show began lampooning politicians, particularly presidents and presidential candidates, during its first season in 1975. Many of the political skits since then, particularly those in election years, have been among the most memorable in the show's history.

Chevy Chase's portrayal of Gerald Ford as a bumbling, clumsy oaf was not necessarily a close imitation of the president, but it resonated with many viewers (including the former president himself[27]), as we discuss in Chapter 3. Opposite Chevy Chase's Ford in *SNL*'s parody of the 1976 presidential debates was Dan Aykroyd, playing a hip and slick Jimmy Carter.[28] In 1992, Dana Carvey played both Ross Perot and George H. W. Bush in a debate; Carvey continually repeated Bush's "stay the course" and "thousand points of light" campaign slogans.

In 2000, Phil Hartman's portrayal of Bill Clinton (gorging on fast food at a McDonald's) and Darrell Hammond's Al Gore (drawling the phrase "lock box"), along with Will Ferrell's George W. Bush impersonation, were all classics of the genre. In fact, Gore's own campaign staff showed their boss Hammond's impersonation to make him aware of his weaknesses as a speaker and debater. Last but decidedly not least, few will forget Tina Fey's uncannily accurate depiction of Sarah Palin in 2008 (partly because Fey's sketches were played again and again on YouTube following the airing of the episodes and are still preserved on YouTube and other social media sites).[29]

There have been many other late night talk shows on television, most of which aired only briefly, in the decades since the 1950s. During the 1990s alone, these included such now-forgotten programs as *The Pat Sajak Show, Keenan Ivory Wayans, The Chevy Chase Show,* and *The Magic Hour.* However, because the programs we have discussed above have provided a consistent presence on late night for a long period of time, we will restrict our attention to these.

WHY LATE NIGHT TALK AND POLITICAL HUMOR MATTER

Most people experience the political world through the mass media. To be sure, some of our political experience is direct. Casting a vote, sending a letter or e-mail to a member of Congress, and having a conversation with a local government official are all examples of direct political experiences. These experiences, in turn, help shape our understanding of politics. In addition, our interactions and conversations with friends and acquaintances influence what we know and how we think about politics. Nonetheless, much of our understanding of politics is secondary, because it is mediated primarily through mass communication channels.

For previous generations this meant that the bulk of their understanding about politics and the political world came from news organizations, via newspapers, newsmagazines, radio, or television. On television, this meant tuning in to a local news broadcast, usually at 6:00 p.m., or the nightly news on one of the three national broadcast networks—ABC, CBS, or NBC—at 6:30 p.m.

Since the 1990s, however, increasing numbers of news consumers have turned away from these more traditional forms and sources of news. In particular, far fewer people today read a daily newspaper or watch the nightly news on broadcast network television. By 2008, one study reported that only 29 percent of those surveyed claimed to watch nightly broadcast network newscasts regularly. This figure is less than half of what it was in 1993 (60 percent). The same report noted that "fewer than half [46 percent] of all Americans report reading a daily newspaper on a regular basis. . . . [This number] was as high as 71% in 1992."[30]

So, what is replacing traditional news organizations as news sources? Increasingly people of all ages, but especially younger adults, are turning to what is referred to as "soft news" for information about public affairs. While exact definitions vary among those who study this subject, all agree that soft news is a blend of entertainment and news, with a distinct emphasis on the former.[31] The main purpose of soft news is to entertain, but public affairs are at least mentioned. Soft news includes a wide variety of television programming, including daytime talk shows (e.g., *Ellen* and *The View*), newsmagazine shows (e.g., *60 Minutes* and *20/20*), and tabloid television (e.g., *Hard Copy* and *Inside Edition*). Soft news also includes late night talk and comedy shows. As Table 2.1 shows, a significant number of people tune in to these programs.

In short, fewer Americans are depending on traditional news outlets for their understanding of the political world, relying to some degree on late night talk and political comedy shows instead. What makes this shift especially important is the fact that, as research has clearly demonstrated, these types of programs have an effect on how people understand politics. Over the past decade, many political scientists and communication scholars have argued that political humor affects the political learning, knowledge, and participation of those who view it.

Political Humor's Effects on Political Learning, Knowledge, and Participation

There is evidence to suggest that political humor may have a positive effect on political learning for its viewers. Although this finding is disputed by some, it is well established that moderate levels of viewership

Table 2.1 Viewership of Late Night Talk Comedy

	PERCENTAGE WHO WATCH REGULARLY		
	Late Night Talk (Leno, Letterman, O'Brien)	The Daily Show	The Colbert Report
GENDER			
Male	13	7	9
Female	9	3	3
AGE			
18–24	12	14	26
25–34	14	7	8
35–44	10	7	5
45–54	10	5	5
55–64	10	2	4
65+	12	1	1
RACE			
White	11	5	7
Black	10	5	2
Hispanic	5	7	6
EDUCATION			
None, or grades 1–8	8	0	0
High school, incomplete	8	0	2
High school graduate	10	4	4
Technical/trade school	14	0	0
Some college	14	7	9
College graduate	13	7	8
Postgraduate	8	4	7
INCOME			
Less than $30,000	11	5	7
$30,000 to under $50,000	12	3	3
$50,000 to under $75,000	12	6	6
$75,000 to under $100,000	11	6	9
$100,000 to under $150,000	8	7	6
$150,000 or more	13	6	6

Source: A. Kohut, D. C. Doherty, M. Dimock, and S. Keeter, "Key News Audiences Now Blend Online and Traditional Sources," Pew Research Center Biennial News Consumption Survey, 2008.

of late night political humor are associated with higher levels of political knowledge. In other words, viewers of political humor seem to be better informed on matters of politics and public affairs. This is especially true for *The Daily Show* and *The Colbert Report* viewers.[32] The likely explanation is that such programs are more focused on politics and, therefore, attract viewers who are more politically interested and knowledgeable than the audiences of traditional late night talk shows.

It is also true that political humor leads viewers to believe they are better informed—regardless of whether this is actually the case.[33] Many people report learning something about politics from these shows. For example, as we noted in Chapter 1, nearly a third of all Americans said they learned about the 2012 presidential campaign and candidates from late night humor. In an earlier study, the Pew Research Center determined that this was particularly the case among younger people. During the 2008 presidential primary season, 46 percent of eighteen- to twenty-four-year-olds (compared to 20 percent of those over forty) claimed that they learned something about the candidates or the campaign from "comedy programs such as *Saturday Night Live* or *The Daily Show with Jon Stewart*." Similarly, 43 percent of eighteen- to twenty-four-year-olds (compared to 23 percent of those over forty) reported such learning from "late night TV talk shows such as *David Letterman* and *Jay Leno*."[34]

Less clear is whether viewers actually learn from political humor or whether these programs simply attract politically knowledgeable viewers. In other words, are people really learning about politics and public affairs as the result of viewing late night comedy, or are viewers already knowledgeable about politics and seeking out shows that reflect their interests? Some earlier studies on the effects of watching late night talk shows found that viewers may learn mainly about facts and ideas that are less relevant to actual issues and public policies.[35] However, most of the studies that examine this issue suggest that late night political humor engages viewers, increasing their attentiveness to particular issues.[36] In addition, when presidential candidates appear on the program, viewers' attentiveness to the candidates increases.[37]

Beyond this—given that increased attention may not necessarily lead to greater learning—there is evidence that some learning occurs as a result of viewing late night talk shows and political comedy.[38] This is true both for viewers who rely heavily on political humor for information about public affairs and for those who pay little attention to politics.[39] Such learning may result from the fact that, after seeing a candidate or hearing an issue discussed on one of these programs, people become interested and seek out more information from traditional news sources.[40] It might also occur because some political information is usually presented on these programs. Even if people tune in just to be entertained, they may still come away better informed. This process is what communication scholars refer to as the "incidental by-product" model of learning.[41]

Late night humor may also affect the likelihood that viewers will participate in politics (e.g., by voting). Some research suggests that late night political humor may actually have a negative effect on political participation.[42] However, most studies on this subject point in the opposite direction. Researchers have found positive associations between viewership and various forms of political participation,[43] including attending political events, joining a political organization,[44] discussing politics with others,[45] and paying attention to news about politics.[46] This relationship seems to be especially strong among those who are already more interested in politics.[47] The increased attention and participation may be the result of either an increased interest in politics or an increased confidence in viewers' own understanding of political complexities.[48]

However, most of these studies do not conclusively establish that viewing late night comedy causes higher levels of political participation, merely that the two are associated. It is also quite possible that (similar to the relationship between late night humor viewing and political knowledge) more politically interested individuals watch late night talk. If this is the case, we could conclude that it is the higher level of political interest—rather than viewing late night political comedy—that causes increased political participation.

The Negative Effects of Political Humor

In addition to its effects on political learning, knowledge, and participation, televised political humor has been shown to have a negative effect on the political attitudes and opinions of viewers. In part this is due to a simple and obvious fact about political humor: it is overwhelmingly negative in nature. Straightforward political humor, such as the jokes told during the monologues of hosts like Leno or Letterman, is primarily constructed around the faults, foibles, and deficiencies—whether perceived or actual—of individual politicians. Presidents are most often the focus of this type of humor, although in an election year, presidential candidates receive a good deal of attention as well.

Although researchers have various explanations for why this occurs, it is now well established that the more common forms of political humor (i.e., satire, sketch comedy, jokes delivered by stand-up comics) have a negative effect on audience perceptions and opinions about the individuals, institutions, and processes being targeted.[49] For example, if Jay Leno were to target George W. Bush in a series of jokes, some of those who saw and heard these jokes would lower their opinions of Bush, if only slightly.

In addition, comedians' constant roasting of the political world lowers our evaluations of political institutions (including the news media) and makes viewers somewhat more cynical about politics than nonviewers.[50] In short, the barrage of negativity that is found in most forms of late night political humor lowers the audience's opinions of the political world. So late night comedy may lead viewers to think more about politics while thinking less of politicians. (Of course, this is true in the aggregate. The perceptions of many individual viewers will remain unaffected.)

There are a few exceptions to this rule. One is that viewers' opinions of political candidates become more favorable when the candidates appear as guests on these programs.[51] This is likely the result of a couple of factors. First, most political humor is directed by the comedian toward others. But self-deprecating humor, in which politicians poke fun at themselves, seems to have a positive effect on audience perceptions. The benefits of self-deprecating humor are intuitively understood by many politicians (e.g., Ronald Reagan was a master at self-deprecating humor) and have been confirmed by recent research.[52]

Second, appearing on talk shows to chat with the host in an easygoing manner about personal habits, likes and dislikes, and so on seems to humanize political candidates.[53] Both of these factors can make the candidate seem more likeable.

Another seeming exception to the rule that late night political humor has a negative effect on attitudes is Comedy Central's *Colbert Report*. Stephen Colbert's portrayal of a right-wing talk show host confuses some viewers into believing that he actually is conservative.[54] In his routines, Colbert seems to be explicitly critical of liberals and the Democratic Party while supporting conservatives and Republicans.

For example, when roasting President George W. Bush at the White House Correspondents Dinner in 2006, Colbert appeared to be lavishing praise on the president with the following statement: "The greatest thing about this man is he's steady. You know where he stands. He believes the same thing Wednesday that he believed on Monday, no matter what happened Tuesday. Events can change; this man's beliefs never will."

As this comment illustrates, on the surface Colbert may seem to praise a politician, but his presentation is so absurd that most in the audience can see that he is really being critical. However, some viewers are apparently persuaded by his explicit (pro-Republican, anti-Democratic) message, rather than by the implicit (and intended) message.[55] As a result, their opinions of Republicans are raised while their opinions of Democrats are lowered—presumably contrary to Colbert's intentions.

A final note about the effects of late night comedy: while viewing political humor seems to lower opinions of its target and of the system in general, some political humor seems to raise viewers' internal political efficacy—that is, confidence in their abilities to understand politics and meaningfully participate.[56] This may reflect the fact that a viewer who "gets" the joke ends up feeling smarter, or more in the know. Whatever the cause, viewing political humor seems to increase feelings of democratic competence among part of the audience. This may counteract the cynicism associated with viewing political comedy, which by itself may reduce the likelihood that an individual will participate in politics.

CONCLUSION

Late night talk has come a long way since its beginnings over a half century ago as an entertainment genre that delivered humor while avoiding controversy. The topical focus of *The Tonight Show* made it all but inevitable that politics would be included in the nightly discussion from time to time. All the same, political references on the show, while sometimes biting, were relatively innocuous.

This began to change in the 1990s, perhaps due to the expanded volume of late night talk and other politically oriented comedy and talk shows. These shows have become increasingly important in, and to, the world of politics. Moreover, research has shown that the political humor of these late night programs affects the ways that viewers, especially younger adults, understand politics. It may increase their knowledge of politics, and it almost certainly increases their cynicism toward politics.

In the next chapter we turn to the content of these programs—the jokes themselves. Using data collected from 1992 to 2012, we focus on the highest-profile targets in American politics: sitting presidents, vice presidents, and candidates for these offices.

NOTES

1. Donald Rieck, "Late-Nite Talk Shows Were Road to White House," Center for Media and Public Affairs, December 29, 2008, http://www.cmpa.com /media_room_12_29_08.html.

2. Bernard Timberg, *Television Talk: A History of the TV Talk Show* (Austin: University of Texas Press, 2002); see also Ben Alba, *Inventing Late Night: Steve Allen and the Original Tonight Show* (Amherst, NY: Prometheus Books, 2005).

3. Timberg, *Television Talk*.

4. Paul Corkery, as quoted in Timberg, *Television Talk*, pp. 59–60.

5. Timberg, *Television Talk*.

6. Ibid.

7. Daniel Kurtzman, "About.com" (no date). http://politicalhumor.about.com /od/funnyquotes/a/johnnycarson.htm. Accessed March 11, 2013.

8. Laurence Leamer, *King of the Night: The Life of Johnny Carson* (New York: William Morrow & Co., 1989), 263.

9. Timberg, *Television Talk.*

10. Michael Kranish, "With Antiwar Role, High Visibility," *Boston.com,* last modified June 17, 2003, http://www.boston.com/globe/nation/packages/kerry/061703.shtml.

11. Timberg, *Television Talk.*

12. Ibid.

13. Ibid.

14. Elizabeth Kolbert, "The 1992 Campaign: Media," *New York Times,* last modified June 5, 1992, http://www.nytimes.com/1992/06/05/us/the-1992-campaign-media-whistle-stops-a-la-1992-arsenio-larry-and-phil.html.

15. Timberg, *Television Talk.*

16. Ibid.; Bill Carter, *The Late Shift: Letterman, Leno, and the Network Battle for the Night* (New York: Hyperion, 1994).

17. Ibid.

18. Bill Carter, *The War for Late Night: When Leno Went Early and Television Went Crazy* (New York: Viking, 2010).

19. Jody Baumgartner and Jonathan Morris, "Stoned Slackers or Super-Citizens? 'Daily Show' Viewing and Political Engagement of Young Adults," in *The Stewart/Colbert Effect: Essays on the Real Impacts of Fake News,* ed. Amarnath Amarasingam (Jefferson, NC: McFarland & Co., 2011), 63–78.

20. Jody Baumgartner and Jonathan Morris, "One 'Nation' Under Stephen? The Effects of *The Colbert Report* on American Youth," *Journal of Broadcasting and Electronic Media* 52 (2008): 622–643.

21. Michael Scherer, "The Truthiness Hurts," *Salon.com,* last modified May 1, 2006, http://www.salon.com/2006/05/01/colbert_10/.

22. Kenneth P. Vogel, "S.C. Dems Reject Colbert Candidacy," *Politico,* November 1, 2007, http://www.politico.com/news/stories/1107/6674.html.

23. Douglas Stranglin, "Colbert Seriously Jokes to Congress About Migrant Agricultural Work," *USA Today,* last modified September 24, 2010, http://content.usatoday.com/communities/ondeadline/post/2010/09/stephen-colbert-testifies-to-congress-today-on-immigration/1#.T-2u-7WAHSU.

24. Justin Sink, "Colbert Creates Shell Corporation to Lampoon Karl Rove's Groups," *The Hill,* last modified September 30, 2011, http://thehill.com/video/in-the-news/184755-colbert-creates-shell-corporation-to-lampoon-rove-money-laundering.

25. David Carr, "Comic's PAC Is More Than a Gag," *New York Times,* last modified August 21, 2011, http://www.nytimes.com/2011/08/22/business/media/stephen-colberts-pac-is-more-than-a-gag.html?.

26. Timberg, *Television Talk;* Jeffrey P. Jones, *Entertaining Politics: Satiric Television and Political Engagement* (Lanham, MD: Rowman & Littlefield, 2010).

27. James Prichard, "Ford Showed Athletic Prowess at Michigan," *Boston*

Globe, December 27, 2006, http://www.boston.com/news/education/higher /articles/2006/12/27/ford_was_among_most_athletic_presidents/.

28. Doug Hill and Jeff Weingrad, *Saturday Night: A Backstage History of Saturday Night Live* (New York: William Morrow & Co., 1989).

29. Jody Baumgartner, Jonathan Morris, and Natasha Walth, "The Fey Effect: Young Adults, Political Humor, and Perceptions of Sarah Palin in the 2008 Presidential Election Campaign," *Public Opinion Quarterly* 76 (2012): 95–104.

30. Pew Research Center, "Key News Audiences Now Blend Online and Traditional Sources," last modified August 17, 2008, http://www.people-press .org/2008/08/17/key-news-audiences-now-blend-online-and-traditional-sources.

31. Matthew Baum, *Soft News Goes to War: Public Opinion and American Foreign Policy in the New Media Age* (Princeton, NJ: Princeton University Press, 2003); Thomas Patterson, "Doing Well and Doing Good: How Soft News and Critical Journalism Are Shrinking the News Audience and Weakening Democracy—And What News Outlets Can Do About It," John F. Kennedy School of Government, Harvard University Press, http://www.hks.harvard.edu/presspol /publications/reports/soft_news_and_critical_journalism_2000.pdf.

32. Young Min Baek and Wojcieszak Magdalena, "Don't Expect Too Much! Learning from Late-Night Comedy and Knowledge Item Difficulty," *Communication Research* 36 (2009): 783–809; Paul Brewer and Xiaoxia Cao, "Candidate Appearances on Soft News Shows and Public Knowledge About Primary Campaigns," *Journal of Broadcasting and Electronic Media* 50 (2006): 18–30; Xiaoxia Cao, "Political Comedy Shows and Knowledge About Primary Campaigns: The Moderating Effects of Age and Education," *Mass Communication & Society* 11 (2008): 43–61; Christopher Cooper and Mandi Bailey, "Entertainment Media and Political Knowledge: Do People Get Any Truth out of Truthiness?" in *Homer Simpson Goes to Washington: American Politics Through Popular Culture,* ed. Joseph J. Foy (Lexington: University Press of Kentucky, 2008), 133–150; Nojin Kwak et al., "Feel Like Learning? An Analysis of Political Implications of Late Night Talk Shows in the 2004 Presidential Election," paper presented at the annual meeting of the Association for Education in Journalism and Mass Communication, Communication Theory and Methodology Division, San Antonio, TX, August 2005; Patricia Moy, Michael Xenos, and Verena Hess, "The Political Effects of Late Night Comedy and Talk Shows," in *Laughing Matters: Humor and American Politics in the Media Age,* eds. Jody C Baumgartner and Jonathan S. Morris (New York: Routledge, 2008), 295–314. However, Pfau et al. found that viewership of "television comedy (e.g., *Saturday Night Live*)" had a negative effect on a measure of "political expertise which included political knowledge." See Michael Pfau, Brian Houston, and Shane Semmler, "Presidential Election Campaigns and American Democracy: The Relationship Between Communication Use and Normative Outcomes," *American Behavioral Scientist* 49 (2006): 113–134.

33. Dannagal Young and Russell Tisinger, "Dispelling Late-Night Myths: News Consumption Among Late-Night Comedy Viewers and the Predictors of Exposure to Various Late-Night Shows," *Press/Politics* 11 (2006): 113–134.

34. Pew Research Center, "Key News Audiences Now Blend Online and Traditional Sources."

35. Barry Hollander, "Late-Night Learning: Do Entertainment Programs Increase Political Campaign Knowledge for Young Viewers?," *Journal of Broadcasting & Electronic Media* 49 (2005): 402–415; Marcus Prior, "Political Communication," *American Journal of Political Science* 20 (2003): 149–171; Marcus Prior, "News vs. Entertainment: How Increasing Media Choices Widens Gaps in Political Knowledge and Turnout," *American Journal of Political Science* 49 (2005): 577–592.

36. Michael Xenos and Amy Becker, "Moments of Zen: Effects of *The Daily Show* on Information Seeking and Political Learning," *Political Communication* 26 (2009): 317–332.

37. Michael Parkin, "Taking Late Night Comedy Seriously: How Candidate Appearances on Late Night Television Can Engage Viewers," *Political Research Quarterly* 63 (2010): 3–15.

38. Matthew Baum and Angela Jamison, "The Oprah Effect: How Soft News Helps Inattentive Citizens Vote Consistently," *Journal of Politics* 68 (2006): 946–959; Hollander, "Late-Night Learning: Do Entertainment Programs Increase Political Campaign Knowledge for Young Viewers?"; Young Mie Kim and John Vishak, "Just Laugh! You Don't Need to Remember: The Effects of Entertainment Media on Political Information Acquisition and Information Processing in Political Judgment," *Journal of Communication* 58 (2008): 338–360.

39. Baum, *Soft News Goes to War*.

40. This is referred to as the "gateway effect"; see Baum, *Soft News Goes to War*, and Parkin, "Taking Late Night Comedy Seriously."

41. Samuel Popkin, *The Reasoning Voter: Communication and Persuasion in Presidential Campaigns*, 2nd ed. (Chicago: University of Chicago Press, 1994); Baum, *Soft News Goes to War*.

42. Pfau, Houston, and Semmler, "Presidential Election Campaigns and American Democracy."

43. Patricia Moy, Michael Xenos, and Verena Hess, "Communication and Citizenship: Mapping the Political Effects of Infotainment," *Mass Communication & Society* 8 (2005): 111–131; Jody Baumgartner, "Humor on the Next Frontier: Youth, Online Political Humor, and the JibJab Effect," *Social Science Computer Review* 29 (2007): 319–338.

44. Xiaoxia Cao and Paul Brewer, "Political Comedy Shows and Public Participation in Politics," *International Journal of Public Opinion Research* 22 (2008): 90–99.

45. Dannagal Young and Russell Tisinger, "Dispelling Late-Night Myths: News Consumption Among Late-Night Comedy Viewers and the Predictors of Exposure to Various Late-Night Shows," *Press/Politics* 11 (2006): 113–134.

46. Lauren Feldman and Dannagal G. Young, "Late-Night Comedy as a Gateway to Traditional News: An Analysis of Time Trends in News Attention Among Late-Night Comedy Viewers During the 2004 Presidential Primaries," *Political Communication* 25 (2008): 401–422; Xiaoxia Cao, "Hearing It from Jon Stewart: The Impact of *The Daily Show* on Public Attentiveness to Politics," *International Journal of Public Opinion Research* 22 (2010): 22–46.

47. Baumgartner and Morris, "Stoned Slackers or Super-Citizens?"

48. Feldman and Young, "Late-Night Comedy as a Gateway to Traditional News"; Lindsay Hoffman and Tiffany Thomson, "The Effect of Television Viewing on Adolescents' Civic Participation: Political Efficacy as a Mediating Mechanism," *Journal of Broadcasting & Electronic Media* 53 (2009): 3–21.

49. See Jody C Baumgartner, "Editorial Cartoons 2.0: The Effects of Digital Political Satire on Presidential Candidate Evaluations," *Presidential Studies Quarterly* 38 (2008): 735–758; Jody Baumgartner and Jonathan Morris, "The 'Daily Show Effect': Candidate Evaluations, Efficacy, and the American Youth," *American Politics Research* 34 (2006): 341–367; Baumgartner and Morris, "The Fey Effect"; Jody Baumgartner and Jonathan Morris, " Research Note: The 2008 Presidential Primaries and Differential Effects of 'The Daily Show' and 'The Colbert Report' on Young Adults," *Midsouth Political Science Review* 12 (2011): 87–102; Jonathan Morris, "'The Daily Show' and Audience Attitude Change During the 2004 Party Conventions," *Political Behavior* 31 (2009): 79–102; and Robin Nabi, Emily Moyer-Gusé, and Sahara Byrne, "All Joking Aside: A Serious Investigation into the Persuasive Effect of Funny Social Issue Messages," *Communication Monographs* 74 (2007): 29–54. But see also Carrie A. Cihasky, "Who's Laughing Now? Late Night Comedy's Influence on Perceptions of Bush and Gore in 2000," paper prepared for presentation at the annual meeting of the Midwest Political Science Association, Chicago, April 21, 2006; and Michael Pfau, Jaeho Cho, and Kirsten Chong, "Communication Forms in U.S. Presidential Campaigns: Influences on Candidate Perceptions and the Democratic Process," *Harvard International Journal of Press/Politics* 6 (2001): 88–105.

50. Baumgartner and Morris, "The 'Daily Show Effect'"; Baumgartner, "Humor on the Next Frontier: Youth"; Jody C Baumgartner, "No Laughing Matter? Young Adults and the 'Spillover Effect' of Candidate-Centered Political Humor," *HUMOR: International Journal of Humor Research* 26 (2013): 23–43.

51. Patricia Moy, Michael Xenos, and Verena Hess, "Priming Effects of Late-Night Comedy," *International Journal of Public Opinion Research* 18 (2005): 198–210.

52. Baumgartner, "Humor on the Next Frontier."

53. Matthew Baum, "Talking the Vote: Why Presidential Candidates Hit the Talk Show Circuit," *American Journal of Political Science* 49 (2005): 213–234.

54. Heather LaMarre, Kristen Landreviller, and Michael Beam, "The Irony of Satire: Political Ideology and the Motivation to See What You Want to See in *The Colbert Report*," *International Journal of Press/Politics* 14 (2009): 212–231.

55. Baumgartner and Morris, "One 'Nation' Under Stephen?"

56. Baumgartner and Morris, "The 'Daily Show Effect.'"

Chapter 3

A Funny Thing Happened on the Way to the White House

Some presidencies have a defining moment that crystallizes their historical significance for posterity—Washington's Farewell Address, Lincoln's Gettysburg Address, Nixon's White House tapes, Clinton's White House trysts. But Gerald Ford was the first president to be defined by a pratfall. It started in 1975, when a television camera caught Ford briefly stumbling as he walked down the stairs from the presidential airplane Air Force One. The clip appeared on the national news and, as Ford later wrote in his memoirs, every time he subsequently "stumbled or bumped [his] head or fell in the snow, reporters zeroed in on that to the exclusion of almost everything else."[1]

But it wasn't TV news that cemented Ford's reputation as a stumblebum. It was late night TV comedy. Ford's stumble happened during the first season of NBC's comedy/variety show *Saturday Night Live*. Cast member Chevy Chase launched each show by taking a pratfall onstage (known as the "fall of the week") before cheerfully announcing "Live from New York, it's Saturday Night!" Chase turned Ford's falls into a running gag in which he bumped into or knocked over various unlikely objects, such as the Oval Office desk.

Ironically, the real Ford was anything but clumsy. In fact, he may have been the most athletic of all recent US presidents. He played center and linebacker for a University of Michigan football team that went undefeated and won national titles in 1932 and 1933.[2] He was also named to the 1935 Collegiate All-Star football team; after graduating he received offers from the Detroit Lions and the Green Bay Packers.[3] But the real-life All-Star athlete couldn't compete with the bumbling comic creation of *Saturday Night*'s weekly skits.

While the public perception that he was clumsy bothered Ford somewhat,[4] he was good-natured about Chase's portrayal of him as a klutz. In 1986 he reflected: "On occasion I winced. But on the other hand, Betty and I used to watch 'Saturday Night Live' and enjoyed it. Presidents are sitting ducks, and you might as well sit back and enjoy it."[5] In reality, Chase eventually became friends with the Fords. In a nice karmic touch, he even rehabbed at the Betty Ford Clinic for treatment of drug and alcohol abuse.

Gerald Ford was only the first in a long line of presidents whose image suffered from the darts thrown by late night comedians. And you can't help wonder whether he would be so forgiving in the current comic environment, when presidential punch lines pour forth every night on broadcast and cable shows and are endlessly recycled on political humor websites and YouTube videos. Presidents are still sitting ducks, but there are a lot more duck hunters out there taking potshots at them.

As political humor becomes more central to political discourse, presidents must pay attention to how their media images are shaped not only by the reporting of journalists but also by the stand-up routines of talk show hosts. In this chapter we turn to our analysis of late night jokes, focusing on the highest-profile targets in American politics: presidents, the vice presidents who serve with them, and the major party nominees for these high offices.

PRESIDENTS AS TARGETS OF LATE NIGHT HUMOR

Sitting US presidents are the most frequent target of late night comedians and talk show hosts. This should come as no surprise, on several counts. Presidents are the most powerful individuals in the country and, arguably, in the world. They are also the country's most visible individuals, as well as the focal point of our political system. Not a day goes by without major news organizations reporting on the president's activities. If a president takes a break from work, his vacation is news.

If he's out sick from work, his illness is news. As a result, even the most apolitical Americans know at least a little about who he is and what he is doing. And the first principle of topical humor is that the audience has to know enough about the topic to get the joke.

In addition to being the most closely watched and widely recognized political figures in the country, presidents are the most consequential. They may need the help of Congress to raise taxes or declare war. But presidents embody the political system, and people often personalize their grievances or suspicions about politics and government in the form of negative feelings toward them. As a result, presidents attract the lion's share of attention not only from late night comedians but from political cartoonists and satirists as well.

In fact, heads of state around the world have historically drawn heavy attention from critics who use humor to give bite to their critiques. Even under dictatorships, where making jokes about the ruler can carry a stiff penalty, people have long poked fun at their leaders in furtive whispers and samizdat literature.[6] Consider the following jokes, which came from Hitler's Germany, Stalin's USSR, and Castro's Cuba, respectively:

Hitler visits a lunatic asylum. The patients give the Hitler salute. As he passes down the line he comes across a man who isn't saluting. "Why aren't you saluting like the others?" Hitler barks. "Mein Fuhrer, I'm the nurse," comes the answer. "I'm not crazy!"[7]

Stalin reads his report to the Party Congress. Suddenly someone sneezes. "Who sneezed?" Silence. "First row! On your feet! Shoot them!" They are shot, and he asks again, "Who sneezed, Comrades?" No answer. "Second row! On your feet! Shoot them!" They are shot, too. "Well, who sneezed?" At last a sobbing cry resounds in the Congress Hall, "It was me! Me!" Stalin says, "Bless you, Comrade!"

Fidel Castro is suffering from insomnia. He goes to his doctor and complains. He says to the doctor, "I cannot sleep, no matter what I do! What should I do?" The doctor replies, "Try reading your own speeches."

Given the universal urge to make fun of the powerful, even when it is risky to do so, it is not surprising that presidents should top the target list of late night comedians. After all, they have little to lose and much to gain, in the form of attracting audiences and publicity. That said, some presidents have attracted more jokes than others over the years, and different presidents have attracted different kinds of jokes.

Out of approximately 102,000 jokes that were told by late night comics from 1992 through 2011, more than 15,000—one out of seven—were directed at sitting presidents. If anything, this figure is conservative, because many jokes targeting the White House, the administration, the First Family, presidential transitions, ex-presidents, and so on were excluded from our calculations unless they explicitly targeted a president while he was in office.

How did the comic treatments of presidents play out over the course of these two decades? Table 3.1 shows the three most frequent targets of late night comics during each year from 1992 through 2012. The percentage of jokes directed at sitting presidents during this period never fell below 7 percent (Barack Obama in 2011), and it rose as high as 33 percent (Bill Clinton in 1998).

Sitting presidents were the most frequently targeted individuals in seventeen of the twenty years we examined. The only exceptions were ex-presidents and failed presidential nominees. In 1996, Bob Dole, the Republican candidate for president, was the butt of 18 percent of all late night jokes, compared with President Bill Clinton's 14 percent. In 2001, 19 percent of the jokes were directed toward outgoing President Clinton, exceeding the 16 percent targeted at incoming President George W. Bush. Finally, in 2008, Republican presidential candidate John McCain won top honors as the target of 10 percent of late night jokes, surpassing President Bush's 9 percent.

Thus, even in the years when the president was not the most frequent target, he was the runner-up. With the exception of 2008, the proportion of jokes directed at the president in these years was close to the twenty-year average of 15 percent. Of the sixty top-three finishers (first-, second-, or third-most frequent joke targets each year for twenty years), twenty-seven—almost half—were presidents or ex-presidents. An additional seven were candidates for president, and

Table 3.1 Late Night Comics' Most Targeted Individuals (1992–2012)

	1st Most Targeted	Number (Percentage)	2nd Most Targeted	Number (Percentage)	3rd Most Targeted	Number (Percentage)
1992	George H. W. Bush	612 (16.3%)	Bill Clinton	421 (11.2%)	Dan Quayle	353 (9.4%)
1993	Bill Clinton	440 (16.3%)	Ross Perot	75 (2.8%)	Bob Packwood	67 (2.5%)
1994	Bill Clinton	552 (16.2%)	Ted Kennedy	85 (2.5%)	Tonya Harding	77 (2.3%)
1995	Bill Clinton	397 (13.3%)	O. J. Simpson	230 (7.7%)	Kato Kaelin	112 (3.8%)
1996	Bob Dole	839 (17.5%)	Bill Clinton	657 (13.7%)	O. J. Simpson	377 (7.8%)
1997	Bill Clinton	808 (27.0%)	O. J. Simpson	260 (8.7%)	Al Gore	103 (3.4%)
1998	Bill Clinton	1,717 (32.6%)	Monica Lewinsky	303 (5.8%)	Kenneth Starr	145 (2.8%)
1999	Bill Clinton	1,317 (29.1%)	Monica Lewinsky	342 (7.6%)	Hillary Clinton	292 (6.5%)
2000	George W. Bush	905 (18.3%)	Bill Clinton	803 (16.2%)	Al Gore	546 (11.0%)
2001	Bill Clinton	657 (19.2%)	George W. Bush	546 (15.9%)	Gary Condit	227 (6.6%)
2002	George W. Bush	314 (10.1%)	Bill Clinton	193 (6.2%)	Martha Stewart	93 (3.0%)
2003	George W. Bush	406 (15.2%)	Bill Clinton	241 (9.0%)	Arnold Schwarzenegger	158 (5.9%)
2004	George W. Bush	1,169 (22.3%)	John Kerry	505 (9.6%)	Bill Clinton	320 (6.1%)
2005	George W. Bush	657 (20.4%)	Michael Jackson	439 (13.6%)	Bill Clinton	116 (3.6%)
2006	George W. Bush	1,213 (18.9%)	Dick Cheney	430 (6.7%)	Bill Clinton	195 (3.0%)
2007	George W. Bush	784 (15.0%)	Paris Hilton	256 (4.9%)	Dick Cheney	192 (3.7%)
2008	John McCain	1,358 (10.2%)	George W. Bush	1,160 (8.7%)	Barack Obama	768 (5.8%)
2009	Barack Obama	936 (8.5%)	George W. Bush	466 (4.2%)	Dick Cheney	406 (3.7%)
2010	Barack Obama	728 (7.6%)	Sarah Palin	298 (3.1%)	George W. Bush	266 (2.8%)
2011	Barack Obama	270 (6.9%)	Herman Cain	180 (4.6%)	Rick Perry	132 (3.4%)
2012	Mitt Romney	1,061 (16.5%)	Barack Obama	401 (6.2%)	Newt Gingrich	368 (5.7%)

six were vice presidents or nominees for that office. There's not much room for doubt that the nation's top political office attracts the lion's share of attention from late night humorists, even when compared to long-standing comedic lightning rods of the period such as O. J. Simpson and Michael Jackson.

So what is it that makes presidents so susceptible to comic ridicule? What are all these presidential jokes about? Generally speaking, the humor tends to be nonpolitical, in the narrow sense. Most jokes that lampoon presidents (and other political figures, for that matter) focus on scandal, incompetence, personal foibles, or inadequacies. Relatively few jokes are concerned with issues of public policy, although this is more true of the hosts of broadcast network talk shows, such as Jay Leno and David Letterman,[8] than of the politically savvy satirists encamped on Comedy Central—Jon Stewart and Stephen Colbert.[9] We discuss the topical focus of jokes at length in Chapters 4 and 5. But the best way to understand why presidents have proved such juicy comic targets is to examine the late night treatment of each one in turn.

Bill Clinton (1993–2000)

In recent times no political figure has been able to excite the imagination of comedians more than William Jefferson Clinton. Dubbed "our first cartoon president," Clinton is in a class by himself in terms of the apparent ease with which late night comics made him the target of their ridicule. The comedians themselves freely give the former president his due. In 2001, after Clinton left office, Conan O'Brien recalled:

> Clinton was wildly generous to the comedic mind. . . . Comedians will soon have to build their own Clinton Presidential Library just to catalogue the thousands upon thousands of joke variations made possible by his two terms. He made our job so easy it was a challenge not to feel irrelevant.[10]

To say that Bill Clinton was targeted the most out of the four presidents included in our study would be an understatement. He was the

Figure 3.1   Percentage of Jokes Targeting President Clinton, by Year (1993–2000)

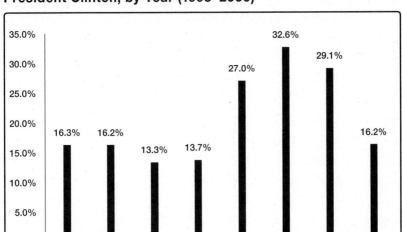

butt of over one out of every five political jokes (21 percent) told by late night comics during his two terms of office from 1993 through 2000. In 1998, against the backdrop of his impeachment by the House of Representatives, Clinton was the target of one out of every three late night jokes, a whopping 33 percent of the overall total (see Figure 3.1). That number was up from 27 percent the previous year, when the Monica Lewinsky scandal was in full bloom, and it carried over to 29 percent the following year.

In fact, Clinton proved such a popular target for comedians that they stayed on his trail even after the end of his presidency. Despite leaving office in January 2001, he outpaced incoming president George W. Bush that year to retain his number-one ranking as a joke target. That marks the only year in the course of the study in which the top spot was occupied by someone other than a president or presidential nominee. In 2002 and 2003 Clinton was the second-most-joked-about individual, and from 2004 through 2006 he ranked third. If you're counting, that makes fifteen straight years in which Bill Clinton was the gift that kept on giving to comedians, as one of the three most-joked-about political figures in America. In all, Clinton personally accounted for nearly one out of ten jokes about politics and public affairs over the entire two decades of our study.

In addition to President Clinton himself, late night comics frequently targeted people associated with him and the various scandals in which he became embroiled. These individuals include long-suffering First Lady Hillary Clinton; the president's half brother and sometimes bad boy Roger; various women associated with Clinton's sex scandals, including Monica Lewinsky, still Washington's most famous intern; Linda Tripp, who was responsible for leaking news of the Lewinsky affair; Kenneth Starr, the Independent Counsel (essentially a special prosecutor) who dug into Clinton's financial and sexual affairs; and Susan and James McDougal, who were associated with the Whitewater real-estate scandal in Arkansas, where Clinton served as governor prior to his presidency. In all, jokes lampooning these Clinton-related individuals add another 7 percent to the study's overall joke total.

What types of jokes were directed at this president? What made him such a rich target? A whopping 50 percent of jokes about President Clinton (well over three thousand) centered on various aspects of the sex scandals that surrounded him from the spring of 1992, when he was still a candidate for president, throughout his entire eight years in office. Clinton was involved in at least four separate sex-related scandals. Two of these were from his days as governor of Arkansas, although they came to public attention at different times. The first involved Gennifer Flowers, who went public about her alleged twelve-year relationship with Clinton during the 1992 primary campaign season.[11] The second was with Paula Jones, who brought a sexual harassment lawsuit against the president in 1994 for unwelcome advances that then-Governor Clinton allegedly made in 1991.[12] The third was the Lewinsky affair. The fourth (less visible) sex scandal involved allegations of sexual assault made by Kathleen Willey, a volunteer White House aide, during the Paula Jones case in 1998.[13]

The most popular joke topic—by far—during the Clinton presidency was his relationship with White House intern Monica Lewinsky. The affair, which took place between 1995 and early 1997, reportedly did not actually include sexual intercourse, although it did produce a national debate over precisely what activities qualify as "having sex." This scandal broke as the result of Lewinsky's denial under oath that she and the president had such a relationship, when she was legally deposed in connection with Paula Jones's sexual harassment lawsuit against Clinton.

At this time Lewinsky was working in the Pentagon, having been transferred out of the White House because of presidential staff concerns about her proximity to Clinton. She confided details about the alleged affair to a coworker, Linda Tripp, who secretly taped some of their phone conversations. Tripp subsequently gave these tapes to Independent Counsel Kenneth Starr, who had been conducting a long-running investigation into the Whitewater affair.

This information became public in January 1998, when Internet journalist Matt Drudge scooped more squeamish mainstream news organizations by breaking the story. But the rest of the media quickly began to make up for lost time by venturing into areas of personal relations where few "respectable" journalists had gone before. For the next year, affairs of state played second fiddle in the press to affairs of the chief of state.

In a nationally televised news conference in August, Clinton repeatedly denied any involvement with Lewinsky. He declared forcefully on camera: "I did not have sex with that woman—Miss Lewinsky." However, Clinton's denials became progressively less convincing in light of such lurid evidence as a DNA analysis of a semen-stained dress kept by Lewinsky. In December the Republican-dominated House of Representatives voted to impeach the president for lying under oath to a grand jury and for obstruction of justice. However, he was acquitted on both charges two months later by the Democrat-dominated Senate.[14]

As this brief and somewhat expurgated chronicle suggests, jokes about Clinton's affair with Lewinsky were popular for obvious reasons. First, although the Senate ultimately voted not to remove the president from office, news concerning different aspects of the affair, the president's statements about it, and the subsequent impeachment proceedings dominated media coverage throughout nearly all of 1998 and early 1999. In the process, major news organizations found themselves charting new territory that they had previously ceded to supermarket tabloids like the *National Enquirer.* Television anchors sometimes felt compelled to begin their reports with parental advisories that the latest developments in the story might not be suitable for children.

These days it may seem that sex scandals are irresistible to news organizations. They are covered in great detail, largely because audiences like to follow them.[15] After all, people weren't just reading about and watching the Clinton sex scandal, they were discussing the latest developments around watercoolers at the office and dinner tables at home (after the kids were excused). At the time, however, there was considerable conflict in newsrooms over how or even whether the more salacious aspects of this story should be covered. In fact, from Gennifer Flowers's allegations of an extramarital affair with candidate Clinton to ex-president Clinton's settlement of Paula Jones's sexual harassment lawsuit, the Clinton scandals pushed much franker discussions of sexual behavior into political discourse.

Once this juicy material became part of the news agenda, it also became fair game for comedians everywhere, including those on television. There was so much material for late night comics to work with—a surfeit of scandalous riches. These included highly explicit details about the alleged affair that were featured in the report issued by Independent Counsel Kenneth Starr in September 1998. Clinton's repeated public denials about the affair only added fuel to the fire. Box 3.1 provides a sampling of the various sex scandal jokes made about the former president.

BOX 3.1
Late Night Sex Scandal Jokes Targeting President Bill Clinton

"Scientists at the University of Rome have discovered that the average person burns six calories with a passionate kiss, a hundred calories in foreplay, and over two hundred fifty calories when they make love. Or as Bill Clinton would say, 'Give me a week, I'll take off the weight!'" —*Jay Leno*

(continues)

BOX 3.1 CONTINUED

"And in a town meeting in Rhode Island, Bill Clinton said there are 'powerful forces' threatening to bring down his administration. I think they're called 'hormones.'" —*Jay Leno*

"Do you know about Paula Jones, the woman who claimed . . . a sexual harassment suit against President Clinton? She's saying she can describe the president's genitalia. You know what I think would be more amazing? A woman from Arkansas who couldn't describe Clinton's genitalia." —*David Letterman*

"Last week President Clinton's approval rating shot up to 48 percent. Although . . . this is great news for the president . . . [aides] have cautioned him, 'Wait 'til it hits 50 percent before you start dating again.'" —*David Letterman*

"[President Clinton] was [in Los Angeles] last night . . . raising about a million dollars for his reelection campaign. . . . He took his motorcade to the House of Blues night club right over here on Sunset. . . . There's a press secretary's nightmare, huh? Bill Clinton in a limo, at midnight, with a million dollars on Sunset Boulevard!" —*Jay Leno*

"Quite a week in Washington, DC. Let's see, we got a Middle East peace agreement, we got a budget deal, we got educational funding. You know, it's amazing how much work President Clinton gets done when he's not dating anyone." —*Jay Leno*

"It seems President Clinton and Hillary have canceled their annual vacation to the Virgin Islands this year. I wonder what happened? Actually the real reason, after Clinton left last year? No more virgins." —*Jay Leno*

"You know, with Bill Clinton as president, I finally understand why they celebrate President's Day with a mattress sale. Our forefathers were able to see ahead to this day." —*Jay Leno*

"A new survey shows 5 percent of American women have had fantasies about having sex with President Clinton. Actually, for a lot of those women it's not fantasizing, it's just reminiscing." —*Jay Leno*

In addition to jokes about sex scandals, late night comedians lampooned various aspects of Clinton's personal demeanor, including his volatile temper, his eating habits, his relationship with First Lady Hillary Rodham Clinton, his having experimented with marijuana (reportedly without inhaling), as well as Whitewater and other nonsexual scandals. For example, his appetite for junk food became a running joke, as the following zingers illustrate:[16]

> Kind of exciting today is the first day [in office] for President Clinton. . . . And today he gave his first presidential order: It was two Big Macs, fries, and a large Coke. —*Jay Leno*

> Number Two on the "Top Ten Things Clinton Had to Do on His First Day" list: "Figure out jogging route that goes past McDonald's and Dunkin Donuts." —*David Letterman*

> It was reported today that fast food sales are up $10 billion since 1992. I was thinking, who says President Clinton has had no effect on the economy? —*Conan O'Brien*

By the time Clinton left office amid controversy over his last-minute pardoning or commuting of the sentences of several former supporters and associates (including his own half brother Roger), we needed a scorecard to keep track of all the scandals. But even between scandals, Clinton provided a treasure trove of material for late night comics with his personal foibles, his physical appearance, and his checkered past—just about everything except his policies, which weren't nearly as easy to make fun of. On a slow news day, Jay Leno paid him a backhanded compliment that was surely in the minds of his fellow comedians as well: "I wish Clinton would get another girlfriend. We need some jokes. Where is our president when I need him?"

George W. Bush (2001–2008)

Clinton was a tough act to follow, but George W. Bush managed to provide the late night comics with considerable material of his own

Figure 3.2   Percentage of Jokes Targeting President George W. Bush, by Year (2001–2008)

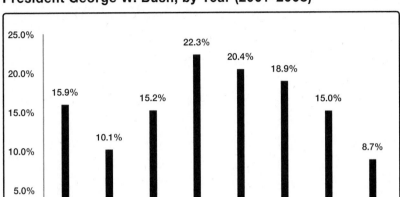

to work with. While Bush was lampooned less often than Clinton, he was the most frequently targeted politician in six of the eight years of his presidency (2002–2007), and he placed a very respectable second in 2001 and 2008 (again, see Table 3.1). Bush's joke totals peaked in 2004, the year he ran for reelection, when he was the target of 22 percent of the jokes in our study. This figure is higher than Clinton's average for his own eight years in office, although nowhere near his 33 percent peak in the year of the Lewinsky scandal. The following two years were good ones for Bush as well (or bad ones, depending on your perspective), putting him on the receiving end of 20 percent (in 2005) and 19 percent (in 2006) of late night jokes. Figure 3.2 shows the distribution of jokes targeting Bush from 2001 to 2008.

Bush's early joke totals were held down by a unique historical circumstance: the terrorist attacks on September 11, 2001, which occurred only eight months after he took office. In the immediate aftermath of the attacks, the late night talk shows went off the air for several nights. Even after they returned, the nation was too shocked and devastated to go back to one-liners as usual. For example, in his return to the airwaves on September 17, New York City–based David Letterman spoke at length about the attacks with a somber tone and not a hint of humor, plaintively asking his audience how any part of what happened "made any goddam sense."

In the longer run, the attacks produced a rally-round-the-flag effect across the country that made it seem churlish, if not unpatriotic, for comedians to make fun of the commander-in-chief of the war on terror. The effects can be seen in Bush's annual joke totals. As a presidential candidate in 2000, he was the target of 18 percent of all jokes, finishing ahead of incumbent president Bill Clinton as well as his Democratic opponent Al Gore. In 2001 as an incoming president, his share dropped to 16 percent, lower than the 18 percent aimed at Clinton, who left office in January; the difference reflects a sharp falloff in Bush jokes after September 11. This paucity of punch lines carried over into 2002, when only 10 percent of all jokes were aimed at Bush, the lowest annual total for any president to date. By 2003 things had returned to normal, with 15 percent of all jokes aimed at Bush.

What did late night comics target in their lampooning of Bush? A popular perception of Bush was that he was less than highly intelligent, or, as one analysis of the media frames that emerged in the 2000 campaign put it, an "inexperienced dolt."[17] Combined with (and partly because of) his folksy manner of speaking and his occasional problems with the English language, this caricature proved irresistible to comedians. They may have lost an easy target for fat jokes and sex jokes when Clinton stepped off the public stage, but they made up for it with a stream of jokes about the intelligence of his successor. Over 2,300 jokes, 38 percent of all Bush jokes, revolved around this single theme. Box 3.2 provides some examples of these jokes.

Another 9 percent of the jokes targeted other aspects of his personal demeanor, such as his youthful drinking habits. Only 5 percent were about the wars in Afghanistan and Iraq, which eventually became politically unpopular and hence easier to joke about. Other jokes targeted the 2000 election results (especially the controversy over the Florida recount) and the lengthy summer vacations he took at his ranch in Crawford, Texas.

All in all, while perhaps not as rich a target as Clinton, Bush proved to be a pretty fair replacement for late night comics in search

BOX 3.2

Dumb Guy? Late Night Jokes Targeting President George W. Bush

"Both candidates now are trying to lower expectations for how they'll do on the debates. For example, Kerry tried to lower expectations for himself by saying Bush has never lost a debate and that he is a formidable opponent. Then Bush lowered expectations for himself when he said, 'Hey, what does formable mean?'" —*Jay Leno*

"Democrats are saying that President Bush is refusing to take part in a town hall debate with John Kerry because Bush is worried about the questions the audience will ask him. After hearing this, the president said, 'That's ridiculous. I'm not worried about the questions, I'm worried about the answers.'" —*Conan O'Brien*

"In his press conference last night, President Bush said he could not remember a single mistake he had made in the last two years. The president's exact quote was: 'I ain't make none mistakes ever.'" —*Conan O'Brien*

"John Kerry says that foreign leaders want him to be president, but that he can't name the foreign leaders. That's all right, President Bush can't name them either." —*David Letterman*

"One critic in the *L.A. Times* said John Kerry looks like he is thinking too much. Well this is one place President Bush has him beat." —*Jay Leno*

"People are still talking about President Bush's use of a four-letter word at the G-8 Summit. It's not a big deal, President Bush using a four-letter word. Now if President Bush used a four-syllable word, that would be unbelievable." —*Jay Leno*

"At a Washington museum, a new exhibit is about to open that features a first-grade report card of President Bush's where he received straight A's. This sounds impressive, but President Bush was twenty-three at the time." —*Conan O'Brien*

of presidential humor. And, as they did with Clinton, they occasionally expressed their gratitude. For example, David Letterman ad-libbed during the course of one monologue: "The good news is the White House is now giving George W. Bush intelligence briefings. . . . Some of these jokes actually write themselves."

Barack Obama (2009–2011)

Barack Obama took office on January 20, 2009, and our analysis covers the first three years of his term through the end of 2011. Although he was the most frequently targeted politician in each of these three years, the percentage of jokes told about him was significantly lower than the percentage told about either Clinton or Bush. Overall, Obama was targeted in only 8 percent of the jokes from 2009 through 2011, little more than a third as many as Clinton. Figure 3.3 provides the breakdown by year.

While most of the jokes about Obama (11 percent) focus on aspects of his personal demeanor, none of these traits stand out as being low-hanging fruit for comedians to pluck. In fact, it is exceedingly difficult to point out any particular theme as being noteworthy. There were, for example, jokes early in his presidency about his cool, calm,

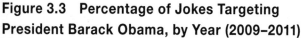

Figure 3.3   Percentage of Jokes Targeting President Barack Obama, by Year (2009–2011)

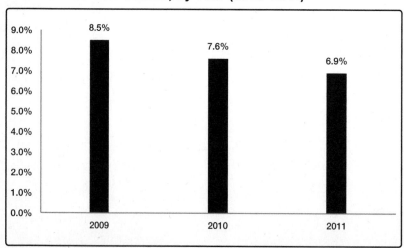

and collected persona. Other jokes poked fun at his "rock star" popularity. Only 3 percent targeted his personal appearance, in sharp contrast to both his predecessor Bill Clinton and his primary campaign opponent Hillary Clinton.

Quite simply, Obama has never developed a clear and consistent comic persona. For that matter, some of the jokes directed his way were really backhanded slaps at his critics. As we discuss below, this treatment of Obama as president follows the pattern established in 2008, when as a dark-horse candidate Obama skyrocketed to victory. One difference is that, as president, Obama began to attract zingers that skewered his policies, including his failure to return the nation to economic prosperity. The economy and health care reform each accounted for 9 percent of the jokes about President Obama. Here are some examples of these and other themes:

> I don't like this new Obama who hunts Muslim extremists. I like the old Obama who *was* a Muslim extremist. —*Stephen Colbert*

> President Obama, I guess, is starting to confess to some of his anxieties. In a recent interview, President Obama said, "I miss being anonymous." He said, "In the old days, I could blend in with all the other Hawaiian Barack Hussein Obamas." —*Conan O'Brien*

> President Obama laid out his plan to reduce the $14 trillion national debt. Unfortunately for Sasha and Malia [the president's daughters], it involves selling a lot of Girl Scout cookies. —*Jimmy Kimmel*

> I tell you, the economy is in bad shape. In fact, the economy is so bad, President Barack Obama's new slogan is "Spare Change You Can Believe In." —*Jay Leno*

> Barack Obama said yesterday that the economy was "going to get worse before it gets better." See, that's when you know the campaign is really over. Remember before the election? "The audacity of hope!" "Yes, we can!" "A change we can believe in!" Now it's, "We're all screwed." —*Jay Leno*

Figure 3.4   Percentage of Jokes Directed at Presidents, by President and Year in Office (1993–2011)

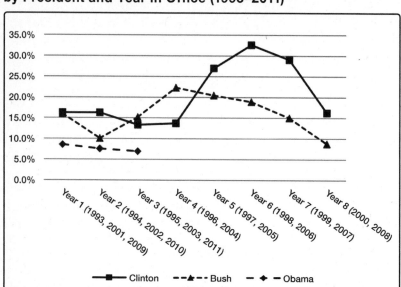

Despite the gradual accumulation of jokes like these, we cannot entirely preclude the possibility that the late night talk show hosts simply feel more positively toward President Obama than they did toward his predecessors. (See Figure 3.4 for the percentages of jokes directed at each president from 1993 to 2011.) A comment by David Letterman illustrates the plight of a comedian who finds himself in the unfortunate position of admiring a man he's supposed to be zapping: "How about President Barack Obama's first prime-time press conference last night? He was cogent, eloquent, and in complete command of the issues. I'm thinking to myself, what the hell am I supposed to do with that?"

VICE PRESIDENTS AS TARGETS OF LATE NIGHT HUMOR

If humorists love to poke fun at presidents because they are so powerful and visible, vice presidents offer tempting targets for the opposite reason—the second-highest office in the land offers its occupants no power (except that delegated by their boss) and little publicity. But it's not just comedians who have seen the vice presidency as a humorous institution, which exists mainly to provide a replacement for a president who dies or is incapacitated. Political observers, too, have been quick to ridicule both vice presidents and the office of the vice presidency. Even those who held the position often regarded it as a joke. John Adams, our first vice president, called it "the most insignificant office that ever the invention of man contrived or his imagination conceived." Harry Truman once observed: "Look at all the vice presidents in history. Where are they? They were about as useful as a cow's fifth teat." Probably the most famous put-down came from John Nance Garner, Truman's predecessor as Roosevelt's vice president, who compared the office unfavorably to "a warm bucket of spit."

The title of a book on the vice presidency sums it up nicely: *Bland Ambition: From Adams to Quayle—The Cranks, Criminals, Tax Cheats, and Golfers Who Made It to Vice President.*[18] To be fair, vice presidents often live up to this poor reputation. Richard Nixon's first vice president, Spiro Agnew, resigned in disgrace while facing federal bribery charges. And Dan Quayle, George H. W. Bush's vice president, was known for his tendency to make misstatements and gaffes. Many more examples can be found going back to the nineteenth century.[19]

With this kind of comic material available, it may seem ironic that vice presidents are targeted by comedians far less frequently than are presidents—or, for that matter, many other public figures. For a joke to be funny, however, the audience has to have some basic knowledge or understanding of the subject matter. Yet, in one recent test, 29 percent of Americans could not even name the vice president of the United States.[20] Woody Allen once said that 90 percent of life is just showing up. The problem for vice presidents is that they show up with nothing to do, so nobody notices them. Truman's vice president, Alben Barkley, was fond of telling a story about a mother who had two sons—one went to sea and the other became vice president, and neither was ever heard from again.

The numbers from our study bear this out. From 1993 through 2000, an average of only 3 percent of the late night jokes we analyzed were directed toward Vice President Al Gore. However, in 2000 Gore ran for president, and most of the jokes made about him that year were

Figure 3.5   Percentage of Jokes Directed at Vice Presidents, by Vice President and Year in Office (1993–2011)

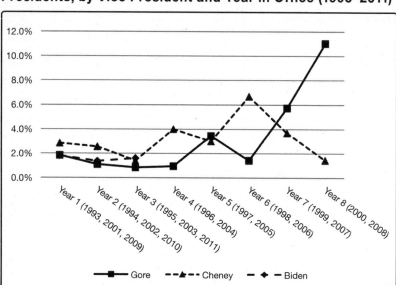

about presidential candidate—rather than Vice President—Gore. If we eliminate the year 2000 from the calculation, his average goes down to only 2 percent. Similarly, George W. Bush's vice president, Dick Cheney, was targeted by 3 percent of the jokes told from 2001 through 2008, despite charges by his political opponents that he wielded great power behind the scenes. Joe Biden, Barack Obama's vice president, is the least targeted of the three vice presidents in our sample, having been the butt of only 1.6 percent of late night jokes from 2009 through 2011—only about half the proportion aimed at Gore and Cheney. Figure 3.5 shows the percentage of jokes directed at each, by year in office.

Almost half of the jokes about Al Gore focused on either his personal demeanor (allegedly stiff, boring, and overbearing) or his family (his wife "Tipper" crusaded against vulgar language in popular music). However, nothing about Gore made for particularly rich comedic targets. Approximately 40 percent of the jokes about Joe Biden centered on his personal demeanor as well, particularly his weakness for verbal gaffes—eyebrow-raising or head-scratching comments that left listeners wondering "Did he really say that?"

One of the more memorable gaffes from the 2008 presidential campaign occurred when Biden told Katie Couric of *CBS Nightly News* that "when the stock market crashed, Franklin D. Roosevelt got on the television and didn't just talk about the, you know, the princes of greed. He said, 'Look, here's what happened.'" Apparently Biden forgot that Roosevelt was not yet president when the stock market crashed, and that television wasn't widely available until years after his death. (Roosevelt's "fireside chats" with the American public were broadcast over the radio.) Similarly, during a campaign stop in Columbia, Missouri, Biden hailed state senator Chuck Graham, who was in a wheelchair, with the following: "Stand up, Chuck, let 'em see ya."

The gaffes continued after the campaign and into his vice presidency. When talking about the swine flu on the *Today Show* in April 2009, Biden said: "I wouldn't go anywhere in confined places now. . . . When one person sneezes it goes all the way through the aircraft. That's me. I would not be, at this point, if they had another way of transportation, suggesting they ride the subway." And as Biden and Barack Obama were preparing to sign the president's signature health care reform bill in March 2010, Biden turned to Obama and, unaware that their microphone was on, told him, "This is a big f***ing deal!"

Apart from Biden's tendency to put his foot in his mouth, the easiest vice presidential late night joke target during the past twenty years was Dick Cheney's "hunting incident." In February 2006, Cheney was quail hunting with friends on a ranch in Texas. While one friend, seventy-eight-year-old Harry Whittington, was retrieving a bird he had downed, Cheney accidentally shot him. Bird shot hit Whittington in the face, neck, and upper chest. He suffered a minor heart attack, and was briefly hospitalized, but made a complete recovery. Nonetheless, this was considerably more serious than even the most cringe-worthy of Biden's verbal gaffes. Commentators struggled in vain to recall another vice president who had actually shot someone since Jefferson's vice president, Aaron Burr, dueled with Alexander Hamilton in 1804.

Making the story even better (i.e., more scandalous) was the fact that Cheney did not release any information about the incident to the press until the next day, and even then, only to a local reporter. This made it appear as if he had something to hide.[21] Cheney's demonstration of poor marksmanship accounts for the spike in the number of jokes told about him in 2006 (as seen in Figure 3.5) and almost one-quarter of all the Cheney jokes in our study. The following are typical examples:

> See, this is why Republicans have to commit white-collar crimes to steal money. They're just not good with guns, they don't know how to handle them. —*Jay Leno*

> America remaining obsessed, fascinated, appalled, by what is being called "Dick Cheney Shot a Guy in the Face–Gate." —*Jon Stewart*

> The real question now is, is this a one-time thing, or will the vice president try to kill again? —*David Letterman*

> Vice President Dick Cheney accidentally shot a man during a quail hunt, making seventy-eight-year-old Harry Whittington the first person shot by a sitting veep since Alexander Hamilton. Hamilton, of course, [was] shot in a duel with Aaron Burr over issues of honor, integrity and political maneuvering. Whittington? Mistaken for a bird. —*Jon Stewart*

> Good news, ladies and gentlemen, we have finally located weapons of mass destruction: It's Dick Cheney. —*David Letterman*

> You know what they say, if Dick Cheney comes out of his hole and shoots an old man in the face, six more weeks of winter. —*Jimmy Kimmel*

PRESIDENTIAL CANDIDATES AS TARGETS OF LATE NIGHT HUMOR

Every four years the media spotlight on the presidency widens to include those who aspire to take over the job in the next election. In some cases this quadrennial contest provides comedians with fresh new targets. In others it just means that the sitting president does double duty as a candidate to succeed himself. At a minimum, there is at least one fresh face representing a major party's choice for president, and the daily routine of campaigning inevitably offers a natural focus for late night humorists, just as it does for political journalists.

Our analysis of this material differs from the rest of this book in one respect: our study period formally ended in 2011. However, because the following year was an election year, we tracked the targets (but not the topics) of jokes in 2012, in order to add a sixth data point to our analysis of campaign humor. So for this section only, we can view the joke parade across nearly a quarter century, from 1992 through 2012. As we shall see, the most recent results mainly reinforced our findings from earlier elections.

In fact, although lampooning presidential candidates on late night talk shows has a rich history, many viewers (and voters) have now come to expect the hosts of these shows to provide comic relief from what are increasingly long campaign seasons. As a result, presidential and vice presidential candidates account for a more substantial chunk of jokes on late night talk shows than presidents in election years.

Collectively, the Republican and Democratic presidential and vice presidential nominees were the unwelcome recipients of nearly one out of every three jokes (32 percent) during the six elections from 1988 to 2012. There wasn't much variation from one election to the next until 2008, which saw a downturn in candidate humor that was repeated in 2012 for reasons we discuss below. By election year, the breakdown is as follows:

- 1992: 38 percent
- 1996: 33 percent
- 2000: 34 percent
- 2004: 38 percent
- 2008: 22 percent
- 2012: 25 percent

The six election years in our study offered a variety of matchups. Four elections featured a sitting president up for reelection, split evenly between the two parties—Republicans George H. W. Bush in 1992 and George W. Bush in 2004, and Democrats Bill Clinton in 1996 and Barack Obama in 2012. A fifth included a vice president in the previous administration moving up to the head of the ticket (Gore in 2004). And 2008 offered the public and the comedians a choice between two nonincumbents—old Washington hand John McCain and newcomer Barack Obama.

Even more intriguing than how much attention the candidates received collectively is the question of which candidates were most often in the comics' crosshairs. Since sitting presidents are so central to political humor in nonelection years, you might expect them to attract the lion's share of jokes in election years as well. Conversely, since their opponents are new faces (or familiar ones raised to new prominence), you might expect comedians to take advantage of new targets. In fact, neither of these scenarios played out on the campaign trail. Instead, what mattered most was a candidate's political party.

Table 3.2 lists the Republican and Democratic presidential and vice presidential candidates for each election year during this period, the percentage of total jokes told about each during that year, and the percentage of jokes told about each party's presidential and vice presidential candidates combined. The table shows that Republican candidates were consistently targeted with greater frequency than Democrats. Although the evidence comes from a relatively small number of election cycles, the pattern holds true not only for all six elections but also for ten out of the twelve pairings of presidential and vice presidential candidates. Every GOP presidential candidate was joked about more often than his Democratic counterpart. The same was true for four of the six vice presidential candidates. The exceptions were 1996, when Jack Kemp and Al Gore each garnered less than 1 percent of all jokes, and 2012, when sitting Vice President Joe Biden's 1.8 percent doubled the 0.9 percent of jokes about relative unknown Paul Ryan.

Across all six elections, weighted equally, Republican presidential candidates averaged 16.9 percent of all jokes, compared to 9.6 percent

Table 3.2 Percentage of Late Night Jokes Targeting Presidential and Vice Presidential Candidates During Election Years (1992–2012)

	Pres. Candidate	Percentage of Jokes	VP Candidate	Percentage of Jokes	Pres. & VP Candidates (Total Percentage of Jokes)
1992 Republicans	George H. W. Bush	16.3%	Dan Quayle	9.4%	25.8%
1992 Democrats	Bill Clinton	11.2	Al Gore	1.3	12.6
1996 Republicans	Bob Dole	17.5	Jack Kemp	0.9	18.4
1996 Democrats	Bill Clinton	13.7	Al Gore	0.9	14.6
2000 Republicans	George W. Bush	18.3	Dick Cheney	3.1	21.4
2000 Democrats	Al Gore	11.0	Joe Lieberman	1.1	12.1
2004 Republicans	George W. Bush	22.3	Dick Cheney	4.0	26.3
2004 Democrats	John Kerry	9.6	John Edwards	1.9	11.6
2008 Republicans	John McCain	10.2	Sarah Palin	5.4	15.6
2008 Democrats	Barack Obama	5.8	Joe Biden	0.8	6.6
2012 Republicans	Mitt Romney	16.5	Paul Ryan	0.9	17.4
2012 Democrats	Barack Obama	6.2	Joe Biden	1.8	8.0

for their Democratic opponents. Among vice presidential candidates, Republicans averaged 4 percent of all jokes compared to 1.3 percent for Democrats. Those figures sum to an average of 20.9 percent of all jokes directed at Republican tickets in election years compared to 10.9 percent directed at Democratic tickets, a margin of almost 2 to 1. In fact, jokes about Republican tickets more than doubled the jokes about Democratic tickets in four of the six elections, including the past three.

The surprising consistency of late night partisan preferences belies the diversity of joke targets and topics in these six elections. This becomes clear from a brief look at each election cycle from 1992 through 2012, highlighting major themes that emerged during the late night comedic "coverage" of each election.

1992: Bill Clinton (Democrat) vs. George H. W. Bush (Republican)

The 1992 election saw incumbent Republican President George H. W. Bush facing Democratic challenger Bill Clinton. Bush had enjoyed extremely high approval ratings throughout the spring and early summer of 1991 as a result of successfully prosecuting the first Persian Gulf War. This popularity scared off some prominent potential opponents and limited the field of Democratic challengers.

Arkansas Governor Bill Clinton emerged as an early front-runner who needed to overcome the fact that he was relatively unknown in national politics. However, his past quickly became all too well-known, as he had to combat several scandalous allegations—that he was a "draft dodger" who avoided military service during the Vietnam War, that he had smoked marijuana as a college student in England, and that, while governor of Arkansas, he had an affair with a woman named Gennifer Flowers. (As noted earlier, this was the first of many allegations of sexual impropriety that dogged him throughout his presidency.) Bill and Hillary Clinton rebutted the Gennifer Flowers story in a joint appearance on *60 Minutes*. He also broke new ground by taking his campaign into the entertainment world, appearing on popular talk shows such as those hosted by Phil Donahue and Arsenio Hall, where he played the saxophone.

Of course, all this was grist for the late night humor mill. Although Clinton lost the first four state nomination contests, he placed second in New Hampshire after being declared politically dead by commentators, and he gave his campaign renewed life by touting himself as the "comeback kid." He eventually secured a hard-fought nomination and selected Tennessee Senator Al Gore, another southern moderate, as his vice presidential running mate.

Despite his success in foreign policy, President Bush faced several challenges in his reelection bid. In addition to facing Clinton, who had established himself as a charismatic politician and skilled campaigner, these included an economy that was in recession (and was widely perceived as being even worse than it actually was); a broken pledge made at the 1988 Republican convention, where he famously promised "Read my lips: no new taxes"; a strong challenge for the nomination from conservative gadfly Pat Buchanan; and an independent candidacy from Texas billionaire H. Ross Perot, who at one point led both major party candidates in the polls and eventually garnered nearly one out of every five votes (19 percent) cast in the general election.

Although the Republican ticket lost at the polls in November, they dominated the 1992 comedy campaign, with twice as many late night jokes (26 percent) as the victorious Democrats (13 percent). Considering the wealth of material offered by Clinton's scandalous past and outsized personality, and the novelty of the Democratic ticket compared to the current office-holders, it seems remarkable that Bush outpaced Clinton in the joke race by 16 percent to 11 percent. One possible explanation is that the incumbent Bush was in the spotlight throughout the entire year while Clinton was initially one of several Democratic contestants during a lengthy primary season. And presidents, as noted above, regularly dominate the late night joke totals (as would President Clinton in 1993, 1994, and 1995).

The GOP's lopsided margin in the joke totals also owed something to the fact that late night comics still had Vice President Dan Quayle to kick around. Since his introduction as the vice presidential candidate in 1988, Quayle had been painted by critics and comics alike as an intellectual lightweight. His reputation was saddled with a string of misstatements throughout his term of office. For example, in a speech to the United Negro College Fund, he mangled the group's slogan, "A mind is a terrible thing to waste," saying instead, "What a waste it is to lose one's mind or not to have a mind is being very wasteful. How true that is."

As if this weren't enough, Quayle gave joke writers everywhere an unexpected gift in June 1992. During a spelling bee at an elementary school in New Jersey, Quayle incorrectly corrected a student's spelling of the word *potato* by suggesting that the student add an *e* to the end of the word. While Quayle claimed he was simply reading from the materials that the school had given him, the story fit existing perceptions of him as stupid.[22] Partly as a result of his newfound reputation as "Mr. Potatoe Head," nearly one out of ten political jokes told during 1992 were aimed at Quayle, with many focusing on his inadequacies as a speller or a thinker. For example:

> Vice President Quayle today unveiled his new literacy program. It's called "Just Spell No." —*Jay Leno*

> Gore could spell trouble for a lot of Republicans, which puts him one up on Dan Quayle, who can't spell nothin'. —*Arsenio Hall*

> Reporters asked Dan Quayle what would be the solution to global warming and he replied, "central air conditioning." —*David Letterman*

> President Bush [then in Europe] was greeted by people shouting "Long live Bush." So, apparently the Europeans know all about Dan Quayle, too. —*Jay Leno*

> If Dan Quayle were a woman, he'd be pointing at dinette sets on a game show. —*Johnny Carson*

It is little wonder that Quayle's comic value far outpaced that of the mostly ignored Al Gore, who was targeted in only 1 percent of all jokes. Jay Leno alluded to the vice president's value to comedians everywhere, as well as to their opinion of him, with an unusually partisan barb: "People have said that every comedian's dream is to poke fun at Vice President Dan Quayle. I think it's every comedian's dream to poke fun at ex-vice president Dan Quayle."

1996: Bill Clinton (Democrat) vs. Bob Dole (Republican)

In 1996, incumbent Bill Clinton was running for reelection against former Senate Majority Leader Bob Dole. By March, Dole had effectively won the Republican nomination after a relatively tame fight. At the Republican National Convention that summer he selected Jack Kemp, a former professional football player and conservative member of the House of Representatives, as his running mate.[23]

In comedy as in politics, 1992 proved a tough act to follow. For most of the year Dole trailed Clinton in the polls. By the traditional Labor Day kickoff of the general election campaign, Clinton held a commanding lead. Many of the jokes throughout the campaign reflected this, focusing on how far behind Dole was in the polls, how hopeless his campaign was, and so on. But, as is typically the case in an election cycle, a dominant frame emerged that helped shape perceptions of each candidate.[24] Clinton's image as a philanderer and a man with big appetites had already been well established. Dole didn't offer much help in this regard, with his dignified and sometimes dour demeanor and an apparently happy marriage to Elizabeth Dole, a polished political wife and future senator in her own right.

Nonetheless, the comic script eventually coalesced around Dole's alleged grumpiness and his undeniable age. If the most memorable theme of the 1992 comedy campaign was "Mr. Potatoe Head," the main theme of 1996 was grumpy old Bob Dole. At the age of seventy-three, Dole was the oldest first-time presidential candidate in history (Ronald Reagan was a few months older when he ran for reelection in 1984). Nearly two out of five late night jokes (39 percent) about Dole focused on his age, while another 12 percent involved the idea that he came off as grumpy or grouchy at times. These two characteristics accounted for a majority of all jokes about Dole, as the following examples illustrate:

Over the weekend Senator Bob Dole was in town. People thought he was here campaigning. He was not campaigning. . . . Turns out Disneyland pays him to come here once a year to give scowling lessons to Grumpy. —*Jay Leno*

Bob Dole admitted that he uses brown tint in his hair. . . . He said it's like a Grecian formula kind of thing. Not the product Grecian Formula you buy in the store. He actually got his from an ancient Grecian. —*Jay Leno*

2000: George W. Bush (Republican) vs. Al Gore (Democrat)

The 2000 election pitted Vice President Al Gore against George W. Bush, the governor of Texas and son of former President George H. W. Bush. Although he faced an early challenge from Senator John Mc-Cain, Bush won the Republican nomination handily. That summer he announced his selection of Dick Cheney as his vice presidential running mate. Cheney had previously served as a congressman from Wyoming, as George H. W. Bush's secretary of defense, and as Gerald Ford's chief of staff. In spite of the fact that only two sitting vice presidents in American history had ever won election to the presidency (Martin Van Buren in 1836 and George H. W. Bush in 1988), Gore was thought to have a very good chance of victory. After all, he had been an important part of the Clinton administration, which had presided over eight years of peace and prosperity.[25]

In 2000, the dominant frame defining George W. Bush was that he was intellectually challenged.[26] As with virtually all frames that emerge to define a politician, there was some basis for the emergence of this theme. In particular, Bush was known for making frequent misstatements and mispronouncing words. On the other hand, Bush—a graduate of both Yale and Harvard Business School and an accomplished politician—was no dummy, and he was shrewd enough to allow his political opponents to underestimate his abilities.

Al Gore, on the other hand, was seen as having a dull personality and condescending manner and as someone who took license with the

facts when it was in his interest to do so. In fact, Gore was not the natural politician that Bill Clinton was, and he often seemed ill at ease on
the campaign trail. Moreover, some of his claims and anecdotes during
the campaign were arguably dubious or self-serving enough that they
allowed Republicans to paint him as a serial exaggerator. For example,
in an interview in 1999, Gore claimed that while in Congress he "took
the initiative in creating the Internet." His political opponents used this
statement to suggest that Gore claimed to have "invented" the Internet.
Late night comics used both of these tropes in lampooning Gore during
the campaign. A full 50 percent of the jokes targeting Gore focused on
his boring, stiff personality, while another 5 percent took aim at his
alleged exaggerations, as you can see from the following examples:

> You think if you get elected, Gore will try to take credit for it? —*Jay
> Leno to George W. Bush*

> Al Gore is very excited for round number two of the debates. He
> says . . . he's prepared five brand-new made-up stories. —*David
> Letterman*

> A man in Florida made history this week by staying awake during
> his own open-heart surgery. Did you see this on the news, this guy?
> Was awake during his own open-heart surgery. Tonight, he broke
> his own record when he stayed awake during Al Gore's acceptance
> speech. —*Jay Leno*

> Al Gore took this week off. I'm trying to imagine Al Gore on a holi-
> day. How boring would those vacation slides be? "Here I am next to
> a tree. I'm the one on the left." —*Jay Leno*

> Tonight is the second presidential debate between Al Gore and
> George W. Bush. And yesterday . . . Gore said that this time he
> will try not to be long-winded and condescending. . . . Then [he]
> spent the next forty-five minutes explaining what "condescending"
> means. —*Conan O'Brien*

The Republican convention so far has been dull, very, very dull. It's so dull in fact, tonight, Al Gore is speaking. —*David Letterman*

The folks who make Sudafed [recently] introduced a brand-new non-drowsy Al Gore. —*David Letterman*

Al Gore says . . . if he's elected to president, he will put a 24-hour television camera inside the oval office. And you thought this show was dull. —*David Letterman*

2004: George W. Bush (Republican) vs. John Kerry (Democrat)

The presidential election of 2004 featured the incumbent George W. Bush against Democrat John Kerry. A senator from Massachusetts, Kerry fought off several challengers to win the Democratic nomination. His main threat was a freshman senator from North Carolina, John Edwards, who eventually agreed to be Kerry's running mate. (Earlier in the campaign, Edwards gained notoriety by announcing his own presidential candidacy on *The Daily Show*. This prompted Jon Stewart to remind him acidly that he was on a *fake* news show.)

The fall campaign revolved around a number of issues, but national security dominated. The wounds to the American psyche were still fresh from the terrorist attacks of September 11, 2001, and the United States had an active military presence in both Afghanistan and Iraq. The same focus on national security had helped the Republicans (who typically benefit when security and defense are the dominant issues) win control of both houses of Congress in 2002.[27] Some of the tropes or themes that dominated in campaign ads and news coverage concerned Bush's decision to go to war with Iraq. However, most of the late night jokes simply continued in the vein of his being an unqualified country bumpkin who stumbled his way through the presidency.

By contrast, three separate themes emerged from the comedy campaign against Kerry. First, he was perceived as being somewhat boring on the campaign trail. Second, he was criticized for shifting his positions on policy issues. Members of Congress are frequently forced to take nuanced positions on complex issues and vote multiple times on different versions of various bills. But Kerry suffered from his unfortunate phrasing in explaining his position on a military appropriations bill by saying, "I actually did vote for the $87 billion [appropriation] before I voted against it." His opponents rephrased this more succinctly as "I voted for the bill before I voted against it." Finally, Kerry was labeled as a gold digger of sorts, inasmuch as his former and current wives—Julia Thorne and Teresa Heinz, respectively—were both very wealthy. The former Mrs. Heinz was heir to a portion of the Heinz ketchup fortune. Spouses are bound by federal limitations on political contributions just like everyone else. However, Kerry's affluent lifestyle helped Republican efforts to portray him as a limousine liberal.

Nearly one-third (32 percent) of all Kerry jokes were about his personal demeanor, and many of these centered on the idea that he was a boring candidate. Another 12 percent targeted the fact that he seemed to flip-flop on policy issues, and 11 percent concerned his personal and marital finances. Here are some examples of the jokes that late night comedians made at Kerry's expense:

Kerry scored many points with voters and pundits by finally putting to rest criticism that he's a flip-flopper. Kerry said, "I have one position on Iraq: I'm forgainst it." —*Amy Poehler,* Saturday Night Live's *"Weekend Update"*

Kerry was here in Los Angeles. He was courting the Spanish vote by speaking Spanish. And he showed people he could be boring in two languages. —*Jay Leno*

We make jokes about it but the truth is this presidential election really offers us a choice of two well-informed opposing positions on every issue. OK, they both belong to John Kerry, but they're still there. —*Jay Leno*

In his big victory speech last night, Senator Kerry said that he wanted to defeat George Bush and the "economy of privilege." Then he hugged his wife, Teresa, heir to the multimillion-dollar Heinz food fortune. —*Jay Leno*

Shrek 2 made over $120 million during its first week. In a related story, John Kerry asked Shrek to marry him. —*Conan O'Brien*

2008: Barack Obama (Democrat) vs. John McCain (Republican)

By 2008 the country was ready for change, a sentiment echoed by the Democratic candidate's campaign slogan. President Bush's job-approval ratings were at near-record lows. There was widespread public disapproval of the continuing military presence in Iraq, as well as uncertainty about how and when the military effort in Afghanistan would end. Then, in the middle of the fall election campaign, the near-collapse of several leading financial institutions presaged the worst economic downturn the country had seen since the Great Depression.[28]

The battle for the Democratic nomination saw the field quickly winnowed to two candidacies with historic dimensions: first-term Illinois Senator Barack Obama and New York Senator (and former First Lady) Hillary Clinton. For the first time in either major party's history, a presidential nomination would go to either a female or a black candidate. After a battle that was fought nearly to the end of the nomination season, Obama prevailed to become the nominee. His selection of veteran Delaware Senator Joe Biden was intended to bring experience, particularly in foreign policy, to the ticket.[29]

On the Republican side, Senator John McCain from Arizona won the nomination in relatively easy fashion. His vice presidential selection, announced the day after the Democratic National Convention ended, was Alaska Governor Sarah Palin. Although Palin was relatively unknown at the time, two things became clear in short order. First, her selection was strategically sound, because it excited the social conservative base of the party, which was still lukewarm toward the more moderate McCain. Second, Palin was vulnerable to criticism that she was unprepared for the vice presidency.[30]

The joke parade that fall marched in a brand-new direction. For the first and only time during our study, one of the major party nominees (and the eventual winner, to boot) failed to finish either first or second in the race to lead the late night monologues. Republican nominee John McCain led the pack with 10 percent of all jokes, followed by outgoing president George Bush with 9 percent. Barack Obama finished a distant third with only 6 percent of all jokes.

Nearly as noteworthy as Obama's low total was the strong fourth-place finish of GOP vice presidential nominee Sarah Palin. She attracted more than 5 percent of all jokes measured over the entire calendar year, despite the fact that she first stepped onto the public stage in late August, when she was McCain's surprise choice as his running mate. In short, Palin attracted nearly as many jokes in four months as Obama did throughout the entire year.

By contrast, Obama's running mate Joe Biden attracted the fewest jokes of any vice presidential candidate in our study—fewer than 1 percent of the total. The absence of jokes about Biden belies his longtime reputation for verbal gaffes, which continued during the campaign, as we discussed earlier. At one point an exasperated Jon Stewart commented, "Senator Biden, there is no law that says that the things that are bouncing around in your skull have to come out through your pie hole." But this callout was the exception, as Biden mostly got a pass from the comedians during the campaign.

The combination of a GOP ticket featuring two heavily-joked-about candidates and a Democratic ticket that was the reverse produced the greatest partisan difference in jokes that we encountered. During the period from the start of the party conventions in late August until election day in early November, McCain more than doubled Obama's joke total, as did Sarah Palin. In fact, Palin's joke total during this period nearly equaled that of McCain. Together they attracted well over three times as many jibes as did their Democratic opponents (32 percent vs. 9 percent of all jokes, respectively).

The paucity of Obama jokes could be attributed to the lack of any central comic theme related to him. Unlike the other presidential candidates in our study, the comedians never settled on any aspect of his personality, lifestyle, background, or physical appearance as a reliable source of humor. There may have been some reluctance by white comedians to make fun of the first black major-party presidential nominee, for fear of seeming racist. But it is also true that Obama's laid-back personality and the absence of scandalous material from his past involving sex, drugs, and so on limited the available comic possibilities. (It was not until 2012 that a biographer documented his heavy marijuana use as a teenager. So Obama was spared a repetition of the many jokes in 1992 about Bill Clinton's admission that he once smoked marijuana but didn't inhale.)

To a surprising degree, in fact, jokes that were nominally about Obama were also aimed at his perceptions by others. This was true of some of the more extreme charges by opponents. Consider, for example, Stephen Colbert's criticism of Obama's flip-flopping on his willingness to accept public funding for his campaign: "Obama rejects public financing—so he's not only a secret Muslim, he's a secret hypocrite." Of course, this kind of joke was a good fit with Colbert's comic persona of a blowhard conservative talk show host, whose pompous pronouncements were actually intended as parodies of the kind of statements made by Bill O'Reilly, Rush Limbaugh, and other conservative talk show hosts.

More frequent were jokes about Obama's being the object of extreme adulation by his supporters or the center of a cult of personality. For example, in his "fake news" report on Obama's trip to Israel in July 2008, Jon Stewart said that he "would be stopping in Bethlehem to visit the manger where he was born." This type of joke extended to criticism of the reporters who were covering him. Studies show that Obama's news coverage was far more positive than that of his opponents in both the nomination and general election seasons.[31] Stephen Colbert also weighed in on the same trip to Europe and the Middle East, saying: "The big story is Obama's world tour. Today he made history by being the first man to travel around the world in a plane propelled by the media's flash photography." However, some of the criticism was aimed directly at Obama's own campaign, as in Jay Leno's zinger: "Barack Obama's infomercial . . . went very well. I especially liked the end where Barack rose to the heavens on a cloud."

By contrast, jokes about McCain followed well-ploughed fields. They focused heavily on the fact that, at age seventy-two, he would be the oldest individual ever to assume the presidency. McCain's candidacy gave comedians a chance to dust off the old-geezer jokes that had been sitting around since Bob Dole's 1996 run, waiting for a similar target to appear. Over one-third (36 percent) of the late night McCain jokes throughout the campaign targeted his age. Below are a few examples:

> Barack Obama said today that he is going to fight for votes in all 50 states. Yeah. That's what he said. Meanwhile, John McCain said he's going to fight for votes in all 13 colonies. —*Conan O'Brien*

> Barack Obama's staff and John McCain's staff are busy now negotiating when the presidential debates will take place.... Obama wants them to be in September, and McCain wants them to be after his nap, but before *Wheel of Fortune*. —*Conan O'Brien*

> Senator McCain, running for president, is in Iraq. Of course, he remembers Iraq when it was known as Mesopotamia. —*David Letterman*

> Senator John McCain has unveiled a new campaign slogan, "Ready to Lead America into the 21st Century." ... This is a lot better than his old slogan, "I've Been Around Since the 19th Century." —*Conan O'Brien*

However, the most noteworthy feature of the 2008 comedy campaign was the number of jokes aimed not at either presidential candidate but at a previously unknown vice presidential candidate (at least in the "lower 48"). The polarizing Ms. Palin was an instant revelation to her supporters and an abomination to her opponents. But to comedians she was manna from heaven. Not since Bill Clinton had a politician given professional humorists so much material to work with. Depending on your perspective, Sarah Palin was sexy, folksy, volatile, clueless, charming, or irritating.

Palin was eloquent in her scripted comments and gaffe-prone in her unscripted remarks, unprepared to discuss public policy issues, and ill-prepared to cope with the heat of the national media spotlight. She also came with a large and colorful family, some of whom leveraged their share of the spotlight into becoming minor celebrities themselves. A few one-liners will suffice to capture the range of the jokes that Palin attracted:

> I just got my 2009 Sarah Palin calendar. Pretty hot stuff. In one, she's all sudsy with a sponge working on a moose. And in April, it's Sarah Palin in a bikini firing a state trooper. —*David Letterman*

> Tomorrow night, Sarah Palin will be on "Saturday Night Live." When they told her, she said, "What night is that on?" —*Jay Leno*

> Yesterday she referred to Afghanistan as our neighboring country. Apparently, she can see bin Laden's cave from her house. —*David Letterman*

> Sarah Palin said she's a life-long member of the National Rifle Association. Which may explain why she's in favor of shotgun weddings. —*Conan O'Brien*

> Sarah Palin and McCain are a good pair. She's pro-life and he's clinging to life. —*Jay Leno*

In addition to providing fodder for the talk show monologues, Sarah Palin helped *Saturday Night Live* bring about its greatest impact on a politician's public image since Chevy Chase was doing his Gerald Ford shtick. Former *SNL* comedian Tina Fey returned to the show and created a Sarah Palin imitation so dead-on that, when the real Palin later appeared onscreen with her, it was difficult to tell who was who.

In the most devastating of a series of sketches, Fey parodied Palin's recent interview with Katie Couric on the *CBS Evening News,* in which Fey-as-Palin seemed unprepared and offered ill-informed or simplistic responses. Part of the dialogue in the skit was quoted verbatim from

Palin's actual answers, an indication that the *SNL* writers found her own words unintentionally funnier than anything they could think up. However, the unabashedly liberal Bill Maher had the last word on the GOP ticket of McCain and Palin, as far as political humorists were concerned: "This isn't a presidential ticket, this is a sitcom."

2012 Barack Obama (Democrat) vs. Mitt Romney (Republican)

Due to our limited resources, we were not able to code for the topics of jokes about candidates in 2012. As a result, we are unable to say which aspects of the candidates were responsible for the most jokes. Impressionistically, Republican nominee Mitt Romney was often joked about as a rich white guy who didn't understand the concerns of ordinary people, a theme that peaked in the wake of his notorious comments about the "47 percent" of Americans who preferred government assistance over taking personal responsibility for their lives. For example, Jimmy Fallon commented: "A new poll found that only 47 percent of voters find Mitt Romney to be trustworthy. Then Romney was like, 'Well, I hope it's not the same 47 percent I don't care about.'"

Romney was also seen as somewhat stiff and less than dynamic in his campaign style. After the first presidential debate, widely viewed as a victory for Romney, David Letterman asked, "Say what you will about Mitt Romney. Last night I thought he was energetic, he was crisp, he was dynamic. What have you done with the real Mitt Romney?"

By contrast, 2012 was déjà vu for Barack Obama. Once again, the most notable thing about Obama jokes was their absence. Despite occupying the presidency, Obama attracted almost as few jokes in 2012 (6.2 percent) as he did in 2008 (5.8 percent). And once again, many of the jokes were not really aimed at him personally. Consider this gem from Conan O'Brien: "The Atheist Party has endorsed Obama for president. When told the news Obama said, 'Thank God.'"

However, the president did attract a flurry of jokes after his poor performance in the first presidential debate. For example, Jay Leno opined: "Close to 60 million people may have watched the debate. In fact, the only person who didn't tune in was President Obama." For the most part, however, Obama lived up to his reputation as the least joke-worthy president—or presidential candidate—in memory.

CONCLUSION: PRESIDENTIAL PUNCH LINES

Our study shows that presidents are the favorite targets of late night humorists, but not all presidents are berated equally. As we saw in Figure 3.4, which illustrates the rise and fall of presidential humor throughout the terms of three chief executives, Bill Clinton emerges as the jester-in-chief—the object of more jokes than anyone else during every year of his administration except for the election years of 1996 and 2000. He even held on to the top spot in 2001, despite leaving office in January.

Even the years in which Clinton slipped to second place in the joke race were a backhanded testament to his domination of late night humor. In 1996 comedians took advantage of his Republican opponent Bob Dole to dust off their jokes about old geezers. These had been in storage while the Oval Office was occupied by the relatively young, famously virile, and occasionally oval Clinton. In 2000 they did the same with George W. Bush, getting new mileage out of the doofus jokes that had accumulated since Dan Quayle departed DC in 1993. Nobody ever suggested that Clinton was stupid, although he sometimes seemed too smart for his own good.

With his election in 2000, George W. Bush became the new whipping boy of late night humor, although he never approached Clinton's dominance in terms of the sheer number of gags at his expense. Whereas Clinton's joke totals rose along with his sexual peccadilloes, Bush's totals declined during the solemn national mood that followed the 9/11 terrorist attacks. They surged after his decision to invade Iraq before gradually declining again during his second term. (We explore these trends in greater detail in Chapter 5.) Finally, if Clinton showed just how much of center stage a president can occupy, Barack Obama demonstrated that a president could step offstage by limiting the available joke topics and, arguably, extending his personal appeal to include the late night comics.

More generally, the evidence in this chapter suggests that humorists have a much easier time when there is an obvious theme or trope to target. These tropes typically contain a grain of truth but have been exaggerated by critics, the media, and humorists themselves to the point where they become caricatures. In some cases the tropes are based on well-known foibles or character traits. In others they revolve around scandals or gaffes. In still others, they are manufactured by political opponents attempting to portray an adversary in a negative light.

In the case of Bill Clinton, humorists targeted his various sex scandals, his eating habits and weight, and so on. George W. Bush's occasional difficulties with the English language and public policy nuances translated into the perception that he was no intellectual. On the other hand, humorists seem to have had difficulty developing a simple trope with which to lampoon Barack Obama, resulting in fewer jokes told about Obama than about his predecessors.

In contrast to presidents, vice presidents get short shrift from the late night comics. Vice presidents exercise little power and rarely make headlines—most people don't know, or care, much about them. Lacking material and audience interest, comedians have little incentive to poke fun at them. Of course, they make exceptions for vice presidential behavior that lends itself to ridicule, such as Dick Cheney's accidental shooting of a fellow hunter.

Indeed, one vice president developed such a strong comic persona that he became what entertainers call an "evergreen," a target who never steps far out of range. That would be Dan Quayle, who is represented in our study period mainly by his misspelling of the word *potato* during the 1992 presidential election campaign, but whose verbal stumbles and fumbles made it easier for comedy writers to meet deadlines throughout the presidency of George H. W. Bush. Quayle's tally of nearly one out of every ten political jokes during the humor-friendly election year of 1992 illustrates the comic potential of a politician who lives up to his late night caricature.

In sum, election years put political humor on steroids. Candidates (including presidents running for reelection) try to make news each day, and their every move is parsed and critiqued by the news media.

They are also engaged in a high-stakes contest, which increases public interest in their activities. As a result, presidential candidates are the second favorite targets of late night comics, and they can even surpass sitting presidents during election years.

Not surprisingly, the themes and topics of candidate humor echo those of presidential humor. However, an unexpected finding was that Republican candidates were joked about more than Democrats. This was true in all six of the elections we studied. Overall we coded nearly twice as many jokes about Republicans as about Democrats. However, this pattern didn't extend to jokes about sitting presidents. Any reluctance to joke about President Obama was more than balanced by the glee that the late night comics displayed in going after his Democratic predecessor Bill Clinton. Whether there is a more general partisan imbalance in late night humor is an issue we will address in subsequent chapters. But first we turn from the question of *whom* the humorists target to *what* they target—the personal traits, behavior, topics, and issues that are the most frequent subjects of political humor.

NOTES

1. Gerald Ford, *A Time to Heal: The Autobiography of Gerald R. Ford* (New York: Harper & Row/Reader's Digest, 1979), 289.

2. Will Perry, *No Cheers from the Alumni: The Wolverines: A Story of Michigan Football* (Huntsville, AL: The Strode Publishers, 1974).

3. Mark Hatfield, *Vice Presidents of the United States, 1789–1993* (Washington, DC: US Government Printing Office, 1997).

4. Ford, *A Time to Heal*, 289.

5. James Prichard, "Ford Showed Athletic Prowess at Michigan," *Boston Globe*, December 27, 2006, http://www.boston.com/news/education/higher/articles/2006/12/27/ford_was_among_most_athletic_presidents/.

6. Ilan Dajoux, "Reconsidering the Decline of the Editorial Cartoon," *Political Science* 40 (2007): 245–248; Elliott Oring, "Risky Business: Political Jokes Under Repressive Regimes," *Western Folklore* 63 (2004): 209–236; Alexander Rose, "When Politics Is a Laughing Matter," *Policy Review* (2001): 59–71.

7. Rudolph Herzog, *Dead Funny: Humor in Hitler's Germany* (Brooklyn, NY: Melville House, 2011).

8. David Niven, S. Robert Lichter, and Daniel Amundson, "The Political Content of Late Night Comedy," *Harvard International Journal of Press/Politics* 8

(2003): 118–133; David Niven, S. Robert Lichter, and Daniel Amundson, "Our First Cartoon President: Bill Clinton and the Politics of Late Night Comedy," in *Laughing Matters: Humor and American Politics in the Media Age*, eds. Jody C Baumgartner and Jonathan S. Morris (New York: Routledge, 2008), 151–170.

9. Paul Brewer and Emily Marquardt, "Mock News and Democracy: Analyzing *The Daily Show*," *Atlantic Journal of Communication* 15 (2007): 249–267; Julia Fox, Glory Colon, and Volcan Sahin, "No Joke: A Comparison of Substance in *The Daily Show* with Jon Stewart and Broadcast Network Television Coverage of the 2004 Presidential Election Campaign," *Journal of Broadcasting and Electronic Media* 51 (2007): 213–227.

10. Niven, Lichter, and Amundson, "Our First Cartoon President," 151.

11. Dan Froomkin, "Time Line," *Washingtonpost.com*, December 3, 1998, http://www.washingtonpost.com/wp-srv/politics/special/pjones/timeline.htm.

12. Ibid.

13. David Van Biema and Viveca Novak, "Clinton Crisis: Sparking the Scandal," *Time*, February 2, 1998, http://www.time.com/time/magazine/article /0,9171,987743,00.html.

14. Ryan Barilleaux and Jody Baumgartner, "Victims of Rogues: The Impeachment of Presidents Bill Clinton and Boris Yeltsin in Comparative Perspective," *White House Studies* 4 (2004): 281–299; Irwin Morris, *Votes, Money, and the Clinton Impeachment* (Boulder, CO: Westview Press, 2002).

15. Larry Sabato, Mark Stencel, and S. Robert Lichter, *Peepshow: Media and Politics in an Age of Scandal* (Lanham, MD: Rowman & Littlefield, 2000).

16. Many thanks to Daniel Kurtzman, who, among other things, maintains the website *politicalhumor.about.com*. The site is an all-purpose repository for political humor, and we drew liberally from his collection of late night jokes about a variety of subjects.

17. Kathleen Hall Jamieson and Paul Waldman, *The Press Effect: Politicians, Journalists, and the Stories That Shape the Political World* (New York: Oxford University Press, 2003).

18. Steve Tally, *Bland Ambition: From Adams to Quayle—The Cranks, Criminals, Tax Cheats, and Golfers Who Made It to Vice President* (San Diego, CA: Harcourt Brace Jovanovich, 1992).

19. Jody Baumgartner, *The American Vice Presidency Reconsidered* (Westport, CT: Praeger, 2006).

20. Andrew Romano, "How Dumb Are We?" *Newsweek*, March 20, 2011, http:// www.thedailybeast.com/newsweek/2011/03/20/how-dumb-are-we.html.

21. Paul Farhi, "Since Dick Cheney Shot Him, Harry Whittington's Aim Has Been to Move On," *Washington Post*, October 14, 2010, p. C1.

22. Paul Mickle, "1992: Gaffe with an 'e' at the End," http://www.capitalcentury .com/1992.html.

23. James Ceaser and Andrew Busch, *Losing to Win: The 1996 Elections and*

American Politics (Lanham, MD: Rowman & Littlefield, 1997).

24. Jamieson and Waldman, *The Press Effect*.

25. James Ceaser and Andrew Busch, *The Perfect Tie: The True Story of the 2000 Presidential Election* (Lanham, MD: Rowman & Littlefield, 2001).

26. Jamieson and Waldman, *The Press Effect*.

27. James Ceaser and Andrew Busch, *Red over Blue: The 2004 Elections and American Politics* (Lanham, MD: Rowman & Littlefield, 2005).

28. James W. Ceaser, Andrew E. Busch, and John J. Pitney, Jr., *Epic Journey: The 2008 Elections and American Politics* (Lanham, MD: Rowman & Littlefield, 2009).

29. Ibid.

30. Ibid.

31. Stephen Farnsworth and S. Robert Lichter, *The Nightly News Nightmare: Media Coverage of U.S. Presidential Elections, 1988–2008* (Lanham, MD: Rowman & Littlefield, 2010); Pew Research Center, "Winning the Media Campaign: How the Press Reported the 2008 General Election," 2008, http://www.journalism .org/node/13307; Pew Research Center, "The Invisible Primary—Invisible No Longer," 2007, http://www.journalism.org/node/8187.

Chapter 4

Politicians Behaving Badly

Up to now we have focused on jokes about America's most visible or influential political figures—presidents, vice presidents, and presidential candidates. We have seen how comedians zero in on the more dubious traits of political leaders—their alleged character flaws, intellectual deficits, advanced age, physical shortcomings, and the like. In fact, jokes about personal characteristics accounted for almost one out of every eight jokes (13 percent) that we catalogued for all politicians.

For the political class as a whole, however, the leitmotif of political humor is the scandalous behavior of politicians. Scandals are easily the most popular late night joke topic. One out of every ten jokes that we catalogued over two decades concerned a politician or public figure charged with some sort of scandalous behavior. These include jokes about sexual peccadilloes, drug and alcohol abuse, influence-peddling, graft, and otherwise unseemly, unethical, or illegal behavior.

Scandals are inherently personal, and most of the individuals they revolve around validate the widely held sentiment that politicians behave badly and can't be trusted. While the effects of scandals are often dark and depressing, late night comics focus on the humor involved when a person of power gets caught with his pants down or with a hand in the cookie jar. In other words, a good scandal joke has a cathartic effect. It brings the powerful down a notch and lets audiences feel morally superior to the high and mighty.

LATE NIGHT COMEDIANS AND POLITICAL SEX SCANDALS

Late night comedians benefited immeasurably from changes in media mores that brought the private lives of politicians out of the shadows and into the limelight just in time for our study. Scandalous personal behavior certainly occurred behind closed doors before the late 1980s in Washington, but it was almost never reported to the general public. For example, in 1921 Warren Harding had sex in a White House coat closet with his twenty-four-year-old mistress (and the mother of his illegitimate daughter) while a Secret Service agent prevented an angry Mrs. Harding from entering his office. When Franklin D. Roosevelt died, he was with not his wife Eleanor but his longtime friend and sometime companion Lucy Mercer, with whom he had an extramarital affair even before he became president. And of course John F. Kennedy made Bill Clinton look like a piker in sexual matters.

So it's not as if this kind of behavior were new—it just wasn't news. The public learned about all these incidents well after the fact, when they were published in tell-all books or more serious historical accounts. All this changed in 1987, when reporters caught Democratic presidential candidate Gary Hart in a sexual liaison with model Donna Rice and broadcast the news in a very public scandal that led to Hart's withdrawal from the race. Once the dam broke, politicians' private lives increasingly became public knowledge, and salacious rumors quickly migrated from the supermarket tabloids to the mainstream media. With reporters serving as "character cops," the public became exposed to the steady stream of titillating tales that we now take for granted.

We can only guess at the hay that comedians would have made of President Kennedy's well-documented sexual exploits if this information had been considered fit for public consumption. For the bad behavior of Kennedy's more recent successors, however, little is left to the imagination. Of course, sex among Hollywood's rich and famous is also fodder for late night comedy. But sex among Washington's powerful and hypocritical has become its own distinctive comic genre.

Bill Clinton's Sexcapades

Just as clearly as scandals are the leading topic of political humor, the top scandal topic is sex. In our study, jokes about sex scandals make up over three out of four (78 percent) jokes about scandals of all kinds. This partly reflects the fact that Bill Clinton was president during eight of the twenty years covered in our study. And he has stayed in the public eye ever since, due to his own activities as well as to his wife's Senate career, presidential candidacy, and tenure as secretary of state under President Obama.

Even in the absence of publicly named paramours since he left office, Clinton remains a ready target for any joke about sexual escapades that crosses the mind of a comedy writer. In fact, 70 percent of all sex scandal jokes in our study were linked in some way to one or more of Clinton's trysts. The most frequent were jokes about his relations with Gennifer Flowers, Paula Jones, and, as Clinton famously called her, "that woman, Miss Lewinsky."

Nearly one out of every four sex scandal jokes (23 percent) that we tracked over two decades focused on some aspect of the Lewinsky affair, which dominated the news agenda for a relatively brief but intense period in 1998 and early 1999. The cast of characters who provided comic material included not only the principals but also such supporting players as Lewinsky-confidant-turned-informer Linda Tripp and Independent Counsel Kenneth Starr. Starr was originally appointed to investigate the Clintons' financial involvement with the Whitewater Development Corporation in Arkansas, but he later expanded his investigations to include Paula Jones's sexual harassment case against Bill Clinton as well as the Lewinsky scandal. Unfair as it may seem, late night comics even pulled poor Mrs. Clinton into the mix. But no one ever said comedy was fair (see Box 4.1).

Ironically, the Clinton sex scandals backfired on his Republican critics, in a development that might be called "Hypocrite-gate." During the impeachment proceedings against Clinton, the online magazine *Salon* discovered that House Judiciary Committee chairman Henry Hyde, one of Clinton's most vocal critics, had an extramarital

BOX 4.1

A Sampling of Hillary Clinton Jokes

"Today is the First Lady's birthday. Happy birthday to her. It must be kind of strange for Bill Clinton giving gifts to a woman he's not having sex with." —*Jay Leno*

"Hillary is on the *Today Show* tomorrow. She is going on these news shows defending her husband. God bless this woman. You got to admit he's good. . . . Not only did he convince his wife he didn't have an affair, he got her on the road defending him." —*Jay Leno*

"To celebrate the birthday yesterday, President Clinton and Hillary shared a quiet dinner, to be followed by another quiet dinner, followed by another quiet dinner, followed by another quiet dinner." —*David Letterman*

"Hillary Clinton goes up to Yale and she's addressing a class there in the Divinity College and the topic of the speech is 'How to Avoid a Man Who Commits Sexual Harassment.' Honestly. Step one. Don't marry him. That would work." —*David Letterman*

"Would you mind having sex with Hillary once in a while?" —*David Letterman, Number Two on the "Top Ten Questions in the White House Press Secretary Job Interview" list*

"Yesterday Hillary Clinton attended a poetry competition at a Washington high school. . . . She agreed to go after aides assured her that nothing rhymes with Lewinsky." —*Conan O'Brien*

"Hillary Clinton refused to answer any questions about her private conversations with President Clinton, . . . [saying] 'It's no one's business what we talk about while I'm punching him in the head.'" —*Conan O'Brien*

relationship with a married woman in the 1960s, before he was elected to Congress. Hyde suffered damage to his reputation, but he was re-elected to Congress and reconciled with his wife.

Some of Hyde's GOP colleagues didn't fare as well. At about the same time that Hyde was defending his reputation to his constituents,

Larry Flynt, the publisher of *Hustler* magazine, took out a full-page ad in the *Washington Post* offering $1 million for evidence of sexual peccadilloes by Republican members of Congress who were pursuing articles of impeachment against President Clinton. Soon thereafter, Republican Speaker of the House–elect Bob Livingston resigned his seat after he was forced to admit to an extramarital affair. Livingston's House seat was taken by David Vitter, who won a special election. Vitter moved to the Senate in 2004, and in 2007 he was identified as the client of a prostitution service in Washington, DC. Nonetheless, he was reelected to the Senate in 2010. You can't make this stuff up.

Hijinks and Low Blows: Other Politicians' Sex Scandals

Of course, Bill Clinton and his foes were not the only targets of sex scandal jokes on late night television in the past two decades (though it sometimes seemed that way). Most such scandals during this period fit the relatively banal mold of a politician being unfaithful to his wife with someone less salaciously intriguing than a twenty-something White House intern. Interestingly, none of these scandals involved female politicians being unfaithful to their husbands, although South Carolina governor Nikki Haley was subjected to unproven allegations of adultery from political opponents during her successful campaign for that office in 2010.

But a few "lucky" individuals later emerged as worthy successors to Bill Clinton in this sphere. In order of the number of jokes they inspired, these included former New York Governor Eliot Spitzer in 2008, Representative Gary Condit of California in 2001, Representative Anthony Weiner of New York in 2011 and again in 2013, Senator John Edwards of North Carolina from 2007 to 2010, Governor Mark Sanford of South Carolina in 2009 (he was Nikki Haley's immediate predecessor), Governor Arnold Schwarzenegger of California in 2003 and 2011, Bill Clinton's political adviser Dick Morris in 1996, and Speaker of the House Newt Gingrich in 1999.[1] Compared with the number of jokes told about Bill Clinton, of course, these individuals are mere mortals. However, the scandals they became involved in were easily as titillating.

New York Governor Eliot Spitzer (2007–2008), who made a name for himself as New York's law-and-order attorney general, was found to have paid thousands of dollars to a prostitution ring.[2] Spitzer was tripped up by federal laws requiring banks to report suspicious cash transactions to the IRS, after he transferred over $10,000 to a front company that paid his paramours. Another New York politician, the unfortunately named Representative Weiner, was forced to resign his House seat after the unlucky public was exposed to the sexually explicit photos that he tweeted to women both before and after his marriage. Weiner proved himself a glutton for punishment when he ran for mayor of New York City in 2013. New messages and photos soon emerged, showing that he had continued his activities well after he publicly pledged to his wife and his constituents that he would sext no more.

Representative Gary Condit's adulterous affair with his twenty-three-year-old intern Chandra Levy was a much darker tale. Ms. Levy's disappearance became a major ongoing news story in 2001. Condit's tight-lipped responses to police inquiries, including an initial denial of their sexual relationship, led both Levy's parents and the DC police to suspect he knew more than he was saying. (The animated TV series *South Park* even ran an episode that hinted at his involvement in her death.) The young woman's body was eventually found, and another man was convicted of her murder. Long before then, however, Condit's heavily publicized behavior had undermined his public support back home, and he lost a primary challenge in 2002.[3]

Former South Carolina Governor Mark Sanford disappeared from public view for almost a week when he was allegedly hiking on the Appalachian Trail. After reporters determined that neither his aides nor his wife knew where he was, Sanford revealed that he was having an affair with a woman in Argentina.[4] Despite getting a divorce from his wife and being censured by the South Carolina House of Representatives, Sanford served out his term as governor. Two years later, campaigning with his onetime mistress and current fiancée, he won a special election to represent South Carolina's First Congressional District. The Democratic opponent he defeated was Elizabeth Colbert Busch, the sister of Comedy Central's Stephen Colbert. Did we mention that you can't make this stuff up? Box 4.2 provides a small sample of the late night jokes told about these individuals.

A few other sex scandals are worthy of mention for going beyond standard-issue marital infidelity or incorporating a salacious twist. In 2007, Republican Senator Larry Craig from Idaho was arrested in a men's restroom at the Minneapolis–St. Paul International Airport and charged with "lewd conduct." According to the arresting officer, who was sitting

---

BOX 4.2

Selected Sex Scandal Jokes: Gary Condit, Eliot Spitzer, and Mark Sanford

On Gary Condit:

"Gary Condit lost his bid for reelection. Know what this means? He may actually have to go back to having sex with his own wife." —*Jay Leno*

"Republican Minority Leader Trent Lott has said Condit should step down if he had an improper relationship with the intern. Bill Clinton said, 'Step down? This guy should run for president!'" —*Jay Leno*

"According to the latest poll in Northern California, 60 percent of voters say they will not vote for Gary Condit in the next election. Apparently the other 40 percent are dating Gary Condit." —*Conan O'Brien*

On Eliot Spitzer:

"The *New York Times* was able to find Kristen, the twenty-two-year-old prostitute whom Spitzer allegedly paid $1,000 an hour. Her real name is Ashley Dupré. . . . Her MySpace page says her first love is music, she wants to be a singer, and then her second love is having sex with governors for money." —*Jimmy Kimmel*

"It turns out the call girl linked to Eliot Spitzer is also an R&B singer, and she said in an interview that her latest song was inspired by a guy. She didn't say which guy, but the song is called 'Bald Creepy Governor.'" —*Conan O'Brien*

"Do you know what the highest-paid government position in this country is? Anybody know? It is working under New York Governor Eliot Spitzer. It pays like $5,000 an hour." —*Jay Leno*

(continues)

BOX 4.2 CONTINUED

On Mark Sanford:

"Governor Mark Sanford disappeared . . . and it turned out he was in South America. And then it turned out he was down there because he was sleeping with a woman from Argentina. Once again, foreigners taking jobs that Americans won't do." —*David Letterman*

"How dare this man, a married man, in this economy, outsource to a foreign country when there are plenty of slutty women living right here in the United States." —*Jimmy Kimmel*

"Apparently the governor said he wanted to do something exotic. Clearly what he meant was he wanted to do someone exotic." —*Craig Ferguson*

---

in the adjacent stall in the line of duty, Craig attempted to solicit sex by touching the officer's feet and waving his hand under the bathroom stall divider. Craig famously claimed that the contact was the result of his "wide stance" when sitting on the toilet, and that he was just trying to pick up a piece of paper from the floor. The incident likely attracted even more attention than usual because Craig was married and had a history of taking positions opposed to gay rights. Craig later resigned,[5] but not in time to halt an onslaught of late night jokes like the following:

> Senator Craig from Idaho is blaming the media for his guilty plea, especially that cute guy from the Associated Press. —*David Letterman*

> It's kind of ironic. The whole time [Senator Craig] was copping a feel, he was actually feeling a cop. —*Jay Leno*

> But [Senator Craig] did say today that if he is found guilty, he would be willing to do some kind of community service. You know, like picking up papers in the men's room. —*Jay Leno*

Another lurid sex scandal involved Representative Mark Foley, a Florida Republican who sent sexually suggestive messages and e-mails to underage male congressional pages. The political impact of this scandal was especially great because earlier reports of his behavior had been ignored by House Republican leaders, and it became public only about a month before the 2006 midterm elections.[6] Because of the involvement of underage pages, this story prompted open expressions of disgust even from the normally jaded comedians, including:

> The big question now is what should be done with Mark Foley's seat in Congress. I say, spray it with Lysol, boil it, coat it with Bactine, and then maybe you can sit on it. —*Jay Leno*

> Mark Foley has now checked into rehab for alcoholism. Oh, shut up. Like that's the big problem. Who cares if he's addicted to Jack Daniels? He's addicted to little Jack and little Daniel. That's the problem. —*Jay Leno*

> CNN is reporting that former Congressman Mark Foley's instant messages were not only sexually inappropriate but were also full of typos. In his own defense, Foley said, "It's hard to type with one hand." —*Conan O'Brien*

Several political figures came to the attention of late night comedians after being accused of sexual harassment. The most prominent was 1990 Supreme Court nominee Clarence Thomas. He was accused of sexually harassing his assistant, Anita Hill, during his time as her superior in the Department of Education and the Equal Employment Opportunity Commission in the early 1980s. Hill's testimony to the Senate Judiciary Committee about Thomas's alleged behavior involved graphic discussions of pornography and sexual anatomy. During these proceedings Jay Leno mentioned that a new "adult" phone line was being created, and, "For a dollar a minute, you can hear Anita Hill read her Senate testimony." And although Thomas was confirmed by the Senate in a 52-to-48 vote, his name has become inexorably tied to sexual harassment.

Other high-level offenders have also been targeted by late night comics for similar transgressions. For example, after Oregon Senator Robert Packwood was accused of harassment by more than a dozen former staff members, he was forced to submit his diaries to the Senate Ethics Committee during its investigation in 1995. The diaries detailed several affairs, and Packwood eventually resigned. Before the resignation, David Letterman noted: "Senator Bob Packwood wrote in his diary that he had sex with 22 different staff members. Good God, I'm lucky if I can get a cup of coffee." Ironically, Letterman admitted in 2009 that he had multiple affairs with his own female staff members at CBS.

In 2013, over a dozen women came forward to accuse San Diego Mayor Bob Filner of sexual harassment. Filner was accused of everything from crude comments to groping. Among the victims who came forward were former staffers, a sixty-seven-year-old great-grandmother who worked at City Hall, and women he met at a function for female members of the armed services who had been sexually assaulted while on active duty. Although Filner initially tried to keep his job, even undergoing therapy, he was eventually forced to resign. Late night comics took notice of his bizarre behavior:

> Shark researchers in Florida report that the number of shark attacks on humans is on the rise. What they do is, they spot their victim, they circle, they circle once, and then grab the first part of you they can. I'm sorry, that's the mayor of San Diego. I'm sorry, that's that Bob Filner guy. —*Jay Leno*

> Communications director Irene McCormack Jackson has filed a harassment suit saying Filner is not fit to hold any public office. That is outrageous. If he is fit enough to hold a woman half his age in a head-lock, I think he's fit enough to hold public office. —*Stephen Colbert*

> But it's not all bad news for the former San Diego mayor. Today Bob Filner was offered a new job as a TSA agent at the airport. —*Jay Leno*

MONEY AND POWER SCANDALS

While sex scandals are undoubtedly the most-joked-about type of scandal, presumably because they're the most salacious, scandals relating to financial impropriety, issues of conflict of interest, and drug use also attracted the attention of late night comedians.

Going Back to Bill Clinton . . .

All scandal-ridden roads seem to lead back to Bill Clinton. About one-fifth of the *nonsexual* scandal jokes we recorded in our study focused on this scandalizer-in-chief and allegations of his various and sundry misdeeds, from his days as a college student all the way through to his behavior during his final days in office. These alleged transgressions included:

- dodging the military draft and smoking marijuana (but famously not inhaling) while a college student in England;
- the firing of White House travel office workers who were replaced with Clinton's Arkansas allies, in an affair that became known as "Travel-gate";
- the suicide of deputy White House counsel and close Clinton associate Vince Foster, and the subsequent removal of records from his office;
- Hillary Clinton's association with the Rose Law Firm when Bill was governor of Arkansas, which critics called a conflict of interest because the firm did business with the state; and
- Bill Clinton's pardon of fugitive financier Marc Rich (wanted on tax evasion charges) just before leaving office. Rich's wife Denise had donated large sums of money to the Clinton library and Hillary's 2000 campaign for the Senate.[7]

Finally, both Bill and Hillary were embroiled in a financial scandal that reached back to their days in Arkansas. The scandal, which became known as Whitewater, involved a failed real-estate deal with their friends James and Susan McDougal's Whitewater Development Corporation. Although the development deal ultimately fell through, many details of the case cast suspicion on whether Clinton or his wife had used the office of the governor improperly.

The Whitewater investigation led to Attorney General Janet Reno's appointment of Independent Counsel Kenneth Starr in 1994. Starr's original mandate was to investigate the death of Vince Foster (who had also been working on the land deal). However, he later expanded the scope of his inquiry to include other alleged transgressions, including extramarital affairs. Starr's ever-widening investigations eventually led to revelations that Clinton had been having an affair with Monica Lewinsky. In this sense Whitewater was the mother lode of the Clinton scandals.[8]

Clinton wasn't the only one in hot water with the public and with late night comedians, though. In the following sections, we touch on two of the most visible—Tom DeLay and Rod Blagojevich.

Tom DeLay

An eleven-term Republican member of the House of Representatives (1985–2006), DeLay was the majority whip from 1995 to 2002 and the majority leader from 2003 to 2006. The conservative DeLay was known for his fiery rhetoric and his behind-the-scenes strong-arm tactics in getting other Republicans to fall in line. (His nickname was "The Hammer.") Controversies surrounding DeLay included his association with shady lobbyist Jack Abramoff, questionable campaign contributions, and improperly using a federal agency (the Federal Aviation Administration) to search for Democratic members of the Texas Legislature who had fled to Oklahoma to block his redistricting efforts.

DeLay's congressional career ended with his resignation after being charged with money-laundering in the course of a campaign finance investigation. In short, DeLay seemed to be everything that cynical Americans perceive public officials to be. He was convicted of money-laundering in January 2011 and sentenced to three years in prison but as of this writing is free on bail while appealing his conviction. Here is a sampling of late night comedians' treatment of DeLay:

It's springtime. It was so nice in Washington Tom DeLay was accepting cash in the park. —*David Letterman*

It has now been revealed that a Washington lobbyist personally paid for Tom DeLay's trips using his own credit card. Even more embarrassing, the lobbyist also put the purchase of Tom DeLay on his credit card. —*Jay Leno*

They shut down Pennsylvania Avenue because of a suspicious package, did you hear about that? Turns out it was just a big bag of laundered money for Tom DeLay. —*David Letterman*

Rod Blagojevich

Governor of Illinois from 2003 to 2009, Blagojevich had previously been a representative in both the Illinois and US House of Representatives. As governor he was largely ineffective and unpopular. Under investigation by the FBI since 2005 (as part of a larger investigation), Blagojevich was arrested in 2008 on federal charges of conspiracy to commit mail fraud, wire fraud, and solicitation of bribery. To top it all off, he was charged with trying to auction off his appointment of a US senator to replace Barack Obama after Obama was elected to the presidency.

Blagojevich was impeached by the Illinois House of Representatives in 2009 (in a 14-to-1 vote) and unanimously found guilty by the Illinois State Senate. In 2010, he was convicted of lying to the FBI. The following year he was convicted on seventeen of the twenty conspiracy counts he was charged with, and he began a fourteen-year prison sentence in December 2011.[9]

Late night comics found Blagojevich an easy target:

Blagojevich held a press conference. . . . He quoted the British poet Tennyson, which was weird, because usually he quotes the movie *Jerry Maguire*—"Show me the money!" —*Jay Leno*

Time magazine reports that Governor Blagojevich has an approval rating of 4 percent. That's with a margin of error of 5 percent. That means he could actually disapprove of himself. —*Jay Leno*

Yesterday President-elect Barack Obama called on Illinois Governor Blagojevich to resign. And after hearing this, Blagojevich said, "If he wants to call and talk to me, it's $4.99 a minute." —*Conan O'Brien*

We're not kidding about this economy, which is so bad that Illinois Governor Rod Blagojevich had to mark down the price of a Senate seat 40 percent. —*David Letterman*

SCANDALOUS POLICIES

The bad behavior we have discussed so far falls into the realms of sex, power, and money—the stuff of scandals everywhere. But the world of politics includes another type of scandal—the policy scandal—that late night hosts have been less likely to mine for comic material. It's not hard to imagine why. Relatively few Americans keep abreast of policy debates, so the potential audience for such jokes is smaller. You don't have to be a political junkie to be titillated by stories of a politician with his hand in the till or his foot under the stall. But it's tough to get a laugh when you have to explain what *sequestration* means.

Further, our study period excluded great scandals of the past like Watergate and the Iran-contra affair, which involved illegalities and cover-ups by presidents or high officials acting on their behalf. The closest we came to a policy scandal was a war that was fought under false pretenses: the Iraq War of 2003.

Following the terrorist attacks of September 11, 2001, the George W. Bush administration built a case, based largely on US and British intelligence reports, that Iraqi dictator Saddam Hussein had acquired weapons of mass destruction, which constituted a threat to the United States. Because of Iraq's continued refusal to fully comply with United Nations inspection protocols, Bush and his appointees argued that the use of force was justified to overthrow Saddam and remove the weapons. In March 2003, the United States successfully invaded Iraq and began a long and contentious occupation of that country.

Unfortunately, arduous searches revealed the nonexistence of the weapons whose removal provided the primary rationale for the invasion. It turns out that many of the intelligence reports on which administration officials relied were faulty. Moreover, administration officials seemed to exaggerate the threat posed by Saddam. Bush would later claim that Iraq was better off without Hussein, and the American role shifted to building a democratic system there. However, such assurances failed to alter the fact that Iraq was invaded based on what we now know were faulty premises.[10]

The fact that the president had fooled either himself or the public brought forth volleys of derisive jokes from late night comics.

> Oscar nominations came out. Up for best actor, Sean Penn for *Mystic River,* Jude Law for *Cold Mountain,* and of course George W. Bush for *Iraqi Weapons of Mass Destruction.* —*Jay Leno*

> In Iraq, the terrorists are now firing missiles from donkey carts and working on plans for suicide donkeys. I guess these are the high-tech weapons President Bush was talking about. —*Jay Leno*

> This week President Bush insisted he is absolutely convinced that Saddam had a weapons program. Of course he was absolutely convinced that he won the 2000 election, so I don't know. —*Jay Leno*

CONCLUSION

Bad behavior inside the Beltway is catnip for comedians. Scandals are the juiciest topic of late night jokes, and scandals involving sex and power help gag-writers wring every last drop out of the material. From garden-variety adultery to consorting with prostitutes to soliciting sex in a public toilet, from sexual overtures to underage pages to prurient tweets with constituents, the people's representatives have given viewers of late night talk shows something to stay awake for.

There has also been plenty of old-fashioned political corruption to fill many a slow humor night. High-level office-holders have been accused or convicted of conspiracy, money-laundering, mail fraud, bribery, and perjury. And those are just the felonies. If Mark Twain were here today, he could only marvel at the consistency of America's governing classes across the centuries.

Through this crowded field of miscreants, Bill Clinton easily trumps his competitors as the all-time favorite target of late night comedians. Clinton was accused but never convicted of a wide range of inappropriate, unethical, and criminal activities, which his wife famously attributed to "a vast right-wing conspiracy" to destroy his presidency. The list includes numerous sexual peccadilloes and transgressions, some of them proven, others refuted, still others hotly contested. F. Scott Fitzgerald claimed that there are no second acts in American lives, but Bill Clinton has had more political lives than Socks the cat. As he continues his post-presidential public career, he has no more ardent group of well-wishers than late night comedians, who know a meal ticket when they see one.

NOTES

1. Associated Press, "A History of Political Sex Scandals," *Washington Post,* April 7, 2011, http://www.washingtonpost.com/wp-srv/special/politics/sex-scandal-timeline/index.html.

2. "Eliot Spitzer," *Biography.com,* http://www.biography.com/people/eliot-spitzer-279076.

3. "Gary Condit," *Biography.com,* http://www.biography.com/people/gary-condit-9542435.

4. Randy James, "Straying Governor Mark Sanford," *Time.com,* June 25, 2009, http://www.time.com/time/nation/article/0,8599,1907022,00.html.

5. Patti Murphy and David Stout, "Idaho Senator Says He Regrets Guilty Plea in Restroom Incident," *New York Times,* August 29, 2007, http://www.nytimes.com/2007/08/29/washington/29craig.html?_r=1&oref=slogin.

6. Walter Roche, "Ex-Page Tells of Foley Liaison," *Los Angeles Times,* October 8, 2006, http://articles.latimes.com/2006/oct/08/nation/na-page8.

7. Joe Klein, *The Natural: The Misunderstood Presidency of Bill Clinton* (New York: Broadway Books, 2002).

8. Ibid.

9. "Rod R. Blagojevich," *New York Times,* December 7, 2011, http://topics.nytimes.com/top/reference/timestopics/people/b/rodr_blagojevich/index.htm.

10. Joby Warrick and Walter Pincus, "Bush Inflated Threat from Iraq's Banned Weapons, Report Says," *Washington Post,* June 6, 2008, http://www.washingtonpost.com/wp-dyn/content/article/2008/06/05/AR2008060501523.html.

Chapter 5

What's So Funny?

Although most late night political jokes are directed at the short-comings of particular politicians, late night comics also devote a fair amount of attention to political institutions. Like jokes directed at individuals, these jokes draw on and reinforce preexisting perceptions or stereotypes. In this chapter we first examine jokes about political institutions like Congress, the Supreme Court, and the political parties. We then turn to the general topics and specific policies that are joked about most frequently.

POLITICAL INSTITUTIONS: WHAT CAN YOU TRUST?
Congress

Poking fun at Congress is a time-honored American pastime. No less a luminary than Mark Twain held Congress in open contempt. In fact, some of the most commonly cited historical examples of political humor are quotations from Twain railing at Congress. The following are among the most widely circulated:

> Fleas can be taught nearly anything that a Congressman can. —*What Is Man?*

> Suppose you were an idiot. And suppose you were a member of Congress. But I repeat myself. —*Mark Twain, a Biography*

> It could probably be shown by facts and figures that there is
> no distinctly native American criminal class except Congress.
> —*Pudd'nhead Wilson's New Calendar*

Will Rogers, who was Twain's unofficial successor as America's
comic laureate, picked up the cudgel with some equally coruscating
comments, including "This country has come to feel the same when
Congress is in session as when the baby gets hold of a hammer" and
"Ancient Rome declined because it had a Senate; now what's going to
happen to us with both a Senate and a House?"

Congress is still an institution that Americans love to hate. Since the
1970s the Gallup organization has regularly asked, "Do you approve or
disapprove of the way Congress is handling its job?" Over the past forty
years, the proportion that approves of Congress has averaged just over
30 percent, and it was often much lower. In November 2013 approval ratings failed to break into double digits—a mere 9 percent of the public approved of Congress's performance.[1] By comparison, Gallup polls going
back to the 1940s show that no president in recent memory has ever had
an average approval rating below 45 percent (Truman and Carter), and
the highest approval rating (Kennedy's) averaged over 70 percent.

One source of public disdain is the fact that few people understand
the complexities and nuances inherent to lawmaking in the US Congress.[2] In addition, although the institution itself is widely recognized
by the American public as necessary for democracy, the individuals
who occupy Capitol Hill are seen as shifty and self-interested.[3] And despite the fact that only a small fraction of the thousands of individuals
who have served in Congress throughout history have been demon-
strably corrupt, those are the members who frequently attract the most
attention. These relatively frequent personal transgressions keep alive
popular perceptions that the people's representatives are inept, power
hungry, and corrupt; the laws they pass either fail to improve things or
just make matters worse; and the process of lawmaking is either repre-
hensible or incomprehensible. Not coincidentally, these same themes
recur throughout late night jokes about Congress.

For all this, the institution of Congress (as opposed to individual members) is not an especially popular topic for late night political

jokes. Fewer than 5 percent of the jokes we tracked focused on the institution, and many of these jokes were scandal related. As noted, the lawmaking process seems both complex and opaque to the majority of the American public. People have to know something about a subject in order for a joke to be funny, and late night comics cannot always assume that this is the case regarding the legislative process.

However, the scarcity of late night jokes targeting the institution of Congress is a somewhat misleading finding. Most of the Congress-related jokes lampoon individual members who are in the news. Congress itself becomes the target of ridicule when the nature or amount of individual bad behavior gets enough public attention that the whole institution is pulled into disrepute. Ironically, efforts to reform the institution also generate jokes, because they stimulate public discussion of the questionable behavior that stimulated the reforms. They also provide a reminder that many previous reforms yielded meager results. The following jokes illustrate how late night comics treat Congress as a whole:

Earlier this week the Senate voted 97-to-0 for tougher regulations. For example, when corporations buy a senator, they must now get a receipt. —*Jay Leno*

Vermont Senator James Jeffords is being called a hero today after he chased down a teenager who stole a wallet from his daughter-in-law on Capitol Hill. . . . At one point Jeffords yelled out "Stop thief," and two hundred congressmen froze. —*Jay Leno*

President Obama has signed into law a bill that bans members of Congress from insider trading. However, they are still allowed to mishandle campaign funds, cheat on their wives, and kill the occasional drifter. —*Jay Leno*

The House of Representatives has passed a bill that prohibits people from using welfare money in strip clubs or liquor stores. I agree with that. Strip clubs and liquor stores should be off-limits for people who get government funds—you know, like congressmen. —*Jay Leno*

The Supreme Court

Unlike Congress, a majority of the public typically approves of the Supreme Court.[4] Further, Supreme Court justices are not elected; thus, they tend not to be viewed by most of the public as political figures.[5] Moreover, if people know little about Congress, they know even less about the Supreme Court. For example, a survey conducted in 2010 found that only about one-third of all Americans could name even one member of the Court, and only 1 percent could name all nine members.[6] It is likely that fewer still fully understand that, while the Court's decisions affect public policy, its mandate is solely to interpret the Constitution. Also, because the Court's procedures and deliberation are hidden from the public eye, details of how the justices go about making decisions are likely a mystery to most Americans.

These factors help explain why fewer than 1 percent of the jokes told on late night talk and comedy programs from 1992 to 2011 centered on the Supreme Court. In addition, most jokes about the Court focus in one way or another on the personal characteristics of individual justices, or those being considered for appointment. It is simply safer for comedians to assume that the average late night viewer can understand these types of jokes, rather than more complex humor about the nuances of constitutional law.

In particular, many jokes about Supreme Court justices focus on their advanced ages (all current justices are over age fifty, and four are over seventy) or their demographic characteristics (specifically, that most justices have been white males).

> I guess we're all excited that President Bush announced his nomination to the Supreme Court—John Roberts. Bush searched far and wide before he made the risky choice of a white guy in his fifties. —*David Letterman*

> Chief Justice William Rehnquist was hospitalized last night with a slight fever. Doctors have worked out a compromise so he can still work. They're going to give him a judge's robe that opens in the back. —*Jay Leno*

Sandra Day O'Connor announced she is retiring from the Supreme Court. She is seventy-five years old. That's going to be a drastic life-style change, you know, from sitting in the Supreme Court in a black robe all day to sitting in front of the TV in a flowered robe all day, watching Judge Judy. —*Jay Leno*

Jokes related to the business of the Court are limited to controversial and high-profile decisions, such as the 2000 presidential election or President Obama's health care reform act. For example, during the 2004 presidential election campaign, Jay Leno alluded to the Supreme Court decision in 2000 that ended the Florida recount and effectively delivered the presidency to George W. Bush: "Kerry is well on his way to reaching his magic number of 2,162. That's the total number of delegates he needs to win the Democratic nomination. See, for President Bush it's different—his magic number is 5. That's the number of Supreme Court judges needed to win."

Political Parties

More than citizens in most other advanced democracies, Americans view political parties with skepticism and even disdain. For example, since the 1950s, over one-third of Americans have been unwilling to identify with either of the two major political parties, and the proportion has increased over the years. In one survey, only 56 percent responded that political parties were actually necessary to democracy, and only 38 percent agreed that "political parties care what people think." In short, there is a high degree of anti-party sentiment among Americans, which lends itself to distrust of, and cynicism toward, the activities of both the Democratic and Republican parties.[7] This makes parties ripe targets for late night comics.

Of all the late night jokes in our database, 9 percent target the Republican Party, while 5 percent are focused on the Democratic Party. Many of these jokes are election related and not necessarily focused on the parties as a whole. Still, such findings give some credence to the complaints of conservatives that they and their views are portrayed unfavorably by the entertainment industry.[8] It is no secret that

Hollywood is populated mostly by political liberals, and this may be reflected in the aggregate differences we found in the number of jokes about the two sides.[9]

Jokes about the parties focus on various issue positions that each is known for, their stereotypical supporters, and other common perceptions. For example, many jokes about Democrats focus on the often-fractious nature of the party. Will Rogers once quipped: "I belong to no organized party. I am a Democrat." Others target the difficulties the Democratic Party sometimes has in putting aside principles for the sake of winning elections. Again, from Will Rogers: "You've got to be [an] optimist to be a Democrat, and you've got to be a humorist to stay one."

More recently, comedians have poked fun at Democrats' policies, celebrity followers, and political ineffectiveness. For example:

Today is the anniversary of the Watergate break-in. That's the day the Republicans tried to steal the Democrats' plans. That's also the last time the Democrats had any plans worth stealing. —*Jay Leno*

Because the election was such a disaster for the Democrats, it looks like the leader of the party might be stepping down. But enough about Barbra Streisand. —*Jay Leno*

It's amazing how quickly the news changes. I mean it's hard to believe just ten days ago we believed Osama bin Laden was dead and the Democratic Party was alive. —*Jay Leno*

The Democrats are unbelievable. They are giving up on their tax cut for the middle class until after the election. They have the worst salesmen in the world. They could not talk Lindsay Lohan into a rum and coke. —*Bill Maher*

Not only were there nearly twice as many jokes about the Republican Party and its supporters as there were about Democrats, but the jokes themselves were more pointedly partisan, targeting the party's conservative policies and supporters. The most common jokes were variations on notions that the stereotypical Republican is a wealthy white male and that conservative Republicans deny that human activity is responsible for global warming, are opposed to gay marriage, seem to believe that they have a direct link to God, and are generally less caring than Democrats. Examples include the following:

> The candidates at the Republican debate looked like a town council that was outlawing dancing. They looked like a board of directors that was lying about poisoning a river. —*David Letterman*

> Last night, Fox News aired the second Republican presidential debate. My favorite part was when the white guy went after those two white guys, and three other white guys chimed in. —*Conan O'Brien*

> How many of you saw the Republican presidential debate? There are ten Republicans who want to be president of the United States. Did you see them? I mean, they looked like guys waiting to tee off at a restricted country club. —*David Letterman*

> The Republican presidential debate was held tonight in California, and ten candidates took part. Political experts say that the ten Republican candidates represented all races, creeds, and colors of rich white men. —*Conan O'Brien*

Of course, jokes about political parties are especially common during election campaigns, to which we now turn.

Campaigns and Elections

Elections are the central organizing mechanism in American political life. They act as a kind of secular ritual that renews the public's faith in the democratic process. For this reason, elections (as opposed to the candidates who seek election) are not a particularly promising target for political humor. Americans may be cynical about politics, but they generally accept the outcomes of elections, whether they like them or not. Among the jokes in our late night database, a full 17 percent—more than one out of six—concerned elections. But the vast majority targeted the candidates and political parties who were involved, not the election process itself.

For instance, a good number of election jokes are focused on candidates' policies or status in the race. They are, in other words, not exactly jokes about elections themselves. One example is this one from *SNL*'s "Weekend Update" about the 2008 Democratic primary season: "According to a new poll, Barack Obama has a 24-point lead over Hillary Clinton in North Carolina. Obama is doing particularly well with one important demographic: voters." Another example, also from *SNL*'s "Weekend Update," is about the 2008 Republican primary season: "During last week's Republican debate, three of the ten candidates said they did not believe in evolution, including Kansas Senator Sam Brownback, who added that he would defend his conviction from one edge of the Earth to the other."

On occasion, however, late night comics poke some fun at the institution of elections. There is some precedent for this from Will Rogers, who once quipped: "Politics has got so expensive that it takes lots of money to even get beat with." Late night television jokes about elections sound similarly cynical themes. For example, a common premise is that politicians during an election campaign will say virtually anything to get elected, as illustrated by this Jay Leno joke: "President Obama has been meeting with voters in what he calls 'backyard chats.' He's held these in real people's backyards. . . . I think all politicians should talk to people in their backyards. Then you could take what they say and spread it on the lawn."

There was one exception to the trend of ignoring the election process in late night political humor. That was the thirty-seven-day post-election Florida recount controversy that determined the outcome of the 2000 presidential election. As votes were counted on the night of the election, two facts became clear. First, neither candidate had the 270 electoral votes needed to win. Al Gore (who eventually won the popular vote by approximately one-half of a percentage point) had 255 while George W. Bush had 246. Second, results from three states were still indeterminate: New Mexico, Oregon, and Florida, with 5, 7, and 25 electoral votes, respectively. As the evening progressed, attention focused on Florida, whose votes would give either candidate a victory.

Although some news organizations had predicted a Gore victory in the state earlier in the evening, they retracted this prediction a few hours later. By 2:30 a.m., with most of the votes in Florida counted, Bush was declared the winner by the networks, and Gore called Bush to concede. Within a few hours, however, votes counted in a few heavily Democratic counties made it apparent that Gore was narrowing Bush's slender lead, and Gore called Bush to retract his concession. By morning, although Bush clung to a lead of a few hundred votes, under Florida law a recount of the ballots was required before a winner could be declared and the electoral votes awarded. Gore requested that ballots in four counties be counted by hand.

Both campaigns, and their supporters around the nation, turned their full attention to the recount. Numerous controversies arose, such as how to count ballots that were improperly marked, a confusing ballot in Palm Beach County that likely robbed Gore of votes, allegations of intimidation of African American voters in several counties, and the way that overseas military ballots were tabulated. Aspects of the recount process were challenged in court, and eventually one of the cases made it to the Florida Supreme Court, which ruled in favor of Gore that the recount be continued. The Bush team appealed to the US Supreme Court, which ruled on December 12 that the recounts could not be completed before the legal deadline, and therefore should cease. Bush, who was ahead in the count at that point, was declared the winner.[10]

Late night comics delighted in making light of this unprecedented situation. The main theme of their jokes was that the election process itself had failed. They poked fun at the indeterminate nature of the recount process, the way Florida was handling the recount, and the decision-making of the Florida and US Supreme Courts. Here are a few examples:

They're still counting absentee ballots in some places. Know how slow it is to count these? Well, just today 7 votes came in for Michael Dukakis! [Dukakis was the 1988 Democratic presidential candidate.] —*David Letterman*

Did anyone see the Florida Supreme Court hearing yesterday? The judges kept asking the same question over and over again: "Are you sure you want either of these guys to be elected?" —*David Letterman*

You know, it shows how old I am. I can remember the good old days when the president picked the Supreme Court justices instead of the other way around. —*Jay Leno*

Here's my solution to the election. Bush will be the president of the red states and Gore will be president of the blue states. —*David Letterman*

In light of these events, America is canceled. Citizens are asked to choose between Canada and Mexico by 4:00 p.m. tomorrow. —*from* Saturday Night Live's *"Weekend Update"*

Eventually it began to seem as if life were imitating satire. Discussing the idea to dub Comedy Central's tongue-in-cheek election coverage "Indecision 2000," Jon Stewart said: "Calling this whole thing 'Indecision 2000' was at first a bit of a lighthearted jab, perhaps an attempt at humor. We had no idea the people were going to run with that."

The News Media (and the Special Case of Comedy Central)

The news media are often called the fourth estate, or the fourth branch of government. As an institution that monitors the executive, legislative, and judicial branches, it is as important to the health of our democracy as any of the other three. Thomas Jefferson famously wrote that he would prefer newspapers without a government to a government without newspapers.[11] (Of course, he also pronounced himself "infinitely the happier" for reading newspapers less than once a month.[12])

You might think that the fourth branch of government would attract as much attention from the late night comics as the other three. After all, everybody is a media consumer; just about everyone seems to have an opinion about the media, and most of these opinions are less than complimentary. Polls show that as many as two-thirds of Americans think that "news stories are often inaccurate," and only one-quarter think that news organizations "get the facts straight." Nearly two-thirds (63 percent) believe that journalists are "politically biased in their reporting." Over 70 percent believe that when reporters get their facts wrong they "try to cover up their mistakes." And a majority of all Americans (55 percent) say they have little confidence in the media (specifically, "not very much" or "none at all").[13]

Despite the apparent audience receptivity to jokes about the media, however, fewer than 3 percent of the jokes we catalogued target journalism or the media more generally. So, if the media play a major role in our lives, and many people are highly critical of news organizations, why don't late night talk show hosts target them more often? It may have something to do with the fact that most late night talk show hosts work for broadcast networks that also have news divisions. This is not to suggest that these comics are actively censored by their network executives, but there may be some self-censoring involved.

One media outlet that is disproportionately targeted is the Fox News Channel. Launched in 1996, Fox News claims to be "fair and balanced," in spite of the fact that it is seen by most journalists as having a conservative and Republican-friendly tone. This has led late night comics to take numerous shots at it over the years, as seen in the following examples:

The Bush administration announced that it is starting its own news channel in Iraq so they can deliver the administration's point of view without any interference. Not surprisingly they are gonna call it the Fox News Network. —*Conan O'Brien*

This week in Baghdad, four people were arrested for pretending to be journalists. I'll tell you, this has got all the people over at Fox News nervous. —*Jay Leno*

> CBS News today has fired four employees for wildly fabricating a news story. The good news: they all got jobs over at Fox. —*Craig Ferguson*

> [Dick Cheney] sat down for a one-on-one with Fox News. Very bold choice. Dick Cheney sitting down with Fox News is like Mrs. Butterworth sitting down with the Pancake Channel. —*Jimmy Kimmel*

It may be that the late night hosts enjoy skewering Fox News because of their own political sympathies. The entertainment industry as a whole is solidly left of center in its politics,[14] and many famous performers, such as Sean Penn, Matt Damon, George Clooney, and Angelina Jolie, are well-known activists for, and supporters of, liberal causes and Democratic candidates. Among television talk show hosts, HBO's Bill Maher and Comedy Central's Jon Stewart and Stephen Colbert make no bones about their ideological sympathies. And we have already seen that Republican presidential tickets come in for more ribbing than their Democratic counterparts.

Whatever their politics, however, these comedians were more than ready to ridicule members of the mainstream media who became involved in journalistic scandals. For example, during the final days of the 2004 presidential election, *CBS Nightly News* anchor Dan Rather was involved in developing and reporting a story about President George W. Bush's National Guard service for *60 Minutes II*. The story alleged that President Bush's attendance records were falsified and suggested that his service was effectively a "no-show" job. However, it turned out that the documents Rather and *CBS Nightly News* were relying on were themselves falsified (or at least couldn't be authenticated).[15] The comics joined media critics and Republicans in lambasting Rather, with jokes such as these gems—both by Jay Leno:

> Dan Rather announced today that he's stepping down as anchor of the CBS News. Though Rather said he hasn't been able to verify it yet. So it's not official.

> I'm sure you've all heard about the troubles at CBS, which stands for Can't Back Story, by the way.

The great exceptions to this tendency to leave the major news organizations alone are Comedy Central's *The Daily Show* and *The Colbert Report*. One reason these programs can target major news outlets is easy to understand: Comedy Central does not have a news division. More importantly, both programs are structured differently from late night talk shows on the broadcast networks. *The Daily Show* is modeled as a "fake" news program that satirizes actual news organizations, while *The Colbert Report* is a spoof of right-wing political news talk programs. Thus, both overt and implicit media criticism are built into the DNA of both shows. The success of these two shows can be seen as an indication that there was an underserved market for comic material that makes fun of the media.

For his part, Jon Stewart regularly lambasts news organizations for their sensationalism, pack journalism, focus on trivialities, factual errors, rush to print, and so on. Sometimes his ire takes the form of segments introduced with overly fancy graphics and exaggerated titles, as in his coverage of elections in the "Indecision 2000" segments and of the American occupation of Iraq in "Mess O'Potamia—The Iraq War Is Over." These segments usually begin with an extended introduction accompanied by high-tech, heavily produced, and exaggerated graphics, highlighting the showbiz side of television news. However, Stewart's main tool is his acerbic commentary, which relies on extended diatribes using exaggeration, sarcasm, and reductio ad absurdum. See the following extended excerpt, in which Stewart takes White House correspondents to task for failing in their watchdog function:

> I love watching the White House press conferences, they're very enjoyable. I love watching talented journalists who spent their entire lives to get the point where they're in the White House press corps only to find out they're dictation machines where the White House will tell them what to say. But I'm watching it today and the strangest thing happened, today was the first press conference relevant since they released the president's Vietnam service record and suddenly, it's like there's a whole new attitude. I have just one question for the press corps: Where the f*** have you been? You're starting to ask questions now? Now? All of a sudden, they've got questions and

it's about his Vietnam service. Guys, you're like eight wars behind. Hey! I heard there was a break-in at the Watergate! You might want to check in on that!

Over the years Stewart has also very publicly rebuked major news figures like Bill O'Reilly, Jim Cramer, and the hosts of CNN's *Crossfire* for their journalistic failings.[16] While his jokes about the media often incorporate his own partisan perspectives on American politics, his sense of humor spans the political spectrum.

TOPICAL HUMOR

In addition to the flawed performance of political institutions, many jokes reference the newsworthy topics of the day. For example, the release of government figures on unemployment or inflation might become the news peg for a joke about the poor economy. That might stimulate a follow-up joke about how miserably the president's economic policies are failing or how Congress blithely ignores the economic hardships of ordinary people.

For the most part, however, jokes that are linked to current issues do not directly concern the *policies* put forth by politicians to address those issues. Comedians simply pick up on issues that they can assume audiences are familiar with and build jokes around them.

For example, consider a Jay Leno joke about former Vice President Dick Cheney: "Apparently there's a problem with the paperwork with Dick Cheney's heart operation. The insurance company doesn't want to pay. They say [that] for Cheney being heartless was a preexisting condition." This is most obviously a joke about Cheney's reputation for being tough-minded if not hard-hearted. (He has jokingly referred to himself as Darth Vader.) But there is a subtext of widespread public concern over rising health care costs and battles with insurance companies regarding what procedures they will cover. Such concerns are linked to ongoing public policy issues by continuing partisan debate over implementing Obamacare.

In this context, we can consider the broad issues lampooned on late night talk shows as a backdrop to more narrowly focused jokes that specifically address public policies. And given the topical nature of late night humor, it is not surprising that a list of the most-frequently-joked-about subjects might easily be mistaken for a list of subjects that stimulated the most news coverage. After all, many of these late night jokes were based on the news of the day. Moreover, the topics covered in these jokes are still on the public agenda today, even though they are drawn from a compendium of jokes that extends back two decades.

Table 5.1 shows that, during the period we analyzed, by far the most frequent topics of late night comedy were the economy (6,255 jokes) and terrorism (5,586 jokes), collectively representing nearly one out of every eight jokes in our entire study. Finishing a distant third were issues related to health and health care (1,492 jokes), followed by environmental issues (1,396) and the military and national defense (1,195). No other issue area reached the 1,000-joke mark, which represents roughly 1 percent of all jokes. Rounding out the top ten were the Middle East (886 jokes), outer space and NASA (768), immigration (666), education (609), and issues revolving around the federal budget and taxes (568).

Jokes about the economy tended to vary according to the economy's performance. When times are good, there is less to joke about, but an economist's nightmare is a joke writer's dream. One staple is the put-down of politicians' failure to make things better. For instance, in the midst of economic hard times in 2012, Leno noted sarcastically: "Federal Reserve chairman Ben Bernanke warned that Congress is heading the economy over a fiscal cliff. Which is great news. How many thought we went over the cliff months ago? . . . Huh? You mean we still got some money left? I can't believe that!"

Similarly, Leno made fun of the furloughs that the State of California imposed on state workers to save money. "Today is furlough Friday here in California. The state is so broke, 200,000 state workers have to stay home without pay as a cash-saving measure. This is what I love about California. They make it sound like it's fun. 'Oh, furlough Friday.' What's the next big holiday? 'Selling your blood for money Saturday?' Is that it?"

In his Halloween show on October 31, 2011, Leno picked up on the Occupy movement, which arose as a protest against poor economic conditions and economic inequality: "Earlier tonight a bunch of rich

Table 5.1   Number of Late Night Jokes About Various Issue Areas (1992–2011)

Issue Area	Number of Jokes
Economy	6,255
Terrorism	5,586
Health and health care	1,492
Environmental issues	1,396
Military and national defense	1,195
Middle East	886
Outer space and NASA	768
Immigration	666
Education	609
Federal budget and taxes	568

kids came to my door, took all my candy, and the other 99 percent of the kids in the neighborhood are now occupying my front lawn." Even good economic news can produce a good news/bad news joke. Again, from Leno in 1996: "Folks, some good news from Washington. According to the latest report, prices have come down 0.3 percent. Unfortunately the cost of driving to the supermarket has gone up 298 percent! It kind of balances out."

The grim topic of terrorism may seem an unlikely stimulus for thousands of jokes in late night monologues. But as regulations by the Transportation Security Administration (TSA) became a source of irritation among travelers, and as the Department of Homeland Security persisted in its sometimes heavy-handed actions and apparent underperformance in the government's "war on terror," it quickly became a favorite topic of late night comics and talk show hosts. In 2004, Leno cracked: "The Department of Homeland Security announced today that airport screeners, for the most part, perform their jobs poorly. That's good information for our [Homeland] Security Department to have . . . as long as they don't broadcast it to the rest of the world." In a monologue during the 2004 presidential election campaign, Leno picked up on another news item: "In the war on terrorism, Osama bin Laden's cook and chauffeur have now been captured. You get the feeling this is not the big victory the Republicans were hoping for?"

When former New York City Mayor Rudy Giuliani inexplicably claimed in 2010 that there had been no domestic terrorist attacks during George W. Bush's presidency, Jon Stewart hit the ball out of the park with this gem: "What Giuliani is saying is that even though the worst terror attack in the history of the country took place during Bush's term, that doesn't count. . . . See, 9/11 was a preseason game. Giuliani is making a point about regular season games." Stewart also expressed incredulity over the delay in President Obama's closure of the Guantánamo detention facility. After showing a clip of Obama saying "Guantánamo will be closed no later than one year from now," Stewart commented acidly, "A year? Not to be a jerk, but how much packing does it really take? A mattress, a couple of Korans."

However, a great many jokes that referenced terrorism or terrorists in a lighthearted way were simply intended to let audiences laugh about what is normally a deadly serious topic. Prime examples of this include Jay Leno's one-liner, "It was so hot [in New York today], Al Qaeda was having wet burqa contests," and this joke from Conan O'Brien: "Homeland Security Director Tom Rich announced Al Qaeda has plans to attack buildings in Newark. After hearing this, Al Qaeda said, 'Are you crazy? Even we won't go to Newark.'" And from David Letterman's list of the "Top Ten Things Overheard at the White House Easter Egg Hunt," Number Seven was "Unfortunately the Easter bunny's been detained at Gitmo [i.e., the Guantánamo detention camp]."

As we noted with regard to Vice President Cheney, jokes about health issues and health care provided a pretext for making fun of individual politicians. For example, Conan O'Brien observed: "Earlier today former President Clinton appeared in New York City and launched a campaign against obesity. Not surprisingly Clinton's campaign is called 'No Fat Chicks.'" But jokes about health and health care were also the basis for sharp political commentary, particularly from Comedy Central's hosts. For example, Colbert satirized Republican opposition to Obamacare in the following rant: "[The government's] always trying to tell me what to do. Take Obamacare. Why do I, as a man, have to pay for a woman's OB/GYN services? So to get my money's worth this year, I'm getting a Pap smear."

A similar pattern can be found in the jokes made about the environment, as seen in these two very different riffs on the climate change debate. In 2007, Letterman used this issue as an opportunity to chide then-president George W. Bush: "President Bush says he's really going to buckle down and fight global warming. As a matter of fact he announced he's sending 20,000 troops to the sun." Three years later, Leno turned the same issue into a criticism of hypocrisy by government bureaucrats: "In a world meeting in Cancun on climate change, experts say we must all drastically cut back on our lifestyles. You know, this would carry a lot more weight if they hadn't made the announcement from Cancun. What, all the hotels in Newark were booked, fellows? Let me know how the follow-up in Tahiti goes."

The only foreign affairs issue to make the top ten topics list (apart from the international dimensions of terrorism) was the Middle East. The jokes told in this context often referenced the general political instability and frequent violence in the region, including Israel's often hostile relations with its neighbors. In 2000, Leno noted that President Clinton was in Egypt "working on a cease-fire in the Mideast. We call it a cease-fire. They call it reloading." A decade later, Jon Stewart mentioned in passing: "In keeping with tonight's lighthearted program . . . you know, it's been almost five minutes since we've heard about a senseless act of violence from the Middle East." Some of these jokes traded in Arab stereotypes, as in David Letterman's "Top Ten New Fall Shows on the Al Jazeera Network" list in 2006, which included "How I Met Your Mullah," "SpongeBob SquareTurban," "Welcome Back Kotter from Your Detainment at Gitmo," and "The Man from C.A.M.E.L."

Among these frequently-joked-about topics, the odd man out is outer space and NASA. Why were there so many jokes on this not very topical topic? The romance of America's entry into the space age, culminating in a manned flight to the moon, has long since faded. So has our competition with the former Soviet Union, which provided a significant policy dimension to space exploration. So what were these jokes all about? Some were standard fare about the stupidity of government bureaucrats, which had more bite in this context because they were aimed at an agency staffed by brilliant nerds. For example, when NASA lost track of a satellite that fell out of orbit and plunged toward Earth, Letterman observed: "They don't know where it's going to hit and what to expect. They're not exactly rocket scientists."

More generally, many jokes referenced NASA just to provide a change of pace or a piquant juxtaposition. For example, in discussing the poor showing of American students on standardized tests, Leno lamented: "Math scores down 20 percent, reading scores down 30 percent, science scores down a whopping 50 percent. And that's just at NASA headquarters." And Letterman commented on an international space mission's return to Earth with this joke: "Last week an American, a Russian, and a Spaniard returned to Earth in a space capsule. Experts believe this could be the beginning of a really good joke."

A more obvious source of jokes was the topic of immigration, particularly the long-standing problem of dealing with illegal immigrants or undocumented workers. Many of these jokes concerned the persistent failure of efforts to halt illegal immigration from Mexico, as is evident from this pair of jokes. First Leno:

> It was this week in 1954 that Ellis Island closed after processing more than 20 million immigrants. You know why they went through Ellis Island? Because they didn't realize how easy it was to sneak through Mexico.

Then Letterman:

> It's the anniversary of the Great Wall of China. You look at it now and we think, what's the deal with those Chinese? What were they trying to pull? But in all honesty, since they put up the wall, not one Mexican has sneaked in.

Occasionally, though, there were sharp criticisms of particular policies. Consider this 2010 barb from Letterman: "Have you heard about the new immigration laws in Arizona? If they don't like your looks, they can have you deported. The new law is essentially 'Buy a piñata, go to jail.'"

Finally, there's the endless partisan squabbling over government spending, budget deficits, and taxation, which makes it almost too easy for comedians looking for surefire zingers with audience appeal. After all, who among us has never thought we could do a better job of divvying up the government's tax dollars than the endlessly bickering politicians in Washington? And that's before we total up our own tax returns. As Jay Leno informed audiences in an April 12 monologue (three nights before Tax Day): "The US tax code is now four times longer than the combined works of William Shakespeare—3.8 million words long. In fact, if Romeo and Juliet were alive today and tried to do a joint return, they'd probably kill themselves again."

As for the federal government's chronic budgetary battles, Letterman's "Top Ten Signs the Government Is Running Out of Money" hilariously skewered this subject. Entries included: "State dinners are at IHOP"; "The Witness Protection Program now issues informants a fake moustache"; "The original Constitution is on eBay"; and "The NSA [National Security Agency] can only afford to tap phones during off-peak hours."

A PAUCITY OF POLICY JOKES?

As we have seen, it's easier to make a joke about an individual than about an institution.[17] It's harder to get a laugh from the legislative process than from lechery in the Oval Office. However, one observer has suggested that the personalized nature of late night political humor is more evident in the humor found on the broadcast networks (e.g., Leno, Letterman) than on Comedy Central.[18]

Some of our data seem to bear out this assertion. In 2008, for example, between 86 and 88 percent of the political jokes told by Jay Leno, David Letterman, and Conan O'Brien were directed at individuals. Of these jokes, 36 to 45 percent focused on some personal characteristic. On the other hand, only 64 to 76 percent of the jokes told by Jon Stewart and Stephen Colbert, respectively, were directed at individuals, and only 12 to 15 percent were keyed to a personal characteristic.

These numbers suggest that the political humor of Comedy Central may be more sophisticated and nuanced than that of the stand-up comedians who host late night shows on broadcast networks. This conclusion fits with the praise that is heaped on *The Daily Show* and *The Colbert Report* by many journalists, politicians, and scholars.[19] It is also consistent with the idea that Stewart's and Colbert's audience is more politically sophisticated than the audience of late night television programming on the broadcast networks.[20] With a more politically knowledgeable audience, Stewart and Colbert can focus on more complex joke topics linked to issues, institutions, and processes. Such jokes presuppose a level of political understanding that the hosts of the broadcast network programs cannot assume is true of their audiences.

All this suggests that an examination of late night jokes about institutions and policies might be largely restricted to the late night programming of Comedy Central. But this is not the case. As we made clear earlier in the chapter, jokes about political institutions are not uncommon on late night broadcast network programming. Our data also show that policy-related political jokes, while not the norm, are just as likely to be told by David Letterman as by Jon Stewart.

Our focus in this final section is on jokes about specific public policies, as opposed to the broad topical areas we discussed above. Most of the policy jokes we analyzed fall into one of four general areas: (1) 9/11 and the "war on terror," (2) "rogue states," (3) other world powers, and (4) a smorgasbord of domestic issues.

9/11 and the "War on Terror"

Easily the most-joked-about issue area in terms of specific policies was the US-led "war on terror" that emerged in the aftermath of the 9/11 attacks, including the Iraq War and our continued military presence in Afghanistan. Of the five leading late night hosts (Leno, Letterman, O'Brien, Stewart, and Colbert), O'Brien told the fewest (4 percent of his total jokes), while Stewart told the most (10 percent); the other three hosts averaged 5 percent of their jokes on this subject. While these percentages may seem small, they represent the total of only three (Iraq, terrorism, and Afghanistan) of the several hundred potential topics in our database. In fact, Iraq and Afghanistan are the first- and third-most-joked-about foreign countries. This is all the more impressive when we consider that well over 90 percent of such jokes were told in the years after 9/11.

The relatively large number of jokes told by Jon Stewart can probably be explained by his clear personal outrage concerning the Iraq War (both the way it was conducted and the conditions under which the United States entered the war). By contrast, Leno, Letterman, and O'Brien may have avoided such jokes because of the war's complexity and controversial nature, given their generally larger and more diverse audiences. However, the broadcast network talk show hosts seemed no less likely to joke about policy than Stephen Colbert, and we will see this pattern replicated with respect to Stewart's numbers in other policy areas. In addition, jokes about the aftermath of 9/11 highlight one of the central characteristics of late night talk show comedy: its topical nature.

Jokes about Iraq constitute 2.5 percent of all jokes in our database—more than 2,500 in all. Just over half of these jokes were told in 2003, 2004, and 2006, during the height of hostilities and controversies. Iraq jokes targeted the war itself and the country's subsequent civil war, the lawlessness following the US invasion, Iraqi leader Saddam Hussein, and the attempts to build a working postwar government.

Terrorism policy jokes, which made up slightly less than 2 percent of all jokes, focused on a wide variety of subjects. These included homeland security and defense, the airline industry, Islam, and New York City. Almost half of these jokes were told during 2006, 2009, and 2010. A majority of the jokes about Afghanistan (which constitutes fewer than 1 percent of our entire database) were focused either on terrorism or on the war and civil war. A full 84 percent of these jokes were told during 2001, 2002 (when the United States invaded Afghanistan), and 2010 (a year that saw more US casualties in Afghanistan than any other). See Box 5.1 for a small sampling of the jokes targeting our policies on war and terrorism.

Rogue States

Since the end of the Cold War, a number of states have been identified by US presidents (and often other world leaders) as posing a continuing threat either to their neighbors or to others. These states typically stray in some way from established international norms of behavior

BOX 5.1

Selected Jokes About the War on Terrorism

"The electricity is back on in Baghdad. That is a very climactic moment in any country's liberation, when the lights come back on and you get a good look at what you looted." —*Bill Maher*

"Saddam Hussein was executed last week by hanging. Or, as they call that in Iraq, death by natural causes." —*Jay Leno*

"We have defeated Saddam Hussein and Iraq. The good news is Iraq is ours, and the bad news is Iraq is ours." —*David Letterman*

"More coming out about Saddam Hussein. We now know he takes Viagra and he has as many as six mistresses. No wonder Congress is reluctant to take action against this guy—he's one of their own." —*Jay Leno*

"In a bizarre move, Saddam Hussein has released all prisoners being held in Iraqi jails. Isn't that amazing? Iraq has prisoners that are still alive." —*Jay Leno*

"Iraqi officials are worried about the upcoming election. They think it could lead to a civil war. At this point, wouldn't a civil war be an improvement?" —*Craig Ferguson*

"President Bush admitted that there are four areas of Iraq where it will be very difficult for people to vote: the east, the west, the north, and the south." —*Jay Leno*

"Osama bin Laden has hired ten look-alikes. Now, how hard up do you have to be before you take that job? There's no way to win! If Osama dies, you don't get paid. If you're found, you get killed." —*Jay Leno*

"I read in the paper today this bin Laden guy is the wealthiest guy in Afghanistan. That's when you know your government is no good, when the wealthiest guy in the country lives in a cave." —*Jay Leno*

"The leaders of the Taliban said today that killing bin Laden won't solve the problem. But, you know, it couldn't hurt." —*Jay Leno*

or rules of order. In particular, "rogue states" (the term is somewhat controversial) pursue weapons of mass destruction, support terrorism, and commit extreme human rights abuses on their own citizens. When the term was first coined by Clinton national security adviser Anthony Lake, it was applied only to North Korea, Cuba, Iraq, Iran, and Libya,[21] although Serbia and Montenegro, Syria, Sudan, and Afghanistan later joined the "club."

We have already reviewed jokes about Iraq and Afghanistan, and not enough jokes were told on late night talk shows about Serbia and Montenegro, Syria, and Sudan to warrant including these countries in our discussion. This leaves jokes about Iran, Cuba, North Korea, and Libya, which together make up between 1.3 percent (by Leno) and 2.4 percent (by Letterman) of the jokes in our database. There is little difference between the total percentage of jokes about these countries on Comedy Central programming (1.9 percent) and on the broadcast network programs (1.7 percent).

Jokes about Iran were most frequent in 2009, the year a controversial presidential election was held there, and in 2006 and 2010, years during which debates over Iran's nuclear power and weapon development, and the international tension they caused, were particularly prominent. Most of these jokes focused on the election (which sparked protests in Iran), relations with the United States, nuclear weapons, and controversial Iranian president Mahmoud Ahmadinejad. Late night jokes about Cuba were heaviest in 1994 (the year an agreement was signed to admit a certain number of Cubans per year into the United States), in 2000 (the year of the political controversy over the custody and immigration status of Cuban refugee Elián González), and in 2008 (the year Fidel Castro stepped down as president and his brother Raul took over). About half of all jokes about Cuba focused on refugee and immigration issues, Raul Castro's succession to the presidency, and Fidel Castro's health problems.

North Korea jokes were heaviest in recent years—two-thirds of them were told in 2006, 2009, and 2010. The relatively recent surge of attention reflected heightened international controversy over the country's nuclear development program and increased hostilities with South Korea. North Korea announced it had tested a nuclear weapon for the first time in 2006 and again in 2009. In 2010 the country was charged with sinking the South Korean warship *Cheonan,* although the government denied responsibility. Some jokes also centered on the personal appearance and odd behavior of former North Korean dictator Kim Jong-il.

Finally, Libya attracted the fewest jokes of any rogue state—just 0.2 percent of all jokes. Most of these occurred in 2009, when Lockerbie bomber Abdelbaset Ali al-Megrahi was released from prison in Scotland on compassionate grounds and allowed to return to Libya, where he was greeted like a hero; and in 2011, when longtime Libyan leader Muammar Gaddafi was overthrown and killed. See Box 5.2 for examples of rogue state jokes.

Foreign Policy and Other World Powers

Late night talk show hosts joke from time to time about countries beyond rogue states and countries that the United States is engaged with in armed conflict. Jokes about these other countries, and American foreign policy more generally, are less common than those focusing on domestic issues and policies. This should come as no surprise, since Americans are notorious for their lack of interest in and knowledge about international events not directly involving the United States.[22]

BOX 5.2

Selected Jokes About Various "Rogue States"

North Korea:

"According to Kim Jong-il's biography, they say he has been constantly accused of dishonesty, drunkenness, and sexual excess. So if he lived here, he could be in Congress." —*Jay Leno*

(continues)

BOX 5.2 CONTINUED

"North Korea conducted a nuclear test and the blast was so small that many scientists are saying it was a dud. Apparently, the nuclear bomb didn't work well because it was made in Korea." —Conan O'Brien

"North Korean dictator Kim Jong-il may be stepping down. Yeah, experts in the State Department say he could be replaced by his son, Menta Li III." —David Letterman

"President Bush met with the president of South Korea. Things got off to an awkward start when President Bush asked 'Are you from the good Korea or the bad Korea?'" —Conan O'Brien

Iran:
"The president of Iran has announced, 'We are a nuclear country.' You know what's scary about that? The president of Iran knows how to pronounce *nuclear*." —David Letterman

"Iran said they will inflict harm and pain on the United States if we try to stop their nuclear program. Who's writing their speeches now—Mr. T?" —Jay Leno

"France and Germany warned Iran this week not to pursue their nuclear research program. In fact, France and Germany warned Iran that if they didn't stop their program they would, you know, warn them again." —Jay Leno

Cuba:
"Well, here's some sad news coming from Havana, ladies and gentlemen: Fidel Castro has resigned. A lot of people thought it was because of his health, but, no, he's resigning because he wants to spend more time with his beard." —David Letterman

"He ran Cuba for almost fifty years. And political analysts are now debating what kind of changes the Cuban people will hope for. I'm gonna guess: term limits." —Jay Leno

"Castro took over in 1959. He's the longest-reigning dictator in power currently, if you don't count Martha Stewart. He's going to be eighty years old. He's talking about retiring. You know what that means? He could wind up in Miami." —Jay Leno

As a result, jokes that focus on foreign countries tend to highlight either heavily publicized news events or widely shared stereotypes.

Among the twenty most-joked-about countries, if we exclude those mentioned in the previous two sections, the number of jokes about some of them is so small that they're almost not worth mentioning. For example, between 1992 and 2012, there were only 112 jokes about Japan, or just over 5 per year (out of a total of over 100,000 jokes logged). Jokes about other world powers ranged from a low of 2.7 percent of all jokes told by David Letterman to 4 percent by Conan O'Brien. The five main programs in our study averaged 3.6 percent, and Comedy Central hosts were, on average, no more likely than broadcast network hosts to tell jokes about foreign powers.

The topical nature of late night humor, along with the public's lack of interest in the world beyond our shores, helps explain the lack of any obvious pattern in jokes targeting America's friends and foes abroad. As we've discussed, foreign dictators are popular targets, particularly those with whom our relations are strained—but so are the leaders of our allies, especially those who have personal foibles. In this regard, jokes about foreign leaders and international celebrities are little different from jokes about American politicians and political institutions. Thus, it is not the sheer number of jokes but rather their *tone* that differentiates jokes about friendly and unfriendly countries.

For example, longtime ally Great Britain was the most-joked-about country outside the United States. But the jokes focused mainly on the personal lives of various members of the royal family. The three heaviest years for Great Britain jokes were 1995 (stories about the looming divorce between Prince Charles and Princess Diana), 1996 (the year Charles and Diana as well as Prince Andrew and Duchess of York Sarah Ferguson or "Fergie" got divorced), and 2010 (a bribery scandal involving Fergie). All this attests to the apparently unslakable popular interest in the royals, who frequently grace the covers of supermarket tabloids.

By contrast, consider the tone of jokes about China, the fourth-most-joked-about country in our study. Once again, jokes were keyed to major international news events, such as the 2008 Beijing Olympics, the accidental US bombing of the Chinese embassy in Belgrade in 1999, and a 2001 incident involving a United States Navy intelligence aircraft downed and detained on the Chinese island of Hainan. But these jokes frequently contained biting criticism of government policies, particularly the repression of political dissent, evoking memories of the 1989 Tiananmen Square massacre and the occupation of Tibet.

Jokes about Russia, the fifth-most-joked-about country, focused in particular on the drinking habits and health problems of former Russian President Boris Yeltsin. Just over half of the jokes about Mexico, most of which are of recent vintage (since 2005), focused on immigration. Jokes about the Middle East region were about the peace process, war, and terrorism, while almost one-quarter of the jokes about Israel revolved around its relations with the Palestinians. The relatively few jokes about India focused on the migration of jobs. See Box 5.3 for some examples of jokes about these countries.

Domestic Policy Issues

Most Americans pay considerably more attention to domestic policy issues than they do to foreign affairs. But this does not necessarily mean that domestic policy is a popular topic for late night humorists. Slightly fewer than 3 percent of the jokes in our database focus on domestic policy issues like gay rights, abortion, gun control, the death penalty, taxes and the federal budget, and so on.

Moreover, many of the jokes about public policy target the positions that individual politicians (or political parties) take on an issue, rather than the specifics of the issues themselves. For example, comedians might joke about how the policy stance reflects some characteristic of the politician who holds it. Conan O'Brien joked about Al Gore's book on global warming and the environment by evoking Gore's reputation for dullness: "The first chapter talks about how you shouldn't chop down trees to make a book that no one will read."

Finally, some public policy issues are rarely joked about, despite (or perhaps because of) the passions they provoke from partisans on both sides. There are relatively few jokes, for example, about race relations, abortion rights, and AIDS. Such topics are likely considered to

BOX 5.3

Selected Jokes About Foreign Policy and Other World Powers

China:

"China is getting ready for the Olympics. The official motto for the Olympics is 'One World, One Dream.' Restrictions Apply. Tibet Not Included." —*Jay Leno*

"Beijing skies are so polluted that Chinese authorities are planning emergency measures for the Olympics. For example, protesters will now only be run over with hybrid tanks." —*Jay Leno*

"China has announced that during the Olympics, protesters will be allowed to assemble in designated protest areas. Yeah. Or, as they're commonly called in China, jails." —*Conan O'Brien*

France:

"I don't know why people are surprised that France won't help us get Saddam out of Iraq. After all, France wouldn't help us get the Germans out of France." —*Jay Leno*

"Army personnel in Kuwait unloaded a dozen faulty tanks that only go in reverse. Tanks that only go in reverse—they've been repackaged and sold to France." —*Craig Kilborn*

"American tourists in Paris are reported to being yelled at, spit upon, and attacked by the French. Thank God things are getting back to normal." —*Jay Leno*

The Middle East:

"A lot of trouble in the Middle East right now between Lebanon and Israel. . . . Last night Israel bombed the runways at Beirut's airport, putting a stop on all flights in and out. So I'm sorry everybody, you're just gonna have to cancel that relaxing weekend getaway to Beirut." —*Conan O'Brien*

"Colin Powell's [Middle East] mission was somewhat a success. He came back alive." —*Jay Leno*

"Egypt now says they will no longer recognize Israel. Well of course they don't recognize Israel, people keep blowing it up." —*Jay Leno*

be too serious to be joked about—close to being considered taboo. (As another example, there were few jokes about the 9/11 tragedy itself.)

Bill Maher had firsthand experience with the dangers of dealing with highly sensitive topics; doing so proved taboo even on a show named *Politically Incorrect*. During the first show that aired on ABC after the 9/11 attacks, he rejected President Bush's characterization of the hijackers as "cowards." To the contrary, Maher said, "We have been the cowards. Lobbing cruise missiles from two thousand miles away. That's cowardly. Staying in the airplane when it hits the building. Say what you want about it. Not cowardly." These comments created a national uproar that cost Maher some major advertisers and affiliates and was likely a factor in ABC's decision to cancel the show at the end of the season. However, Maher landed on his feet. In 2003 he began his long-running series *Real Time with Bill Maher* on HBO, which depends on subscribers rather than advertisers for revenue.

Generally speaking, a joke whose success depends on the audience taking a particular position on a controversial issue has lost half the audience (those on the other side of the issue) at the outset. Of course, this is less of a problem for a show that draws its audience from one side of the political spectrum. For example, Bill Maher, Jon Stewart, and Stephen Colbert appeal primarily to political liberals, which makes it easier for them to joke about conservative policies. In fact, we found that Colbert was more likely to joke about domestic policy issues (5 percent of his total jokes) than any of the other hosts. By contrast, Jon Stewart's share of such jokes was below the average (3 percent) of the five top hosts.

Perhaps as a result of such strictures, jokes involving public policy issues often draw on existing stereotypes or noncontroversial positions in order to generate laughs. For example, jokes about gay rights often draw gently on stereotypes of gay men. In a joke about the debate over gay marriage, Letterman asked: "When you're a gay couple getting married, who gets the bachelor party? Who forgets the anniversary?" As we noted earlier, immigration jokes frequently target our inability to deter illegal immigration and the number of illegal immigrants in the country, without directly linking the problem to either party's policies. For example, after President George W.

Bush noted that the United States lacks full control over its border with Mexico, Leno responded: "Full control? If we had any less control, there'd be an EZ Pass lane." And rather than joking that taxes are too high, late night humorists often focus on people's efforts to avoid paying taxes. For example, in a monologue that aired on April 1, Leno joked that on April Fools' Day people try to fool their friends and relatives. Then he added, "Don't confuse that with April 15, when people try to fool the IRS." See Box 5.4 for more examples on domestic policy–related jokes.

BOX 5.4
Selected Jokes About Domestic Policy

The Environment:
"According to a new UN report, the global warming outlook is much worse than originally predicted. Which is pretty bad when they originally predicted it would destroy the planet." —*Jay Leno*

"Yesterday, a group of scientists warned that because of global warming, sea levels will rise so much that parts of New Jersey will be under water. The bad news? Parts of New Jersey won't be under water." —*Conan O'Brien*

"Al Gore said over the weekend that global warming is more serious than terrorism. Unless the terrorist is on your plane, then that extra half a degree doesn't bother you so much." —*Jay Leno*

Immigration:
"The president of Mexico has arrived in the US, thanks to some nifty fence climbing. . . . I thought this was encouraging. He offered to take President Bush's job for $3 an hour cash." —*David Letterman*

"Mexican President Vicente Fox arrived in the US today. So, it's official. He's the last one. Turn out the lights. They are all here now." —*Jay Leno*

"In Orange County, President Bush was talking about immigration. Bush said that massive deportation is unrealistic. He said you can't just move 12 million people to another country. I don't know, Mexico did it." —*Jay Leno*

(continues)

BOX 5.4 CONTINUED

Gay Marriage:

"You know who is really against the president's position on gay marriage? Gay men afraid of commitment. Now they have no excuse." —*Jay Leno*

"Soon we may live in a world where the only people opposed to gay marriage will be gay people who are married." —*Craig Ferguson*

"As of today, same-sex couples may now legally get married in Vermont. So finally, finally, after years of waiting, we'll get to hear these words out of Vermont: 'I now pronounce you Ben and Jerry.'" —*Conan O'Brien*

Budget and Taxes:

"Dick Cheney said he felt terrible about shooting a seventy-eight-year-old man, but on the bright side, it did give him a great idea about how to fix Social Security." —*Bill Maher*

"I'm not going to pay taxes. When they say I'm going to prison, I'll say no, prisons cost taxpayers a lot of money. You keep what it would have cost to incarcerate me, and we'll call it even." —*Jimmy Kimmel*

"The IRS said today anyone with a refund coming from their 2001 taxes will lose it if they don't pick it up by April 15th. If it is more than three years they will just keep it. How come it doesn't work that way with back taxes?" —*Jay Leno*

CONCLUSION

Compared to the comic opportunities offered by the foibles and failings of individual politicians, it is little wonder that political institutions and public policies get short shrift in late night monologues. And even in the few jokes about political institutions and policies, the primary targets are individual inadequacies rather than the issues and policies themselves. Many of the jokes about policies are really jokes about the people who support them. Even jokes about institutions like Congress tend to be based on the newsworthy shenanigans of its individual members.

Jon Stewart is an exception to this rule. He frequently builds his humor around deficiencies of the political system, the election process, and the news media. And his Comedy Central compatriot Stephen Colbert has created a comic persona as a right-wing political talk show host that allows him to do the same. But Stewart and Colbert deal in satire and parody on cable TV, where the narrower audiences are more politically attuned, while the traditional talk show hosts are delivering stand-up comedy meant to appeal to a broader audience.

The topical areas that are referenced most often in late night humor are usually plucked from the day's headlines. As a result, they often resemble the news agenda. When it comes to policies, however, foreign affairs get more attention than domestic debates. Other countries and their leaders are relatively safe targets for comedians, and jokes about foreign countries often reference national stereotypes. The really savage jokes are saved for foreign enemies and terrorists, such as Saddam Hussein and Osama bin Laden. Targets such as these draw audiences together as Americans fighting common enemies, rather than separating them from each other as partisans who differ on domestic policies. As Bill Maher discovered, criticism of American policy is fair game for humorists, but criticism of America can backfire.

We did find some partisan differences, with nearly twice as many jokes about the Republican Party and its supporters as about their Democratic counterparts. This echoes our finding in Chapter 3 that Republican presidents and presidential candidates are joked about more often than Democratic presidents and candidates—a reflection, perhaps, of the left-of-center milieu of the entertainment industry, to which many late night comedians belong. As we saw in Chapter 4, however, these leftward-leaning tendencies certainly haven't kept them from joking about Democrats as well as Republicans who are scarred by scandal, which is by far the richest source material for late night monologues.

However political their material, these are comedians, not candidates. Their goal is to produce the biggest laughs from the biggest audience, and their success is measured in ratings rather than in votes. Comedy Central's Jon Stewart and Stephen Colbert are partial exceptions to these rules, with more consistently political material and a more partisan perspective. Even so, the political humor on late night talk shows is more focused on politicians' bad behavior than on their failed policies.

NOTES

1. The results of this Gallup poll can be found at http://www.gallup.com /poll/166196/congress-job-approval-drops-time-low-2013.aspx.

2. John Hibbing and Elizabeth Theiss-Morse, *Congress as Public Enemy: Public Attitudes Toward American Political Institutions* (Cambridge: Cambridge University Press, 1995).

3. Ibid.

4. Pew Research Center, "Supreme Court Favorability Reaches New Low," 2012, http://www.people-press.org/files/legacy-pdf/5-1-12 (Supreme Court Release.pdf).

5. Rosalee A. Clawson and Eric N. Waltenburg, *Legacy and Legitimacy: Black Americans and the Supreme Court* (Philadelphia: University of Temple Press, 2008).

6. "Two-Thirds of Americans Can't Name Any U.S. Supreme Court Justices," *PR Newswire,* June 1, 2012, http://www.prnewswire.com/news-releases/two -thirds-of-americans-cant-name-any-us-supreme-court-justices-says-new -findlawcom-survey-95298909.html (accessed May 12, 2013).

7. Jody C Baumgartner and Peter L. Francia, *Conventional Wisdom and American Elections: Exploding Myths, Exploring Misconceptions,* 2nd ed. (Lanham, MD: Rowman & Littlefield, 2010); Russell J. Dalton and Steven A. Weldon, "Public Images of Political Parties: A Necessary Evil?" *Western European Politics* 28 (2005): 931–951.

8. Ben Shapiro, *Primetime Propaganda: The True Hollywood Story of How the Left Took Over Your TV* (New York: Broadside Books, 2012).

9. S. R. Lichter, L. Lichter, and S. Rothman, "Hollywood and America—The Odd Couple," *Public Opinion* 6, no. 1 (1983): 54–58; D. Prindle and J. Endersby, "Hollywood Liberalism," *Social Science Quarterly* 74, no. 1 (1993): 136–149.

10. James Ceaser and Andrew Busch, *The Perfect Tie: The True Story of the 2000 Presidential Election* (Lanham, MD: Rowman & Littlefield, 2001).

11. The Founders' Constitution, Volume 5, Amendment I (Speech and Press), Document 8, http://press-pubs.uchicago.edu/founders/documents/amendI _speechs8.html (University of Chicago Press).

12. H. A. Washington, ed., *The Writings of Thomas Jefferson* (New York: H. W. Derby, 1861).

13. Lymari Morales, "Distrust in U.S. Media Edges Up to Record High," *Gallup*, September 29, 2010, http://www.gallup.com/poll/143267/distrust-media-edges -record-high.aspx; Pew Research Center, "Press Widely Criticized, but Trusted More Than Other Information Sources," September 22, 2011, http://www.people -press.org/files/legacy-pdf/9-22-2011 (Media Attitudes Release.pdf).

14. Ernest Giglio, *Here's Looking at You: Hollywood, Film & Politics*, 3rd ed. (New York: Lang, 2010).

15. Howard Kurtz, Michael Dobbs, and James V. Grimaldi, "In Rush to Air, CBS Quashed Memo Worries," *Washington Post*, September 19, 2004, p. A1.

16. Jody C Baumgartner and Jonathan S. Morris, "Stoned Slackers or Super-Citizens?" 'Daily Show' Viewing and Political Engagement of Young Adults," in *The Stewart/Colbert Effect: Essays on the Real Impacts of Fake News*, ed. Amarnath Amarasingam (Jefferson, NC: McFarland & Co., 2011).

17. David Niven, S. Robert Lichter, and Daniel Amundson, "The Political Content of Late Night Comedy," *Harvard International Journal of Press/Politics* 8 (2003): 118–133; David Niven, S. Robert Lichter, and Daniel Amundson, "Our First Cartoon President: Bill Clinton and the Politics of Late Night Comedy," in *Laughing Matters: Humor and American Politics in the Media Age*, eds. Jody C Baumgartner and Jonathan S. Morris (New York: Routledge, 2008), 151–170.

18. Russell L. Peterson, *Strange Bedfellows: How Late-Night Comedy Turns Democracy into a Joke* (New Brunswick, NJ: Rutgers University Press, 2008).

19. Baumgartner and Morris, "Stoned Slackers or Super-Citizens?"

20. Dannagal Young and Russell Tisinger, "Dispelling Late-Night Myths: News Consumption Among Late-Night Comedy Viewers and the Predictors of Exposure to Various Late-Night Shows," *Press/Politics* 11 (2006): 113–134.

21. Anthony Lake, "Confronting Backlash States," *Foreign Affairs* 73 (March–April 1994): 45–55.

22. Pew Research Center, "Key News Audiences Now Blend Online and Traditional Sources," August 17, 2008. http://www.people-press.org/2008/08/17 /key-news-audiences-now-blend-online-and-traditional-sources/.

Chapter 6

Laughing Matters

TV comedians take aim at the most powerful politicians—especially presidents and presidential candidates—and target their weakest points: alleged deficits of intelligence, physical flaws, verbal gaffes and, above all, any sort of scandalous behavior. But does all this really matter? Do viewers really allow their political perceptions or opinions to be influenced by comedy routines?

Certainly many political consultants and campaign staffers think so. And experimental studies have shown that exposure to unflattering comic caricatures does influence the way subjects view political figures.[1] We have all seen instances of how a gaffe or impropriety can quickly turn a politician into a national laughingstock. But a more difficult question is whether political humor can systematically undermine the public image of its unfortunate targets day in and day out.

One way to address this question is to look at presidential election campaigns. Every four years, two candidates—each representing one of the major political parties—engage in a lengthy struggle to win the hearts and minds of voters. They are constantly in the news, and their every move is scrutinized, giving comedians nightly opportunities to make fun of them. Meanwhile, opinion polls are regularly taking the pulse of public opinion, providing information about how their popularity waxes and wanes.

Does the constant barrage of jokes directed at presidential candidates have any noticeable effect on how the public views them over the course of the campaign? We address that question in this chapter by looking at the relationship among jokes, news, and unfavorable ratings in presidential election campaigns.

NEWS, COMEDY, AND PUBLIC OPINION

The focus of late night comedy during national elections has always been mostly on the candidates. This is also the case with news coverage. Television news in particular is heavily candidate centered.[2] Researchers who have examined the effects of candidate-centered news media coverage of presidential election campaigns have found that the manner in which candidates are presented can influence how they are perceived by the viewing public.[3]

This also holds true for the viewing public's response to portrayals of political figures in late night comedy routines. For instance, Dannagal Young determined that late night comedy in the 2000 election was consistently framed around two contrasting caricatures: George W. Bush was stupid and Al Gore was a liar.[4] Exposure to these tropes had a significant impact on viewers with low levels of political knowledge. Other research has highlighted the ways other candidates were framed on late night comedy programs, from the serial philanderer Bill Clinton[5] to the folksy but dim Sarah Palin.[6] Why do such caricatures stick to candidates? Overall, the tone of political humor is inherently negative, these constructions are fairly simplistic and highly repetitive, and they focus primarily on individual candidates rather than on, say, the political parties.[7] Moreover, these tropes gain momentum over time.

None of this should come as a surprise. We have discussed at length just how negative, candidate centered, and repetitive late night humor can be. But ordinary viewers pick up these negative jokes and skits in dribs and drabs over a period of time, and thus the most negative images of candidates in the news are often reinforced. The same jokes and skits are also discussed around the office watercooler and shared with friends through social media. In short, the news media call out a politician, but the entertainment media provide a lingering echo. It took only a single stumble for *Saturday Night Live* to turn Gerald Ford, football All-American, into Gerald Ford, uncoordinated stumblebum. And candidates like Bill Clinton and Sarah Palin gave comedians a lot more to work with than a single stumble.

Measuring Humor and News

Our goal is to examine more systematically the ways in which public perceptions of candidates are related to their targeting by late night comedians. Almost uniformly, previous research on the link between late night jokes and candidate favorability has looked at this relationship on the individual level. That is, researchers have examined how a single individual's late night viewing habits are linked to his or her own feelings about a candidate, often in an experimental setting. By contrast, our data set allows us to look at this relationship on the aggregate level. This gives us the ability to examine large-scale shifts in overall favorability toward a candidate throughout the campaign. We can also see if aggregate opinion changes are related to changes in the number of jokes about a given candidate.

Our measure of humor is the same data set of jokes we have drawn on throughout this book. Since the jokes are highly topical, we included a measure of the tone of election news coverage as well. This measure comes from a series of content analyses done by the Center for Media and Public Affairs for the same election campaigns as the ones studied for the data on late night political humor. These studies classified all positive or negative statements about the candidates on the ABC, CBS, and NBC evening news shows.[8] Even in today's vastly expanded news environment, these programs remain a good proxy for the mainstream media more generally, and they are at their most influential during election campaigns.

Measuring Candidate Favorability and Unfavorability

In order to understand how a candidate for president is viewed by voters, we tracked public opinion polling data in which people report whether they view a candidate favorably or unfavorably. Specifically, we looked at the public's unfavorable ratings of candidates during the five general election campaigns from 1992 through 2008. We chose to track how unfavorably people view candidates instead of whom they say they will or will not vote for, because this better reflects the degree to which a candidate is liked or disliked based on his or her personal traits and behavior on the campaign trail.

Since late night comedy tends to criticize personal traits over policy preferences,[9] we were most interested in how perceptions of candidates' likeability are linked to jokes told at their expense. In addition, unfavorable ratings fluctuate somewhat more than intended voting choice, because they are not closely tied to partisanship or policy positions. Also, in contrast to measures of their voting intention, people can report feeling favorably or unfavorably toward both candidates.

Unfortunately, although favorability and unfavorability are pretty clear concepts, no single measure of it has been consistently used over time. Presidential approval has routinely been measured by Gallup polls since the 1940s with the same question that asks, "Do you approve or disapprove of the way [insert name] is handling his job as president?" Favorability measures are more variable, although they address a similar concept. For example, here are two survey items that were both used during the 2000 general election campaign:

1. I would like to read you the names of several individuals who have been mentioned in the news recently. For each one, please tell me whether you have heard of that person and if so, whether you have a favorable or an unfavorable impression of that person. If you do not recognize the name, just say so. . . . George W. Bush (If favorable/unfavorable, ask:) Would that be a strongly favorable/unfavorable impression or just a somewhat favorable/unfavorable impression?

2. I'd like to rate your feelings toward some people and organizations, with one hundred meaning a very warm, favorable feeling, zero meaning a very cold, unfavorable feeling, and fifty meaning not particularly warm or cold. You can use any number from zero to one hundred; the higher the number the more favorable your feelings are toward that person or organization. If you have no opinion or have never heard of that person or organization, please say so. . . .

George W. Bush (If don't know, ask:) Would you say you are unable to give an opinion of George W. Bush, or have you never heard of George W. Bush?

Strictly speaking, we cannot aggregate these questions to create a single measure of unfavorability, even though both attempt to measure the same concept. Among researchers who have public opinion data problems of this nature, it is common to use an algorithm developed by James Stimson,[10] which constructs a generalized measure of opinion about a person or issue based on multiple unique survey items that all address a similar idea. With this calculation, we were able to construct a single measure of unfavorability over time based on dozens of unique survey items. This approach yielded a generalized measure of the public mood toward a candidate at any given point of time.

In particular, we searched the Roper Center's iPoll data bank for all survey items that contained the term *favorable* and the last name of the candidates in each general election, and we treated the general election campaign as beginning once a candidate became the party's presumptive nominee. (In almost all cases this occurred in March.)[11] This produced over eight hundred questions from dozens of unique question series spanning five elections and ten candidates. Using Stimson's algorithm software, we constructed a single time-series measure of unfavorability for each of the candidates. The unit of analysis was a calendar week from Sunday through Saturday, giving us approximately thirty data points per series, and over three hundred data points when all general election candidates were combined for all campaigns.

Such a broad range of data has never before been used to measure the relationship between political humor and voters' assessments of presidential candidates. Nonetheless, there are significant limitations to the conclusions we can draw from this evidence. First, we are looking at how public opinion as a whole moves in relation to jokes that are aired on late night talk shows. But only a minority of the public watches these shows. Even among this audience, only the most devoted viewers would watch a given show every single night, and no one views all the different shows that are aired each night.

Furthermore, we can't know whether the individuals whose opinions changed in any survey of unfavorability ratings were the same ones who were exposed to these jokes. And we don't know whether the people who watch these shows differ in unknown ways from the rest of the electorate. For that matter, we don't know whether there is a secondary effect on people who didn't see a show but learned about some of the jokes later from friends or the media.

Finally, we have included news coverage in the mix because it is a major stimulus for late night jokes, which are highly topical. But it is difficult to sort out the effects of jokes independently of the news that produced them, because they are so tightly bound together on a daily basis, and the public's feelings about the candidates are typically sampled only once every several days.

On the other hand, all these factors would tend to diminish any observable relationship between jokes and candidate unfavorability ratings. If we find a relationship despite these limiting factors, particularly after controlling for news, it would be highly suggestive, even if it is only preliminary and heuristic rather than conclusive. The ability to sort out all these competing factors is a major advantage of experimental studies, which comprise much of the scholarly literature on the effects of political humor. But these studies also have severe limitations—they examine the responses of a very small number of people, usually for a very brief time period. Moreover, we don't know whether people respond the same ways in a laboratory setting as they would under real-world conditions. Thus, the two approaches are complementary, providing different kinds of evidence.

LATE NIGHT HUMOR TARGETS
AND CANDIDATE FAVORABILITY

In this section, we track the association among candidates' unfavorability ratings, the tone of their television news coverage, and the percentage of jokes told at their expense each week until Election Day through a series of charts (Figures 6.1 to 6.10). In order to make comparisons easier, we standardized all the data sets so that each weekly plot on the graph represents the average deviation from a score of zero. For each election cycle from 1992 through 2008, we discuss how news, jokes, and unfavorability ratings move in relation to each major-party candidate. In what ways were the associations between joke targets and changes in unfavorability scores different? In what ways were they similar? Were there points in the campaign where favorability ratings spiked? If so, how closely was the candidate being targeted by late night comedians at that time?

1992: George H. W. Bush and Bill Clinton

The earliest election for which we have news and joke data is the 1992 contest between President George H. W. Bush and his Democratic challenger Bill Clinton. Figure 6.1 demonstrates the weekly fluctuation in unfavorable ratings toward Bush, as well as changes in the percentage of jokes and negative news stories about him. Overall the figure shows a small amount of variation within each series and little association between them. The percentage of jokes directed at Bush rose sharply during the two weeks at the beginning of August, when the Republican National Convention was dominating the news cycle. This convention was heavily criticized in later years for its negative tone, along with its heavy emphasis on traditional values in the days leading up to the nomination. (A case in point was conservative firebrand Pat Buchanan's "Culture War" speech.) However, President Bush was the man of the hour, and late night comics were more apt to focus on him while the convention was unfolding. Overall, there was a positive correlation between jokes about President Bush and his unfavorability ratings.

Figure 6.2 shows changes in the same data on unfavorability, jokes, and negative news for Bill Clinton throughout his campaign. Compared to Bush, Clinton's shifts were more erratic. (Note that the lines tend to go farther above and below the center point for Clinton than for Bush.) This difference is not surprising. As the incumbent, Bush was much better known to the public, the media, and late night talk show hosts. This familiarity likely mitigated significant swings in media coverage, late night jokes, and mass opinion.

Figure 6.1   Unfavorability Rating, Jokes, and Negative News: George H. W. Bush, 1992

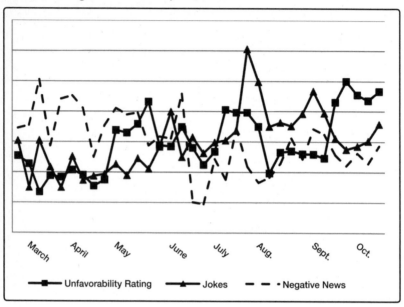

Figure 6.2   Unfavorability Rating, Jokes, and Negative News: Bill Clinton, 1992

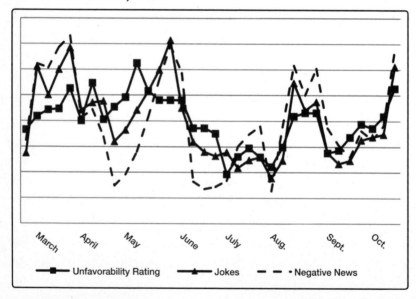

During the Clinton campaign there were four distinct periods in which late night jokes and negative news coverage rose almost simultaneously. The first occurred at the end of March and the beginning of April. Around this time Clinton had been declared by most pundits to be the eventual nominee for the Democratic Party. He had just defeated his remaining opponents, Paul Tsongas and Jerry Brown, in the Illinois and Michigan primaries to effectively clinch the nomination. During this same time, Tsongas dropped out of the race and Clinton secured some major endorsements, including one from the AFL-CIO.

Although these events might seem likely to produce more positive news stories and lower levels of unfavorability among voters, the opposite occurred. In a classic case of the "buyer's remorse" that often occurs at this point in presidential campaigns, many news stories focused on whether or not the Democrats had made a mistake by nominating a relatively unknown candidate with a checkered past, which included charges of draft dodging and extramarital affairs. There was also discussion in the news about new allegations regarding an affair with former Miss America Elizabeth Ward, who was slated to pose nude for the May issue of *Playboy* magazine.

These charges gave late night comics a chance to return to the theme of Clinton's sex life, which had already become a running joke in their monologues. For example, on a day when Clinton was visiting a New York City high school, Jay Leno commented: "He didn't want to give a speech. He just wanted to take advantage of some of those free condoms they're giving away." Meanwhile, Clinton's unfavorable ratings rose slightly but steadily from mid-March to early April, which suggests that the bad press directed at the presumptive nominee was having an effect on public opinion.

Following the initial peak shown in Figure 6.2, there was a clear drop in negative press and late night jokes told at Clinton's expense in April and May. At the same time, however, Clinton's unfavorable ratings increased. During this period, businessman Ross Perot declared his third-party candidacy for the presidency and actually opened a lead over both major-party candidates in the presidential preference polls. This pushed Clinton out of the crosshairs of both the media and late night comics, as they concentrated their attention on the new guy on the block. Unfortunately for Clinton this drop in attention coincided with an increase in unfavorable ratings, which peaked in the third week of May.

The inverse relationship between the media's treatment of Clinton and his unfavorable ratings among the public lasted from late May through mid-June. Then negative media attention started to fall and his unfavorable ratings dropped. The shift corresponded with two major events that were widely discussed at the time. The first occurred when Clinton made a speech to Jesse Jackson Sr.'s Rainbow Coalition criticizing African American song artist Sister Souljah for her comments about race riots that had occurred in Los Angeles. In an interview published in the May 13 *Washington Post,* Souljah reflected on the violence in the riots by commenting: "If black people kill black people every day, why not have a week and kill white people?"[12]

Clinton rebuked Souljah in his comments to the Rainbow Coalition, saying, "If you took the words 'white' and 'black' and you reversed them, you might think [former Klu Klux Klan leader] David Duke was giving that speech."[13] Following the speech, Jesse Jackson was critical of Clinton's harsh comparison. The subsequent war of words between Jackson and Clinton sparked a peak in negative news and jokes about Clinton in the short term. However, the drop in unfavorable ratings seems to indicate the public sided more with Clinton than with Souljah and Jackson.

As the disagreement with Jesse Jackson was playing out, the Clinton campaign underwent an overhaul in strategy that included using nontraditional talk show appearances as a way to bypass traditional journalists and communicate more directly with voters.[14] The most notable of these was on *The Arsenio Hall Show.* Unlike his appearance on *The Tonight Show with Johnny Carson* four years earlier, in which Clinton engaged in damage control over his disastrous nomination speech for Michael Dukakis, he used his *Arsenio Hall* appearance to display empathy and accessibility.

Both the Sister Souljah conflict and the shift in campaign strategy have subsequently been treated as successful campaign maneuvers. The "Sister Souljah moment" (as it later would be called) allowed Clinton to distance himself politically from Jesse Jackson and traditional liberalism,[15] and the *Arsenio Hall* appearance broadened his appeal among less-committed swing voters, who are less likely to watch traditional news.[16] The Sister Souljah episode in particular is regarded as a classic example of a candidate successfully reassuring voters of his own moderate views by rebuking more strident voices within his party.

In June and July, there was a significant drop in all three variables. Negative news and jokes both subsided, and Clinton was viewed much more favorably by the public. Of course, he couldn't stave off criticism from journalists and comedians indefinitely. As was the case with President Bush, Clinton's next burst of negative attention came as his party's national convention approached. And with this attention came another rise in his unfavorability ratings.

Every evening of the Democratic convention, the *Tonight Show with Jay Leno* checked in with *NBC Nightly News* anchor Tom Brokaw, who was leading his network's convention coverage. Although Leno delivered most of the jokes in these discussions, Brokaw sometimes got into the act as well. For example, the night after Clinton accepted the nomination with a fifty-three-minute speech, Brokaw noted: "I did an actual calculation. If [Clinton] had spoken for another 10 minutes, his speech would have been longer than Ross Perot's presidential campaign."[17]

Both jokes and negative news coverage for Clinton peaked during the last full week of the campaign. This was likely due to Clinton's status as front-runner, as well as to the Bush campaign's efforts to portray him as untrustworthy. The late night comics connected the dots more clearly, reminding viewers of the draft-dodging and extramarital-affair allegations that still dogged Clinton. Under this onslaught, his unfavorability ratings soared during the campaign's final days. But it was not enough to change the election outcome, as Bush's unfavorability ratings were also high (see Figure 6.1).

1996: Bill Clinton and Bob Dole

To paraphrase Yogi Berra, it was déjà vu all over again in 1996. As Figures 6.3 and 6.4 demonstrate, the percentage of jokes told, negative news, and candidate favorability again moved in unison during the

Figure 6.3 Unfavorability Rating, Jokes, and Negative News: Bill Clinton, 1996

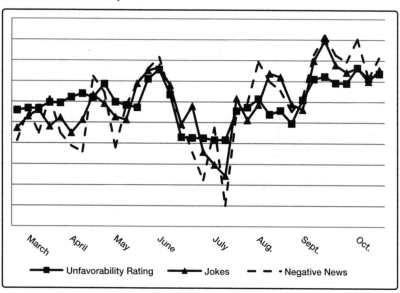

Figure 6.4 Unfavorability Rating, Jokes, and Negative News: Bob Dole, 1996

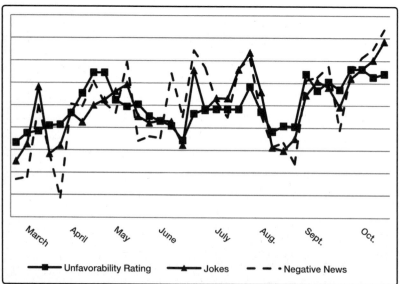

1996 presidential campaign, in which Bill Clinton was challenged by Republican nominee Bob Dole. In fact, these three elements tracked more closely than they had during the 1992 campaign. President Bill Clinton showed less volatility in his joke totals, negative news coverage, and unfavorable ratings than candidate Clinton had four years earlier. This decline in volatility may reflect the fact that Clinton was far better known to voters, journalists, and comedians alike.

Bill Clinton's unfavorable ratings held fairly constant from March until late May, when his negative news, joke totals, and unfavorability all spiked. This development coincided with the fraud and obstruction-of-justice convictions of twenty-four defendants associated with the Whitewater land deal in the president's home state of Arkansas. Among those convicted were Arkansas Governor Jim Guy Tucker and James and Susan McDougal, who were the Clinton family's former business partners.[18] Reports of the convictions coincided with ongoing reports of other investigations by House Republicans and by Independent Counsel Kenneth Starr that were examining the Clinton family's connections to the Whitewater fraud.

Late night comedians reveled in the fraud convictions and Whitewater in general. For example, Leno said of Governor Tucker: "You know who I really feel sorry for, the guys on death row. They are waiting for the governor's call. . . . [They're] walking that last mile, you look in the cell and there he is, he's in the cell right next to you." He also took aim at the Clinton family when he suggested a possible reelection strategy for the president: "[Clinton] frames Hillary, he lets her take the fall for Whitewater so she goes to jail, people feel sorry for him, he gets the sympathy vote, gets reelected, and he's back in the White House as a single guy."

As Whitewater faded from the news, the jokes aimed at Clinton dropped off, and his unfavorable ratings came down as well. In late July, however, all three measures shot upward, following revelations that the Secret Service had stepped up drug testing on twenty-one White House staffers who had admitted to past illegal drug use.[19] Clinton's political opponents jumped at the chance to revive public doubts about his character. For example, House Speaker Newt Gingrich called the event "scandal ridden," and Republican presidential nominee Bob Dole quipped, "No wonder we're losing the war on drugs when you've got a big problem in the White House itself."[20]

The comedians were quick to highlight the drug-testing story in the context of the Summer Olympic Games being held at that time in Atlanta. For example, when Hillary Clinton attended the games, Jay Leno noted: "I guess she wants to meet with the Chinese women's swim team. You know, pick up tips for the White House staff on how to pass a drug test." When President Clinton invited the US team to the White House, Leno said: "Boy, that will be a first, don't you think? It'll be the first time in three years before the White House had any young people in there that could actually pass a drug test."

Following the White House drug-testing scandal, jokes and negative news targeting Clinton fell off for a few weeks, but his unfavorability ratings held fairly steady. In August, however, both jokes and negative news about Clinton increased. This coincides with the mid-August Republican National Convention meeting, where a multitude of criticisms were being leveled against the Clinton administration. It also coincides with the late-August news that Clinton's chief political strategist, Dick Morris, had been enlisting the services of a prostitute. Morris, who was married, was reported to have allowed the prostitute to see advance copies of political speeches and even let her listen in on his conversations with President Clinton.[21]

Because of the scandalous nature of the Morris story, and because the story fit with the preconceived stereotype that President Clinton was a womanizer himself, late night comics piled on the jokes. Jay Leno noted: "She [the prostitute, Sherry Rowland] said at one point, [Morris] has the phone up to her ear and she heard the president talking. In fact she said, 'Bill?' And he said 'Sherry? Is that you?'" That same week, David Letterman weighed in with a "Top Ten" list of Dick Morris's excuses for visiting a prostitute, which included:

- Shouldn't have listened to new campaign adviser Hugh Grant
- Misunderstood when President Clinton asked him to "poll some women"

- Didn't pay for sex—paid for excellent ideas on foreign policy
- Always thought it was okay to screw a taxpayer

As the Dick Morris debacle quieted down, jokes at Clinton's expense tapered off slightly, and his unfavorable ratings held fairly steady (see Figure 6.3). The tone of news coverage also varied little as the candidates moved into the debate season. During this time, the percentage of jokes about Clinton—although down from the height of the Dick Morris scandal—was still as high as at any other time in the campaign. Another Letterman list, "Top Ten Ways Clinton Is Preparing for the Debates," from October 4, gives a good sense of the types of jokes about women, drugs, and weight that were aimed at Clinton—not just in October but across the entire campaign. Jokes on that list included:

- Engaging drive-thru guy in heated "Big Mac vs. Arch Deluxe" debate
- Pulling strings to make sure audience is full of chicks who might want him
- Changing daily routines from: smoke pot, nail hookers, to: nail hookers, smoke pot
- Practicing being persuasive by explaining to Hillary where he was last night at 3 a.m.

Figure 6.4 shows that an association between public unfavorability, jokes, and negative media coverage is also apparent for Clinton's Republican challenger Bob Dole. The attention paid to the Kansas senator increased dramatically once he became the presumptive nominee. The bulk of jokes from this period poked fun at Dole's age. The week that Dole became the likely nominee, Dennis Miller commented on his poor standing in the polls: "I guess Clinton has a fifteen-point lead right now. You know, this wouldn't have happened if Bob Dole were alive." Similarly, in reaction to the news that Dole had visited a kindergarten class, Jay Leno said: "Dole stayed about fifteen minutes, then he had to leave because it was nap time—not the kids'."

Both jokes and negative news coverage of Dole spiked after he quit the US Senate in May, in order to campaign full-time. Dole's resignation from the Senate also coincided with a well-publicized effort by his campaign team to make the candidate appear more youthful. Upon hearing news that Dole was attempting this strategy, late night comics naturally ramped up their attacks. As Dole was campaigning in the popular retirement state of Florida, David Letterman quipped, "That's a good way to reinforce that new youthful image. He quits his job and moves to Florida." Similarly, Jay Leno asked, "Is that the best way to counter criticism that you are too old? First you retire, four days later you move to Florida? What's his next goal? Shuffleboard championship?"

Subsequent weeks showed a steady drop in the percentage of jokes and negative news about Dole. His disapproval ratings also dropped consistently, suggesting that the campaign's effort to show the public a younger and more energetic Bob Dole was working. However, this trend came to an end in late July, when Dole turned seventy-three years old. This birthday gave comics a fresh opportunity to roll out the "Bob Dole is old" jokes. The day after Dole's birthday, Jay Leno noted: "Last night on the news they showed . . . Bob Dole at a picnic. He was eating an apple. At first I thought it was one of those Fixodent commercials."

The frequency of jokes targeted at Dole subsided during August and early September, then increased in mid-September, along with negative news coverage and unfavorable ratings. All three metrics remained high throughout the remainder of the election campaign. There was no major event that could be linked to the elevated joke frequency or the higher levels of unfavorable ratings. Perhaps the late night comics were emptying their cupboards of Dole jokes while they still had him on the campaign trail to kick around, since it was evident from public opinion polls that Clinton would be reelected. In any event, the jokes aimed at Dole went up every week in October, his unfavorable ratings hit their highest levels, and he lost his bid for the White House convincingly.

2000: George W. Bush and Al Gore

The 2000 presidential election is notorious for the electoral controversy surrounding the key swing state of Florida. After an unprecedented legal battle and vote recount that went on for over a month after Election Day, it took a Supreme Court decision to give George W. Bush the victory over Al Gore in Florida, and with it the presidency. Also unprecedented was the amount of election coverage from late night comics. The number of late night comics had increased significantly since 1996 with the addition of Jon Stewart, Bill Maher, and Dennis Miller, and thus the sheer volume of political jokes increased as well.

Overall, as Figure 6.5 shows, there was surprisingly little association between joke frequency and aggregate unfavorability ratings for Al Gore. A notable exception came in early June, when Gore's unfavorable ratings spiked along with jokes about the news that he owned rental property in Tennessee that was in dilapidated condition. For example, Leno quipped: "We've got our own *Survivor* show here at NBC. Apparently a group of people will try to survive for one month living in one of Al Gore's rental properties." Bill Maher, on the other hand, used the story to poke fun at Bush: "Al Gore is in trouble. He is a landowner in Carthage, Tennessee, and the tenants are calling him a slumlord. Of the two of them I thought Bush would certainly be the one running the crack house." And David Letterman debuted his "Top Ten Al Gore Tenant Pet Peeves" list, which included such gems as:

- Request to fix leaky faucet has been sitting in a congressional subcommittee for eleven years
- You put Bush sticker on car, your electricity mysteriously stops working
- Endless stories about how he invented the mailbox
- House is always getting egged by George W. Bush

For candidate Gore, there were a few more instances throughout the campaign in which jokes directed at him surged without accompanying changes in unfavorability. The first occurred in late August during the lead-in and airing of the Democratic National Convention. As typically happens, Gore's public image improved as part of a successful convention "bounce."

Following the convention, jokes about Gore dipped, while George W. Bush and the Republican Party occupied the spotlight during their own national convention. After the Republican convention, the frequency of jokes directed toward Gore began to climb as both campaigns kicked into high gear with an array of media appearances, which for the first time included candidates' visits to the late night comedy programs as well as hour-long interviews with Oprah Winfrey.

The level of jokes directed at Al Gore remained fairly high as the three presidential debates unfolded. Many observers were critical of Gore's performances, and late night comics were no exception. Overall, an increase in jokes about Gore's debate performances coincided with a general increase in his unfavorable ratings by the public as the end of the campaign approached. Summing up Gore's debate performances, David Letterman noted: "The first debate [his staffers] said, 'Al, you're too aggressive. Too aggressive, Al.' The second debate they said, 'You're a little too passive.' So now the third debate . . . I don't know what happened. They apparently got the medication just right."

There was a particularly odd moment in the town hall debate when Gore moved across the stage toward Bush, who was speaking, and appeared to invade his personal space. Naturally, the comics took note of this:

> Gore is like up—right up in his face and he—they're just like backing him off. And Bush, I think, did something smart. He threatened Gore with a lethal injection. —*David Letterman*

> Barbara Bush was on. She said she's—during the debate she was worried that Al Gore was gonna hit George. Remember the—remember when he walked right up to him last night and Bush kind of—yeah, she was worried he was gonna hit him. Yeah. And what better way for Bush to prove he's his own man than have your mom stick up for you like that? Huh? Yeah. —*Jay Leno*

Figure 6.6 shows that the variations in George W. Bush's unfavorable ratings were more closely tied with the number of jokes told at his expense. The limited data on news coverage from July to October indicate that negative coverage of Bush was also associated with unfavorable ratings. From the moment he became the presumptive nominee,

Figure 6.5 Unfavorability Rating, Jokes, and Negative News: Al Gore, 2000

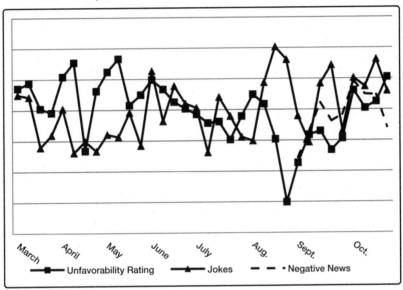

Figure 6.6 Unfavorability Rating, Jokes, and Negative News: George W. Bush, 2000

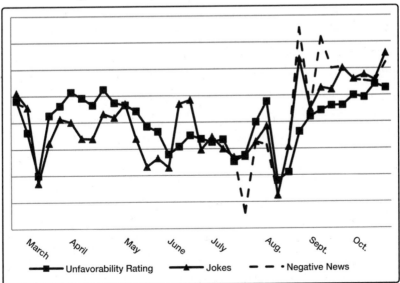

comedians had a field day with jokes about his intelligence, speaking skills, and alleged past drug use. Jokes spiked in late June, following news stories about the high number of executions that took place in Texas while Bush was serving as governor. Jay Leno took a particular interest, with jokes like these:

> It's so hot in Texas, people down there are visiting death row just to feel that breeze coming off the revolving door.

> I guess George W. Bush is handling it now by telling them that he has to act tough, or else he's going to be labeled a wimp. Act tough? They've executed, what, 134 people? How much tougher can he be? Whose record is he going for, Stalin's?

> George W. Bush is taking some criticism for his death penalty policy. This guy has executed so many people—have you heard his campaign slogan? "I see dead people." . . . You think this is going to work against him? You've got Gore and Bush. But at least when Gore puts you to sleep, you wake up again.

Early September brought a dramatic increase in jokes and negative news during the Republican National Convention. Bush's unfavorable ratings were comparatively low during this period, but they increased significantly in the weeks following the convention. As Election Day approached, the level of jokes aimed at Bush remained high, as did his negative news and steadily increasing unfavorable ratings. Like Gore, he was the target of many debate jokes:

> Earlier today, George W. Bush said he has one goal for these debates. He wants to show the American people that he's presidentiamable. —*David Letterman*

> And Bush—interesting—he says he's going to use the same strategy he used to get through Yale University. See, once the debate starts, he's going to push his podium real close to Gore and then cheat off of his answers. —*Jay Leno*

> George W. Bush accused Al Gore of using phony numbers. . . . It wasn't until after the debate that someone explained to Bush that billion and trillion are actually real numbers. —*Conan O'Brien*

> George W. Bush was fighting a cold during the presidential debate last night. Fighting a pretty bad cold, yeah. Afterwards, George W. was quoted as saying, "I haven't sniffed that much since college." —*Conan O'Brien*

Overall, the joke percentages and unfavorable ratings for Bush and Gore followed similar trends in the weeks preceding the 2000 election. An exception was the very last week of the election, when jokes aimed at Bush rose and jokes about Gore fell. This was the result of news that broke just a few days before the election that Bush had been arrested on a DUI violation in 1976. The comedians, of course, took their last and best shot at candidate Bush:

> Let's see what's new with George Anheuser-Busch, ladies and gentlemen. Yeah. The man who put the party back in Republican Party. —*Jay Leno*

> When reporters asked Bush today why he waited so long to come forward about it, he said he was going to write up a press release earlier this year but couldn't spell "DUI." —*Jay Leno*

> According to reports, the arresting officer became suspicious when he noticed George W. wasn't slurring his words. —*Conan O'Brien*

> This is the last day of the presidential race. Or, as George W. Bush calls it, "last call." —*David Letterman*

2004: George W. Bush and John Kerry

The relationship between late night jokes and public favorability ratings for George W. Bush's reelection bid against Democratic nominee John Kerry is illustrated in Figures 6.7 and 6.8. Figure 6.7 shows that both frequency of jokes and unfavorability ratings varied more for President Bush in 2004 than they had in 2000, and that the two variables were not as closely related.

Bush's joke totals spiked at a few notable points. One was in April, when Secretary of State Condoleezza Rice testified before the 9/11 Commission, bringing considerable bad press over the administration's handling of foreign affairs. It also provided comedians with an opportunity to revisit some old themes:

> It was initially reported that President Bush did not watch the hearings yesterday. It turns out that is not true. President Bush watched the TV coverage live from his ranch in Texas. He was able to watch, because yesterday *Spongebob Squarepants* was a rerun. —*Jay Leno*

> In a speech, earlier this week, Senator Ted Kennedy said that Iraq was President Bush's Vietnam. That's what he said. And when he heard about it, President Bush said, "That's not true. I went to Iraq." —*Conan O'Brien*

> All the networks are gonna carry Rice's testimony live on ten-second delay in case she needs a little more time to get her story straight. —*Jay Leno*

During the week of Rice's testimony, unfavorable ratings toward Bush were low, but they did rise in subsequent weeks. The second notable increase in jokes occurred in late May, when President Bush fell off a mountain bike and sustained minor injuries. This allowed comedians to revisit Gerald Ford joke territory, along with some allusions to an earlier mishap when Bush choked on a pretzel. Jay Leno, in particular, had fun with this incident, leading to jokes like "As you know, President Bush fell off his mountain bike this weekend. Luckily, he was not hurt. You know, he was wearing the same helmet he wears when he eats pretzels" and "Did you hear about this? President Bush fell off his bicycle this weekend. You know what's really sad? It was a stationary bike."

Figure 6.7   Unfavorability Rating, Jokes, and Negative News: George W. Bush, 2004

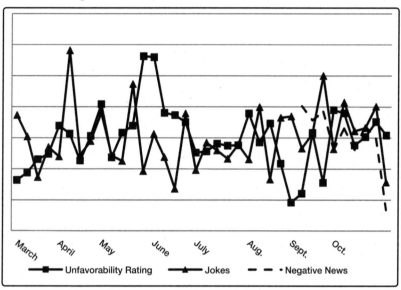

Figure 6.8   Unfavorability Rating, Jokes, and Negative News: John Kerry, 2004

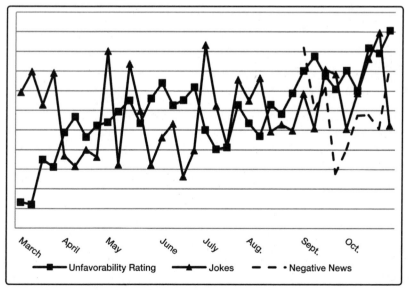

Bush's unfavorable ratings rose dramatically in the weeks following the bicycle incident, but it would take a high degree of cynicism to believe that a presidential fall on a mountain bike would produce an increase in unfavorable ratings among voters. Similar to patterns we saw in the previous campaigns, Bush's unfavorable ratings dropped during convention week, even though the volume of jokes was high. The last spike in jokes about Bush occurred after the initial debate with Democratic opponent John Kerry—a debate in which Bush was widely viewed as the loser:

> Bush didn't have a good night, if you saw it. I think he hadn't choked that bad since the last time he had a pretzel. —*Jay Leno*

> Political experts say Bush was off his game the other night. They said he looked distracted, confused, at a loss for words. Off his game? That *is* Bush's game. —*Jay Leno*

> Experts are saying that if this was a game show, Bush would have gone home with a handshake and a quart of motor oil. —*David Letterman*

For the 2004 election, we have news media data only for the general election from Labor Day to Election Day. In general, the tone of Bush's news coverage moved in tandem with his joke totals. There was a gradual drop in the negativity of his news coverage over the course of the fall campaign, which accelerated during the last week of the campaign. The number of jokes directed at Bush dropped considerably in the final week of the campaign as well.

For Massachusetts Senator John Kerry, the attention from comedians varied somewhat erratically from week to week, and the frequency of jokes about Kerry was less clearly correlated with his unfavorability ratings than was the case with Bush. Ironically, the first spike in jokes occurred in May, when he, too, crashed his bicycle. As they had with Bush, the late night comics linked this event to popular themes in

Kerry's public image, such as his tendency to "flip-flop" on policy issues and his marriage to multimillionaire heiress Teresa Heinz Kerry and subsequent wealth. Here are two examples:

> Thankfully, Senator Kerry was not seriously injured. In fact, when the police arrived, Kerry was well enough to give conflicting reports to the officer about what happened. —*Jay Leno*

> Hey, see this on the news yesterday? Senator John Kerry was out riding his bike, fell off his bicycle. Luckily, he landed on his wallet so he was fine. —*Jay Leno*

Kerry's joke totals and unfavorable ratings continued to rise and fall erratically throughout the general election campaign. Unfortunately for him, however, the jokes reached their highest levels in the last few weeks of the campaign, as did his unfavorable ratings and negative news coverage. It was also unfortunate for Kerry that jokes directed at his opponent, President Bush, did not increase in the same fashion during the last few weeks of the contest.

Although comedians had a few go-to themes for Kerry, none really dominated in their humorous portrayals of him. Some jokes focused on a botched goose-hunting photo opportunity, while others picked up the married-into-money theme. This couldn't have helped Kerry's efforts to fend off GOP attacks on him as wealthy and out of touch with ordinary people. The following are some choice examples of Kerry jokes:

> John Kerry went hunting today. Killed a goose. He didn't bring his wife Teresa along. He's a little rusty. He wanted to make sure he didn't kill the goose that laid the golden egg. —*Jay Leno*

> In Las Vegas yesterday, John Kerry met with the AARP. They were having their convention. Kerry gave a speech, then Kerry introduced his retirement plan, his wife Teresa. —*Jay Leno*

John Kerry went duck hunting and he's doing that to fulfill his campaign pledge to hunt down ducks and kill them wherever they are. —*David Letterman*

Kerry did pretty well, he came back with three ducks and four purple hearts. —*David Letterman*

2008: Barack Obama and John McCain

In 2008 Barack Obama did not become the clear presumptive nominee for the Democratic Party until well into June, much later than in the preceding elections. As we discussed in Chapter 3, Senator Obama was also unique in the lack of attention he received from late night comedians. Figure 6.9 shows how Obama's unfavorable ratings compared to the percentage of jokes and negative news targeted toward him. While most candidates for president—particularly challengers—are targeted more often as the campaign progresses, this did not happen to Obama. There were only two points during the election at which his joke totals spiked. The first occurred in late July, when Obama visited Europe and was warmly greeted by foreign leaders and publics. Late night hosts joked about the fawning over Obama with such zingers as these:

I guess you've heard that Barack Obama was elected chancellor of Germany. —*Jay Leno*

Barack Obama is back from his big European tour. Did you see him in Europe? People were cheering him, holding up signs, blowing him kisses. And that was just the American media covering the story. —*Jay Leno*

But there was one little episode while Barack Obama was overseas. He was in Jerusalem, and he was heckled. And he's not used to being heckled, because everybody likes the guy wherever he goes so nobody heckles him. And this woman was just furious and nasty and heckling him, and finally he said, "All right, Hillary, knock it off!" —*David Letterman*

As these examples illustrate, many of the Obama jokes on late night television weren't really at his expense. Not surprisingly, the week following Obama's trip to Europe brought a noticeable drop in his unfavorable ratings. The tendency of comedians to tread lightly with Obama, and instead focus on those around him, was also evident during the second peak period of jokes about him, the week of the Democratic National Convention. Some examples of this included Jay Leno's joke "As you all know by now, Barack Obama sent out a cell phone text message at 3:00 a.m. on Saturday morning to tell everyone he picked Joe Biden as his vice president. How do you think this makes Hillary Clinton feel, huh? Finally gets a phone call at 3:00 a.m., it's to tell her they picked Joe Biden"; and David Letterman's joke "Joe Biden is Barack Obama's running mate. . . . Yeah, nothing says change like a guy who's been in the Senate for thirty-five years." Letterman's "Top Ten Surprises in Barack Obama's Democratic National Convention Address" list didn't so much make fun of Obama's foibles as make fun of the fact that he seemed not to have any. Examples from that list included:

- Wants to change October to "Barack-tober"
- Outlined plan for America, then took calls about the Broncos' defense
- Kept saying to John Kerry, "Hey, why the long face?" It's funny every time!
- Promised to make Pluto a state
- Also pronounces "nuclear" as "nuc-u-lar"

Initially, unfavorable ratings of Obama did not move in conjunction with either the number of jokes or the tone of his news coverage. For example, in the week following the Democratic convention, jokes about Obama plummeted while his unfavorable ratings increased—a shift that coincides with the Republican convention, where speakers and delegates fired volleys of criticism at him.

In the weeks that followed, however, news, jokes, and public opinion about Obama became more closely related. Following the September 15 stock market crash, both the number of late night jokes about Obama and Obama's unfavorable ratings dropped, as he worked with his Republican opponent John McCain and President George W. Bush to address the economic crisis. But the frequency of jokes about Obama, his negative news coverage, and his unfavorable ratings all increased during the presidential debates, as Obama was targeted by humorists for his encounter with a conservative critic nicknamed "Joe the Plumber," as well as his controversial former spiritual mentor, the Reverend Jeremiah Wright.

If jokes about Barack Obama were few and often toothless, jokes about John McCain were one-dimensional retreads. As we've discussed previously, comedians, for the most part, just dusted off their "old geezer" jokes left over from the 2000 Bob Dole campaign. McCain's advanced age was by far the most frequent theme of late night humor—he turned seventy-two a few days before his nomination at the Republican convention. There were, however, a few exceptions. The first took place in August, when the McCain campaign ran a negative TV ad comparing Senator Obama to celebrities who lack substance, such as Paris Hilton and Britney Spears. Jay Leno told several jokes about this McCain ad, including:

> Well, the campaign's starting to get nasty. . . . Have you seen the new commercial? The McCain campaign compares Barack Obama to Britney Spears and Paris Hilton. And today, the Obama campaign released an ad comparing John McCain to Zsa Zsa Gabor and Bea Arthur.

> Actually, McCain's not backing down. He's defending the commercial where he compared Barack Obama to Paris Hilton as being "all talk and little action." That's what he said. Like Paris, Barack Obama is "all talk and little action." Really? Has he seen her sex video?

Figure 6.9   Unfavorability Rating, Jokes, and Negative News: Barack Obama, 2008

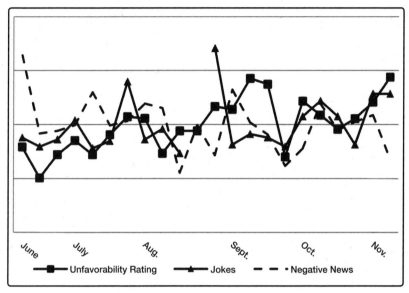

Figure 6.10   Unfavorability Rating, Jokes, and Negative News: John McCain, 2008

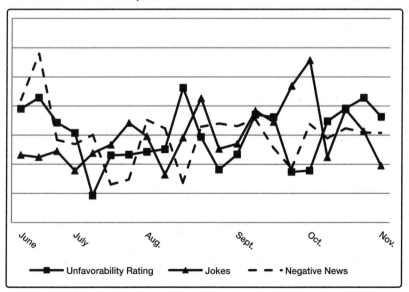

And earlier this week on the Internet, Paris Hilton posted her own ad to spoof the ad John McCain made about her. The McCain camp responded to that by saying Paris Hilton supports McCain's approach to America's energy crisis. You know, how desperate is your presidential campaign when you have to try and convince people that Paris Hilton agrees with you?

The second jump in jokes targeting McCain came in early September, when he nominated the relatively unknown Alaska Governor Sarah Palin as his running mate. Following the announcement, late night comics had a field day, particularly after the revelation that Palin's seventeen-year-old daughter was pregnant. In fact, the controversial Palin's entry proved a welcome development for joke writers. As we saw in Chapter 3, Palin as well as McCain were more productive topics for the late night comedians than Obama was. Nonetheless, McCain's age remained a consistent underlying theme, one that comedians often worked into comparisons of the aging McCain and his youthful running mate, as these two jokes illustrate:

Some question whether a mother of five who's been running the state of Alaska for only two years is the right person to fill out a ticket fronted by a 175-year-old man. . . . And how are you going to be the vice president of the United States with five kids to take care of? Now Palin is going to be a grandmother and she's partnered with John McCain. How many diapers can one woman possibly change? —*Jimmy Kimmel*

No, Governor Palin announced, over the weekend, that her seventeen-year-old, unmarried daughter is five months pregnant. Oh, boy! You thought John Edwards was in trouble before. . . . Apparently, Governor Palin told McCain about the pregnancy weeks ago, but . . . I guess she said it into his bad ear, so he didn't realize. But despite the pregnancy, Republicans think Palin is a pretty good running mate for McCain, because they feel she can bring in . . .

female voters. She also has a good conservative voting record, and she doesn't mind eating dinner at 4:30. —*Jay Leno*

Jokes about McCain increased again in October as the debate season ensued and comics critiqued both McCain's and Palin's debate performances (including Palin asking Biden if she could call him "Joe"). Here are some prime examples:

Did you folks see the second presidential debate? It got off to an awkward start when a confused John McCain said to Barack Obama, "May I call you Joe?" But this was . . . what they call the town hall format. And that means that the candidates get to walk around on stage. And it was pretty successful because John McCain only wandered off twice. —*David Letterman*

During the vice presidential debate, Sarah Palin would wink a couple of times when she delivered a line. Did you see that? She'd kind of wink and . . . try to use a little sex appeal. See, the other candidates could never get away with that. Like if Barack Obama winked, that would be seen as too condescending. If Joe Biden winked, it'd be too creepy. If McCain started winking, everybody would think he was having a stroke. —*Jay Leno*

Wasn't the debate fantastic? It was a town hall format. I like that. Candidates can walk around freely. McCain was prepared. He put new tennis balls in his walker. —*Craig Ferguson*

In short, the relationship between late night jokes and public perceptions of McCain was complicated by the heavy media coverage given to his running mate. At times it seemed as if the order of the Republican ticket had been reversed, with McCain being treated by the media as Palin's running mate. McCain also suffered from a kind of comedic vendetta waged against him by David Letterman after he canceled a scheduled appearance on *The Late Show*. Following the economic crisis hit in September, in particular, news coverage of Mc-Cain remained negative, his unfavorability ratings became more erratic, and the association between the number of jokes told about him and public perceptions of him diminished (see Figure 6.10).

LATE NIGHT HUMOR AND AGGREGATE PUBLIC OPINION

Our narrative account of five presidential election campaigns shows how difficult it is to sort out the relationship among news, jokes, and candidate favorability as they interact with events on the campaign trail. Sometimes these variables seem to move in tandem, at other times they don't, and at still other times some variables seem to be related while other variables are not.

In order to assess whether or not a systematic relationship between jokes and public perceptions exists across all candidates and elections, we calculated the correlation between the percentage of jokes directed at each candidate and that candidate's subsequent favorability ratings, with each individual week within a campaign as the unit of analysis. In fact, we did find a modest but statistically significant positive association between the number of jokes that comedians tell at a candidate's expense and more negative public impressions of that candidate (Pearson's $r = .22$, $p = .001$).

Of course, there is also the possibility that the number of jokes about candidates each night simply reflects their ups and downs on the campaign trail each day. If the jokes follow from the news, then it may be the news that is having the real effect. To find out, we first calculated the same correlation between the tone of news about each candidate and the subsequent favorability ratings of the candidate. The result was almost identical to our previous finding for jokes—a positive association of .23, also significant at the .001 level.

Then we performed a regression analysis that simultaneously predicted favorability ratings from both jokes and news. Both variables contributed independently to the relationship, with standardized beta coefficients of .24 for jokes and .21 for negative news, both coefficients significant at the .01 level. In other words, negative news and jokes did not cancel out each other's effect on favorability ratings—each had an independent influence on the way people evaluated presidential candidates.

These findings suggest that the late night comics may have become a genuine political force—indeed, part of the mix of media that shapes voters' sentiments toward presidential candidates. They may also reflect something that successful politicians already know instinctively: they *do* have to worry about their treatment by both news and entertainment media. More generally, campaign discourse has expanded beyond the morning headlines and evening newscasts to include late night talk shows and shows like *SNL*.

In addition, this analysis may help us to identify the campaign conditions that are more or less conducive to late night humor playing a role in elections. For example, the overall relationship among frequency of jokes, negative news coverage, and unfavorability ratings is probably diluted by a structural aspect of presidential elections—the party nominating conventions that typically take place in late summer. These weeklong events formally introduce the candidates to the public with hoopla, pomp, and circumstance, while providing a kickoff for the general election campaign in the fall. Because the conventions are produced by the parties and highly orchestrated, they typically bring a wave of positive news coverage about the parties' nominees. At the same time, they provide the late night comedians with a week of news centering on the parties' nominees, typically resulting in a surge of jokes at a nominee's expense. This decoupling of the tone of news and entertainment during this period likely minimizes any relationship between late night political humor and public perceptions of the candidates.

Party conventions aside, the steady stream of jokes at the candidates' expense feeds into the generally negative slant of campaign discourse. As we noted earlier, the negative tone of much political news is linked to unfavorable public perceptions of politicians and politics in general. This holds true for presidential elections especially, despite the fact that none of the campaigns we studied featured any scandal of the sort we discussed in Chapter 4.

For social scientists, such findings raise the question of whether the joke parade is just good clean fun at the expense of politicians who deserve it, or whether it might be undermining public support for the political system. Unlike journalists, comedians are under no professional obligation to be fair or balanced with their barbs. Bad news for candidates brings a wave of jokes at their expense; good news for candidates brings nothing.

So, from the point of view of candidates trying to keep their campaigns afloat, the combination of bad press and late night jokes is a kind of double whammy: first the journalists knock them off their feet, then the comics kick them while they're down. In the next chapter, we will see how the candidates try to beat the comedians at their own game.

NOTES

1. Jody Baumgartner and Jonathan Morris, "The 'Daily Show Effect': Candidate Evaluations, Efficacy, and the American Youth," *American Politics Research* 34 (2006): 341–367.

2. Thomas E. Patterson, *Out of Order* (New York: Knopf, 1993).

3. John Zaller, *The Nature and Origins of Mass Opinion* (Cambridge: Cambridge University Press, 1992).

4. Dannagal Young, "Late-Night Comedy and the Salience of the Candidates' Caricatured Traits in the 2000 Election," *Mass Communication and Society* 9 (2006): 339–366.

5. David Niven, S. Robert Lichter, and Daniel Amundson, "The Political Content of Late Night Comedy," *Harvard International Journal of Press/Politics* 8 (2003): 118–133.

6. Jody C Baumgartner, Jonathan S. Morris, and Natasha L. Walth, "The Fey Effect: Young Adults, Political Humor, and Perceptions of Sarah Palin in the 2008 Presidential Election Campaign," *Public Opinion Quarterly* 76 (2012): 95–104.

7. Niven, Lichter, and Amundson, "The Political Content of Late Night Comedy."

8. Stephen Farnsworth and S. Robert Lichter, *The Nightly News Nightmare: Media Coverage of U.S. Presidential Elections, 1988–2008* (Lanham, MD: Rowman & Littlefield, 2010).

9. Ibid.

10. James A. Stimson, *Public Opinion in America: Moods, Cycles, and Swings* (Boulder, CO: Westview Press, 1991).

11. Jim Rutenberg, "TV's Pundits Pronounce Judgment: It's Over," *New York Times,* May 8, 2008, p. A32.

12. David Mills, "Sister Souljah's Call to Arms," *Washington Post,* May 13, 1992, p. B1.

13. Ronald A. Taylor, "Clinton Raps Sister Souljah's Remarks," *Washington Times,* June 14, 1992, p. A4.

14. Dee Dee Myers, "New Technology and the 1992 Clinton Presidential Campaign," *The American Behavioral Scientist* 37, no. 2 (1993): 181–184.

15. Mark White, "Vicissitudes: 1992 and the Road to the White House," in Mark White, ed., *The Presidency of Bill Clinton: The Legacy of a New Domestic and Foreign Policy* (New York: Palgrave, 2012).

16. Richard Davis and Diana Owen, *New Media and American Politics* (New York: Oxford University Press, 1998).

17. "Conventional Humor: When TV Turns Politics into a Laughing Matter," *New York Times,* July 18, 1992, p. A10.

18. R. H. Melton and Susan Schmidt, "For Clinton, Whitewater Woes Continue," *Washington Post,* May 30, 1996, p. A1.

19. Tim Wiener, "21 White House Workers Got Extra Drug Test, Official Says," *Austin-American Statesman,* July 16, 1996, p. A4.

20. Walter Mears, "The Political and Robbed Walt Gets Personal," Associated Press, July 27, 1996.

21. Donald M. Rothberg, "Clinton's Day of Triumph Jarred by Aide's Resignation," Associated Press, August 29, 1996.

Chapter 7

If You Can't Beat Them, Join Them

We have seen how late night television comedians portray politicians as crooks, cads, and clowns. Presidents and presidential candidates are regularly roasted, as are senators and members of Congress, mayors and governors, and many other garden-variety politicians whose behavior opens them up to comic ridicule. Moreover, a wealth of evidence suggests that these jokes affect the way voters view them.

So how do the targets of these jokes—who include some of the most powerful people in America—respond to the torrent of taunts and gibes that may damage their reputations and even their chances for election? Do they sue for slander, demand retractions, or issue press releases denouncing their tormentors? None of the above. Instead, most politicians try to wrangle a guest appearance that lets them join in the fun and show that they're good sports. This strategy is particularly popular with presidential candidates, who are on the political clock and need to repair their reputations before Election Day.

It would seem foolish for presidential candidates to willingly put themselves in the line of late night comedic fire by personally appearing on these programs. It's bad enough that they have already been the butt of jokes. Why risk having to listen to additional insults and irreverent comments in front of a live studio audience and millions of viewers? Furthermore, they have to keep their cool while sitting across from someone who has very recently been ridiculing them.

Of course the reality is that it's now commonplace for presidential candidates to appear on late night talk shows. In the 2008 campaign alone there were more than one hundred such appearances.

How did this come to pass, such that it's become commonplace for future presidents to subject themselves to grilling by comedians as well as journalists? This chapter looks at how and why late night comedy programming is seen as a virtually mandatory stopover on the road to the White House. Why do candidates willingly appear on these programs? What happens when their appearances go well, and what happens when they go badly? But first, to better understand why tête-à-têtes with late night talk show hosts have become an integral part of presidential campaigns, let us begin at the beginning.

TWO CANDIDATES, TWO APPROACHES TO TV ENTERTAINMENT APPEARANCES

The precedent for what has become a virtual "parade of stars" of presidential candidates on late night talk shows was set by two very different presidential contenders—Richard Nixon and Bill Clinton. Two decades separated the two candidates' appearances, and even after Clinton, hitting the late night talk circuit did not immediately become standard practice. Nonetheless, we discuss each of these appearances in some detail, not only because they created precedents but also because they highlight the two different strategies that candidates now employ when they appear on late night television talk shows.

Richard Nixon: "Sock It to Me?"

Richard Nixon was not good on television. His close loss to John F. Kennedy in the 1960 presidential election has been linked by many commentators to his appearance on the first of three televised debates between the candidates. While Nixon had no problem with the substance of his answers, on camera he appeared pasty, sickly, and generally uncomfortable. His opponent, on the other hand, was projecting almost the exact opposite image. Nixon looked pale while Kennedy had a healthy tan, he slouched in a sport jacket that appeared too big for him while Kennedy stood tall in a perfectly tailored suit, and he seemed painfully aware of the cameras while Kennedy was perfectly at ease.

When Nixon declared himself a candidate for president again in 1967, he only begrudgingly embraced television. He viewed it as an artificial medium, one that required an unnecessary amount of work, and one that (most damning of all) played a significant role in thwarting his first bid for the presidency. In preparation for a 1967 appearance on the *Mike Douglas Show*, he quipped to a producer: "It's a shame a man has to use gimmicks like this [television] to get elected." The producer, a young man by the name of Roger Ailes, responded: "Television is not a gimmick, and if you think that it is, you'll lose again." Nixon was so impressed with Ailes's bluntness that he hired him and placed him in charge of the team responsible for crafting his new television persona.[1] (Whatever his other failings, Nixon recognized talent. Ailes later became the mastermind behind both *The Rush Limbaugh Show* on television and the Fox News Channel.)

Under this new team Nixon's televised appearances increased, and he eventually moved beyond standard political programming and into the arena of talk shows. In addition to a greater number of appearances, the campaign team instituted meticulous and rigorous control over every aspect of these appearances. For example, lighting was endlessly manipulated to avoid a repeat of the infamous 1960 debate appearances, and questions had to be pre-cleared by both the team and the candidate himself. This team understood their candidate: Nixon would never do well in the medium unless the situation was perfectly controlled. They also knew that Nixon's previous failures on television went beyond issues of lighting or makeup. As one observer suggested, Nixon's "problem was himself. Not what he said, but the man he was. The camera portrayed him clearly."[2]

Paul Keyes, one of the main players on the Nixon team, had experience working on programs like the *Jack Paar Show* and the *Dean Martin Show*. He had been working for a sketch comedy program called *Laugh-In* just before joining the campaign. *Laugh-In*, which debuted in January 1968, was a fast-paced show built around vaudeville-style humor and a faux-hippy "summer of love" motif—in fact, the title itself was a play on the hippy "love-ins" of the time.[3] Although it adopted the look and sound of the counterculture then popular among young people, it lacked overt political content.

One of *Laugh-In*'s signature lines was "Sock it to me," which was variously used to mean "bring it on" or "let me have it," at times with an underlying sexual connotation. The character who delivered the line was sometimes doused with a bucket of water. Keyes's idea was to drop one of the straightest political figures of the era into the middle of this colorful and vibrant show and deliver the line with self-deprecating confusion: "Sock it to *me?*" In his brief cameo Nixon delivered only those four words, but the scene was meticulously planned, and there were multiple takes to make sure Nixon would deliver the line without coming across as angry or offended.[4]

The most significant aspect of Nixon's cameo was the reaction from the public and the press. With four short words, Nixon was able to present an image of himself that countered what most people thought of him. Indeed, in his study of *Laugh-In*, Hal Erickson made the following claim about Nixon's four-word appearance:

> The Richard Nixon cameo remains the single most famous moment in the entire six-year history of *Laugh-In*—not only because of the ominous connotations taken on by the "Sock it to me" during the Watergate era, but also because so many media analysts have pointed to Nixon's *Laugh-In* appearance as the turning point in his presidential campaign, transforming him from the bitter Gloomy Gus who told the press that they wouldn't have Dick Nixon to kick around anymore after his 1962 California gubernatorial defeat, into a "regular fella" willing to poke fun of himself.
>
> Some have even credited, or blamed, *Laugh-In* for Nixon's election.[5]

While this might be overstating the case, Nixon's cameo certainly proved that presidential candidates can benefit from sending themselves up on a TV entertainment program.

Bill Clinton: Redemption

Bill Clinton's presence as late night talk show comedy fodder predates his run for the presidency. It began in 1988, when then-Governor Clinton was selected to officially introduce Michael Dukakis as the Democratic nominee for president at the Democratic National Convention. His broader task was to introduce the nominee to the larger television viewing audience. In his biography Clinton claimed that the Dukakis campaign team asked him "to take the entire allotted time, about twenty-five minutes," in his introductory speech.[6] This is significant because televised nominating speeches traditionally lasted only five or ten minutes.

Unfortunately for Clinton, his bloated four-thousand-word speech was an unmitigated disaster. As it lumbered along, the delegates quickly lost interest and then began to turn against Clinton. This shift in mood was clearly captured on television, which showed audience members giving Clinton the "cut" sign and audible chants of "We want Mike" from the delegates. ABC cut away to present a biographical piece on Dukakis, and NBC and CBS commentators openly criticized Clinton. NBC's Connie Chung reported that DNC Chairman Jim Wright was personally asking Clinton to cut the speech short. Chris Wallace noted that "[Clinton] has completely lost this crowd. . . . It seems Bill Clinton has overstayed his welcome in this hall."[7] Unfortunately for Clinton, the only positive response from the delegation came when he finally said the words "in closing."

Criticism in the media was harsh during the days that followed the speech. Thomas Edsall of the *Washington Post* wrote: "Arkansas Governor Bill Clinton got his moment in the sun of national television and would not let go until he was in a deep political nightfall." And the *Post*'s David Broder told the *Today Show:* "The only thing the American people are going to know about [Clinton] is he's a guy who can't stop talking."[8] Criticism of Clinton transcended the world of political pundits and made its way into late night comedy. Johnny Carson was especially hard on the governor. The night after the address, Carson put Clinton front and center in his monologue:

> How many of you watched Bill Clinton, the governor of Arkansas, last night do the nomination speech for Michael Dukakis? He was supposed to come out and do 15 minutes. He did 34 minutes. And the surgeon general has just approved Governor Bill Clinton as an over-the-counter sleep aid. What a windbag.

Carson went on:

> Clinton's speech went over about as well [as a] Velcro condom. I tell
> you, people were talking, they were sleeping, and they were eating.
> They didn't listen to this poor man at all. He lost the crowd com-
> pletely. Mary Alice Williams and CNN in the booth had to do a
> striptease just to get the delegates. . . .

And Carson added one more devastating jab:

> I'll tell you, when it comes to television drama, Governor Clinton is
> right up there with the PBS pledge breaks.[9]

The drubbing Clinton took in the news media and on late night
talk appeared to destroy a promising political career before it could
ever take off. One analyst wrote, "So what does this [speech] do to
Clinton's supposed future in national politics? I think it could ruin
it. . . . His main calling card has been that he is known to political in-
siders as this young governor from Arkansas who gives a great speech.
Now he is known to the country as the windbag governor from Arkansas who gave a God-awful speech at the convention."[10] Another said it
was "like watching a political career imploding."[11]

In the midst of this media firestorm came a radical suggestion as
to how Clinton could repair his tattered image. Television producer
Harry Thomason, an old friend of Clinton's, called the governor a few
days after the convention and suggested that Clinton agree to be inter-
viewed by his harshest critic: Johnny Carson himself. Clinton noted in
his biography that "Harry told me I could make silk out of this sow's
ear, but I had to move fast. He suggested that I go on the Johnny Carson show and poke fun of myself."[12]

The decision to appear as a guest on *The Tonight Show* was politically risky, considering that Carson continued his barrage of jokes at
Clinton's expense even after the guest appearance was announced. "It
will be great [having Clinton as a guest]. We won't have to book any
other guests," said Carson. He also joked two nights after Clinton's

address: "Clinton's speech is still going on. Because of the greenhouse effect, it's still trapped in Atlanta."[13] Before the appearance, writer Deborah Mathis noted the delicate balance Clinton would have to strike in appearing on the typically nonpolitical late night talk venue:

> Johnny Carson's job is to make people laugh. The governor, as a guest, will be in an awkward position, doubtlessly having to endure more ribbing (though it may be more subdued face-to-face); and at the same time, having to try to explain himself, even though *The Tonight Show* is not staged for social redemption. It may be his biggest television test to date, because he will have to be both a very important person and a good-sported average guy. If Clinton indulges in too much apologia, he could emerge as an excuse-bearing political weakling. If he laughs too much and tries to be an entertainer, he could appear frivolous and goofy.[14]

Clinton appeared on *The Tonight Show* on July 28, 1988. He was the first political figure ever to appear as a guest of Carson, so it was unclear how the appearance would unfold. However, it was apparent from the monologue that Carson would not be conciliatory. After announcing that Clinton would be the evening's guest, Carson told the audience: "Not to worry, we have plenty of black coffee and extra cots in the lobby." When Carson introduced Clinton, he did so in a long, protracted manner in order to mock his guest.[15] Once Carson finally did get around to bringing Clinton onstage, he asked: "My first question is, how are you?" He then proceeded to turn over an hourglass on his desk.

Faced with this do-or-die situation, Clinton handled himself well. He was not overly apologetic but was comfortable laughing at himself. He did not try to defend his speech, clearly acknowledging he made a mistake, but he was not overly dramatic in admonishing himself. In short, he came across as an average guy and a good sport, precisely as Thomason had suggested.

Even more important than Clinton being a good sport was his mix of self-deprecation and humor. He started by telling Carson that he thought the speech was a success, saying, "My sole goal was achieved.

I wanted so badly to make Dukakis look good, and I succeeded be-yond my wildest dreams." Clinton also jested that he gave the speech purposely, because he always wanted to appear on *The Tonight Show*.

Following a commercial break, Carson mentioned that the gover-nor played the saxophone and asked if he would play. Unbeknownst to the audience, this was planned ahead of time and was actually a condition *The Tonight Show* insisted on. Clinton modestly agreed and said he was "going to play a short song," emphasizing the word *short*. He then played a rendition of "Summertime" on his saxophone ac-companied by the *Tonight Show* Orchestra. The response from the live audience was overwhelmingly positive, and a clearly impressed Carson commented: "The Gov's got some good chops there."

In the following days it became clear that Clinton's appearance was a success. CNN's weekly *Winners and Losers* said that Clinton posted the "fastest turnaround ever," and the Associated Press said that "Arkansas Gov. Bill Clinton has gone from the media dog house to media darling in one short week. All it took was a smile, a few self-deprecating jokes and a song."[16]

Two Different Approaches: Cameos and Sit-Downs

Although they were two very different politicians, the similarities be-tween Nixon's and Clinton's TV entertainment appearances outweigh the differences. First, they were both in uncharted waters, crossing an established line between politics and entertainment, a line that has since become more blurred with each election cycle. Second, both almost instantly rehabilitated their public image by doing the same thing: using self-deprecating humor and appearing like an "average guy" and more good-natured than most Americans imagine politi-cians to be. Finally, their TV appearances set a precedent for future political aspirants. It became clear that entertainment-based television could be exploited for political gain.

There was, however, a key difference between the two appearances: Nixon's was a cameo role while Clinton appeared as a guest on a talk show. The cameo strategy has been used with increasing frequency over the years, particularly on *Saturday Night Live* but on other late night venues as well.

The cameo is intended to highlight what a good sport the candidate is. This was apparent with the high-profile cameos by two markedly different female candidates in 2008. Both Hillary Clinton and Sarah Palin appeared opposite their impersonators—Amy Poehler and Tina Fey, respectively—in order to show that they could take a joke and laugh at themselves.

Palin, for example, went so far as to appear alongside her outspoken critic Alec Baldwin, in the lead-in scene to *SNL*. In the segment, Baldwin "mistakes" Palin for her impersonator (Fey) and implores *SNL* producer Lorne Michaels not to let Tina go onstage with "that horrible woman." Michaels points out that Baldwin is talking in front of Palin—not Fey. Baldwin, unfazed, says to Palin: "Forgive me, but I feel I must say this: you [pause] are way hotter in person." The governor responds to his condescension by thanking him and remarking that his brother (and fellow actor) Stephen is her favorite Baldwin.

Later in the same episode, Palin appears in a cameo on "Weekend Update," the show's faux news segment. However, she refuses to participate in the planned sketch, telling host Seth Meyers: "I've been thinking it over and I'm not going to do the piece that we rehearsed. . . . My gut is telling me it might be a bad idea for the campaign. . . . After a lot of thought, I think it might just cross the line." A disappointed Meyers turns to co-host Amy Poehler and asks if she can fill in. She almost immediately launches into a rap that Palin was (jokingly) supposed to deliver, while Palin smiles and moves to the beat (see Box 7.1).

Hillary Clinton showed what a good sport she is by appearing in a cameo alongside Poehler, as the comedian was impersonating the former First Lady. After complimenting each other on their hair and clothing (which were identical), Clinton told Poehler she wanted her earrings back. This prompted Poehler's impersonation of Clinton's cackling laugh. Clinton responded by smiling and asking Poehler, "Do I really laugh that way?" which got a positive response and big laughs from the audience.

BOX 7.1

Excerpts from *Saturday Night Live*'s 2008 "Palin (Poehler) Rap"

My name is Sarah Palin you all know me,

Vice prezzy nominee of the GOP,

Gonna need your vote in the next election,

Can I get a "what what" from the senior section?

McCain got experience, McCain got style,

But don't let him freak you out when he tries to smile,

'Cause that smile be creepy,

But when I be VP,

All the leaders in the world gonna finally meet me

[. . .]

My country tis of thee,

from my porch I can see,

Russia and such

All the mavericks in the house put your hands up,

All the mavericks in the house put your hands up,

All the plumbers in the house pull your pants up,

All the plumbers in the house pull your pants up

[. . .]

Shoot a mother-humpin moose, eight days of the week,

[three gunshots at Dancing Moose running across stage]

Now yer dead, now yer dead,

'Cause I'm an animal, and I'm bigger than you,

Holding a shotgun walk in the pub,

Everybody party, we're going on a hunt,

la la la la la la la la

[six gunshots]

Yo I'm Palin, I'm out!

Cameos can be useful for politicians, but guest appearances that include sit-down interviews on late night comedy shows probably offer greater opportunity for them to connect with audiences. Bill Clinton's 1988 *Tonight Show* appearance demonstrated this perfectly. Clinton was able to score points with the audience by laughing at his missteps, entertaining with his saxophone, and showing off his personality and wit. We have seen this talk show guest strategy used with increasing frequency ever since.

In 1992, for example, presidential candidate Clinton appeared on *The Arsenio Hall Show*. Again he played saxophone and, importantly, had an opportunity to put his winning personality on display. He quipped with Hall that he would prefer the Post Office honor Elvis Presley by displaying the "young Elvis" rather than the "old Elvis" on postage stamps, saying: "When he got old, [Elvis] got fat, like me." Hall also got serious and allowed Clinton to talk freely about his experience dealing with the impoverished and with young adults in the African American community. In short, the interview format allowed Clinton to show his multiple sides—funny and witty but also serious and empathetic.

The risks of the sit-down interview on late night comedy programs are higher than those of the tightly controlled cameo. But they are still small when compared to the pitfalls involved in traditional political interviews. While late night hosts display irreverence toward political figures during their monologues and skits, they are mostly respectful and deferential to presidential candidates in interviews. And perhaps more importantly, they do not share the sense of professional duty that leads traditional journalists to ask challenging or adversarial questions. This gives candidates an opportunity to highlight their personalities rather than discuss potentially controversial matters associated with their politics and policies.

This last point is a reminder that late night talk shows are primarily nonpolitical. Their main purpose is to entertain, not to inform. With the exception of *Daily Show* and *Colbert Report* viewers, late night talk show audiences are not necessarily highly interested or engaged in politics. However, the fact that late night comedy viewers are less engaged does not mean that they are completely apolitical. A Pew Research Center poll found that 82 percent of those who regularly watch late night TV shows such as *Letterman* or *Leno* reported that they were registered to vote, as were 89 percent of regular *Daily Show* viewers.[17] While these numbers are certainly inflated,[18] they show that the late night comedy audience is not a wholly apolitical group that rarely votes.

Moreover, many members of these audiences feel that they learn something about politics or current affairs from such programs. Another Pew survey, administered during the 2008 presidential election campaign, found that 28 percent of all adults claimed to get at least some information about elections from watching late night talk shows, and the number rose to 39 percent among those under age thirty. Similar proportions said that they learned something about the election from comedy shows such as *The Daily Show* and *Saturday Night Live*.[19]

Thus, it makes sense that presidential candidates would make an effort to reach these viewers. As Matthew Baum notes:

> Clearly, many [television] talk show viewers and politically inattentive individuals vote. One-on-one interviews on *Meet the Press* or *The Jim Lehrer News Hour* [sic] are unlikely to reach these potential voters. In today's increasingly personality-driven political environment, appearances and [television] talk shows afford candidates the best opportunity to communicate with a substantial niche of the electorate.[20]

This "niche" is a group that takes personality more seriously than partisanship and prioritizes likeability over political ideology. Personal characteristics and personality traits are widely employed heuristics that many people use to guide their voting decisions in today's media age.[21] Late night comedy is one of the best venues for presidential candidates to put their personalities on display, so it is understandable that they would exploit the opportunity to do so.

PRESIDENTIAL CANDIDATE APPEARANCES: 1996–2012

Although Bill Clinton successfully used late night talk shows to rehabilitate his image and promote himself in 1988 and 1992, there were few appearances by presidential hopefuls in 1996. Bob Dole, the Republican nominee for president, made a brief cameo on *SNL*'s "Weekend Update" in the week following his loss and told host (and Dole impersonator) Norm Macdonald that "you've had your fun, Norm, now you're out of work . . . unless there's a recount." But for the most part, late night talk shows were limited to poking fun at the candidates rather than hosting them as guests. This would soon change.

The 2000 Election

As the 2000 campaign began to unfold, it became clear that late night comedy would play a more significant role than in any previous election cycle. The Monica Lewinsky scandal of 1998 ushered in open season for jokes directed at President Clinton, his allies and advisers, as well as his opponents.[22] Top contenders for the Republican and Democratic nominations were drawing heavy fire from comics as well, as the new millennium neared.

As the 2000 primary season drew to a close, it became apparent that candidates Al Gore and George W. Bush would take a page out of the Clinton television talk show playbook in an effort to showcase their personal qualities for the electorate. The most significant of these appearances occurred when, for the first time, Oprah Winfrey ventured into the world of politics and invited both Bush and Gore individually onto her program for hour-long sit-down interviews. These interviews were oriented around the personal lives of the candidates; issues, politics, and policy were off-limits.

However, our focus is on late night comedy appearances, and in 2000 these started during the primary season. For example, on March 1, a week before Super Tuesday, George W. Bush and his remaining rival for the nomination, John McCain, appeared simultaneously on late night talk shows—McCain on Leno's *Tonight Show* and Bush on Letterman's *Late Show*. This was the evening that Letterman proclaimed, "The road to Washington runs through me."[23]

These appearances demonstrated that the sit-down interview does not always paint a candidate in a positive light. For example, it probably did not help McCain that he was Leno's second guest of the evening, following actress Neve Campbell. McCain appeared to be a bit uncomfortable, perhaps trying too hard. He referenced the foot problems Campbell had spoken of in her own interview by saying to her,

"I'm very concerned about those bunions. . . . You know, we're looking at a universal health care plan. Perhaps bunion treatment should be one of those."

McCain also did an impression of Leno that did not appear to go over well with the studio audience. Then he drew a hint of derision from Leno himself, when he told the host that he always carries a flat penny, a Hopi feather, and a compass so he can "always know the direction [I'm] heading in." He defended the practice by asking, "What's wrong with . . . being superstitious?" Leno replied, "Oh, nothing wrong. Only a little frightening."[24]

For all its limitations, McCain's *Tonight Show* appearance was a wild success compared to George W. Bush's guest spot on *The Late Show*. Hampered by a satellite connection that had enough of a delay to destroy any comic timing, Bush also made the mistake of trying too hard to be funny. Letterman first complimented Bush by saying: "You look like you've been on vacation. You look like a million damn dollars. I know that campaigning is hard. How do you look so youthful and rested?" Bush, in an attempt to be pithy, answered: "Fake it." This gave Letterman the opportunity to retort: "And that's pretty much how you're going to run the country?"[25]

It got worse for Bush when he attempted to make light of Letterman's recent coronary bypass surgery. In response to Letterman's quip that "the road to Washington runs through me," Bush attempted to make a joke by saying, "It's about time you had the heart to invite me [onto the show]." This drew some laughter, but some groans as well, from the studio audience.[26] Bush returned to Letterman's heart condition when he was asked to explain how he was "a uniter, not a divider." Bush answered, "When it comes time to sew up your chest cavity, we use stitches as opposed to opening it up. That's what that means."[27]

Luckily for Bush, he was able to repair the damage with an in-studio appearance on *The Late Show* later in the campaign. In the course of exchanging pleasantries and chatting about sports, Letterman unexpectedly segued into an interview that might have come from the *CBS News* division. In a persistent but not overly adversarial manner, he asked Bush about a variety of issues, touching on global warming, health care, terrorism, and capital punishment. Bush came across as serious and concerned—folksy, but not to a fault. At one point, the following exchange ensued:

> **Letterman:** I've told jokes about you, I've said unpleasant things, I've just been shooting my mouth off left and right. . . . Does it bother you that I'm always, you know, yakking about stuff?
> **Bush:** No, I'm glad you're saying my name. [This is a variant of the public relations adage that it doesn't matter what they say about you, just so long as they spell your name right—that is, any publicity is good publicity.]

On the Democratic side, Al Gore had more success as a guest on the late night circuit. Gore already had a reputation as someone with a less-than-dynamic personality, so it could be argued that he had more to gain than Bush did by making a good showing on late night talk shows. When he appeared on *The Late Show* on September 14, 2000, Gore joked with Letterman about the much-publicized long kiss between him and his wife onstage at the Democratic National Convention, saying: "For me, that was just a little peck."

Gore also gave Bush a pass on a recent gaffe, in which Bush was caught on an open microphone referring to a reporter from the *New York Times* as a "major-league a**hole." Gore generously suggested, "That kind of thing could happen to anyone." Perhaps his best moment came when he shifted from the sit-down interview into more of a scripted cameo role and delivered Letterman's signature "Top Ten" list for the evening titled "Top Ten Rejected Gore-Lieberman Campaign Slogans," which included the following:

- Vote for me or I'll come to your home and explain my 191-page economic plan to you in excruciating detail
- Remember, America: I gave you the Internet, and I can take it away. Think about it.
- With Lieberman on the ticket, you get all kinds of fun new days off

- Vote for me, and I will take whatever steps necessary to outlaw the term "Whazzzup!"

Just a few days after his *Letterman* appearance, Gore made an unannounced cameo on *The Tonight Show,* appearing onstage during Leno's monologue:

> **Leno:** Now according to the latest polls, Al Gore is the handsomest, smartest, most qualified—What? That doesn't sound like a joke I wrote. But who's the cue card guy? Oh, look who the cue card guy is.
> **Gore [holding cue cards]:** Keep going, Jay. Keep going.
> **Leno:** It's the man who invented the cue card, Al Gore. Wow! Nice to see you sir.

The reference here was to Gore's supposed claim to having "invented the Internet." Gore then went into the audience to shake hands. Although the appearance was brief, he did get a chance to quip to Leno that he liked that evening's abbreviated monologue "because [it] cut short the jokes about me." (In actuality, the program was cut short due to NBC's coverage of the Summer Olympics.)[28]

The 2004 Election

Despite the potential pitfalls highlighted by Bush's early appearance with Letterman in 2000, the candidates seeking the 2004 Democratic nomination to challenge Bush seemed to believe that the late night strategy was worth the risks. While previous election cycles featured a smattering of appearances from a few of the major presidential candidates, 2004 saw a comparative onslaught. All eight major contenders for the Democratic nomination appeared on late night talk shows, most of them on multiple occasions.

The outspoken black activist Al Sharpton was the most active candidate on the late night circuit, with five visits, followed closely by pre-primary campaign front-runners Howard Dean and John Edwards, with four apiece. The eventual Democratic nominee, John Kerry, made three appearances as a guest (on *The Tonight Show, Late Night,* and *The Daily Show*), as did lesser-known candidates Carol Moseley-Braun and Wesley Clark.

On the Republican side, President Bush and Vice President Cheney continued the long-standing norm of sitting presidents and vice presidents not appearing as guests on late night comedy programs. (This tradition was finally broken by President Obama, who appeared on *The Daily Show* in 2009.) Years after Bush's presidency ended, former White House Press Secretary Dana Perino discussed why Bush (like Clinton before him) avoided the late night comedy circuit while in office and running for reelection: "President Bush . . . just didn't think it was a place where the president should be. And also, they're dangerous."[29] Only the president's wife, First Lady Laura Bush, appeared on a late night show, visiting *The Tonight Show* once.

With one exception, there was little variation as to which shows the presidential candidates would frequent. Bill Maher was the most likely to have Democratic guests, hosting ten on his HBO program, *Real Time with Bill Maher.* This is not surprising, considering that Maher's program is the most overtly political and partisan of all the late night talk shows. Among the remaining hosts, Leno and Letterman hosted four candidates each, while Jon Stewart hosted three and Conan O'Brien two (both lesser-known candidates—Sharpton and Moseley-Braun).

Some of the more memorable appearances during the 2004 election season came the year before, during what is known as the "pre–primary" season. For example, on September 30, 2003, Howard Dean made a cameo appearance on *The Tonight Show* in order to explain his early fundraising success relative to his Democratic competitors. Leno showed a film of Dean playing the guitar on a street next to a sign that read "Your change for real change" and "Will strum for presidency," as passersby dropped money into the guitar case.[30] (In reality, it was widely known that Dean's advantage was due to his unprecedented success in raising money from small donors via the Internet.)

The following month John Kerry made an appearance on *The Tonight Show* as well. For the most part the guest spot was a standard sit-down interview in which Kerry tried to highlight his personality, talking about how his (at that point) stagnant campaign had been a "long and humbling experience." What set the interview apart was Kerry's entrance, riding a Harley-Davidson motorcycle onto the stage, wearing a leather jacket, jeans, denim shirt, and helmet.[31]

Some media observers were critical of the appearance. One commented that "Mr. Kerry's arrival on the set astride a Harley-Davidson appeared to have fallen flat, looking awkward and contrived."[32] Leno himself found the incident odd, noting years later: "Yeah, I remember when we had John Kerry on, and he came on a motorcycle and had a beer, and it just seemed like we're pushing a little too hard here. I mean I like John Kerry but I just felt like, "really?"[33]

The appearance, however, took place when Kerry's campaign was at perhaps its lowest point. Considered an early front-runner, he had lost ground to Howard Dean and John Edwards. His poll numbers had fallen into the single digits, his campaign was losing money, and (on the same day as his Leno appearance) his press secretary and deputy finance director quit in reaction to Kerry's decision to fire his campaign manager. *The Tonight Show* spot unofficially marked a restart of the Kerry campaign. Given the fact that he eventually secured the nomination, few would argue that the "motorcycle stunt" did anything but help him.

While Kerry soared in the polls and scored early primary victories in early 2004, the Dean campaign was sinking. Dean's disappointing third-place finish in the Iowa caucuses was compounded by a political miscue in a speech to supporters afterward. In order to assure supporters that the campaign was still on track and moving forward, Dean tried to deliver his concession speech with a high degree of energy and optimism:

> I'm sure there are some disappointed people here. [But] not only are we going to New Hampshire . . . we're going to South Carolina and Oklahoma and Arizona and North Dakota and New Mexico, and we're going to California and Texas and New York. And we're

going to South Dakota and Oregon and Washington and Michigan. And then we're going to Washington, DC. To take back the White House! Yeah!

The "yeah!" at the end of this quote does not capture the tone, tenor, and volume in which it was delivered. It was, in fact, a loud yell. This speech, now famously known as the "Dean Scream" or the "I Have a Scream" speech, was played repeatedly on cable news stations, the radio, and the Internet in the days following the Iowa caucuses. The response of pundits and talking heads on television was that Dean came across as slightly unhinged. Late night comics, of course, did not ignore the situation in their monologues:

> Seriously, I'm starting to worry about Howard Dean. Earlier today, he was debating Dennis Kucinich and he head-butted him. —*David Letterman*

> Did you see Dean's speech last night? Oh my God! Now I hear the cows in Iowa are afraid of getting mad Dean disease. I'm no pundit but it's always a bad sign when at the end of your speech, your aide is shooting you with a tranquilizer gun. —*Jay Leno*

> Did you see Howard Dean ranting and raving? Here's a little tip Howard—cut back on the Red Bull. —*David Letterman*

It would be foolish to assume that Dean's speech alone was the cause of his fall in the polls in January 2004, but it certainly did not help. His slide had begun weeks before and was capped off with the disappointing third-place finish in Iowa. Not surprisingly, the Dean campaign's effort to recover included an appearance on late night television. In late January, Dean made a pre-taped cameo on *Late Night with David Letterman* to deliver a "Top Ten" list titled "The Top Ten Ways I, Howard Dean, Can Turn Things Around," which included such gems as:

- Switch to decaf
- Unveil new slogan: "Vote for Dean and get one dollar off your next purchase at Blimpies"
- Go on *American Idol* and give 'em a taste of these pipes
- Show a little more skin
- Marry Rachel on final episode of *Friends*
- Oh, I don't know—maybe fewer crazy, red-faced rants

But despite Dean's effort to show that he was a good sport, it was too little and too late. By this time, the momentum had switched to Kerry as the most viable option to beat President Bush in the general election, and the senator from Massachusetts eventually secured the nomination.

The 2008 Election

The number of candidate appearances on the late night circuit in 2008 dwarfed that of 2004. This can be explained at least partly by the fact that in 2008, there was no incumbent president seeking reelection and no sitting vice president seeking either party's nomination. The field of candidates was thus larger than usual. In total there were sixteen major candidates for president: eight Democrats and eight Republicans. In addition, the relative explosion of candidate appearances on late night television in 2004 had established the practice as standard operating campaign procedure in presidential politics.

Table 7.1 lists the number of appearances each candidate made on late night talk shows and the number of candidates each program hosted. What's immediately noticeable is the total number of appearances throughout the campaign. Candidates took to the stage as guests over one hundred times on nine different late night comedy programs during the 2008 campaign. Not surprisingly, front-runners were very active in this regard. The eventual nominees, Barack Obama and John McCain, had thirteen and eleven appearances respectively, followed by Hillary Clinton and John Edwards with seven appearances each.

Arkansas Governor Mike Huckabee led all candidates, with fourteen appearances on late night shows. This was especially notable

Table 7.1   Presidential Candidate Appearances on Late Night Talk (2008)

Total Late Night Appearances by Candidate		Total Number of Candidates Hosted	
Huckabee, Mike	14	Jon Stewart	18
Obama, Barack	13	Jay Leno	16
McCain, John	11	David Letterman	14
Clinton, Hillary	7	Stephen Colbert	12
Edwards, John	7	Bill Maher	8
Biden, Joe	5	SNL	5
Paul, Ron	4	Craig Ferguson	3
Kucinich, Dennis	3	Conan O'Brien	3
Thompson, Fred	3	Jimmy Kimmel	1
Dodd, Chris	2		
Giuliani, Rudy	2		
Gravel, Mike	2		
Richardson, Bill	2		
Romney, Mitt	2		
Thompson, Tommy	2		
Hunter, Duncan	1		

Source: Center for Media and Public Affairs.

because Huckabee was largely unknown until his victory in the Iowa caucuses made him a serious contender for the Republican nomination. However, John McCain became the presumptive Republican nominee relatively early in the nomination season, making it even more unusual that Huckabee would appear so many times on late night talk shows. In fact, several of these appearances took place after it was clear that he could not win his party's nomination. Consider, for example, Huckabee's cameo appearance on *Saturday Night Live*'s "Weekend Update" on February 23, 2008 (see Box 7.2 for an excerpt).

Perhaps the funniest part of the cameo occurred when the segment seemed to come to a close, but Huckabee remained onstage even though he had clearly been given the cue to leave. After multiple rounds of applause, the governor smiled and waved, which finally prompted host Seth Meyers to urge him to leave, saying: "Uh, Governor Huckabee . . . I think we're done now, sir." To which Huckabee responded: "Oh, right. . . . Normally I pick up on those things. Sorry." It may be that Huckabee simply had a natural flair for the talk show milieu, which made him popular with their hosts. Since the election he has hosted his own talk shows on ABC Radio Network and the Fox News Channel.

BOX. 7.2

Excerpt from Mike Huckabee's Appearance on "Weekend Update" (2008)

Seth Meyers (Host): After his win in Wisconsin on Tuesday, Senator John McCain pronounced himself the Republican nominee for president. This, despite the fact that his closest rival, Arkansas Governor Mike Huckabee, remains in the race. Here to explain why he has yet to concede, Governor Mike Huckabee.

Mike Huckabee: Hello Seth, Amy [Meyers's co-host].

Meyers: So Governor, you remain in the race despite the fact that it's a mathematical impossibility that you can win, and our question is, why?

Huckabee: Well Seth, the media loves to throw around the term "mathematical impossibility" but no one can ever explain exactly what that means to me.

Meyers: Well let me give it a shot. Basically, it takes 1,191 delegates to clinch your party's nomination, and even if you won every remaining unpledged delegate, you would still fall 200 delegates short.

Huckabee: Wow. Uh, Seth, that was an excellent explanation. But I'm afraid that you overlooked the all-important "super-delegates." Don't forget about them.

Meyers: Well, I won't forget about them, but the super-delegates are only in the Democratic primary.

Huckabee: Uh, they can't vote in the Republican primary?

Meyers: They cannot.

Huckabee: Uh-oh! That's not good news. You know Seth, I was counting on those super-delegates. . . .

One of the strangest events of the 2008 campaign involved Republican nominee John McCain and David Letterman. The two seemed to have a fairly good relationship up to and through the 2008 primary season. McCain jokes during Letterman's monologues were oriented around McCain's age and appearance. The jokes followed a formula that started, "McCain looks like the kind of guy that [fill in the blank]." See the following examples, many of which came from the early primary season:

> But seriously, how about that John McCain? John McCain looks like a guy whose head you can barely see over the steering wheel. . . .

John McCain looks like the guy who thinks the nurses are stealing his stuff.

How about that John McCain, huh? John McCain looks like the kind of guy who brags that his new denture adhesive allows him to eat corn on the cob. He looks like a guy who parked his RV overnight at Wal-Mart.

During an April 1, 2008, broadcast, McCain made his first appearance of the campaign on Letterman to "defend himself" in a cameo appearance during the monologue:

> **Letterman:** You know who I like is that John McCain. . . . He looks like the guy who goes into town for turpentine. He looks like the guy who always [has] wiry hair growing out of new places. He looks like the guy who points out the spots they missed at the carwash. . . .
> [McCain walks onto stage behind Letterman to audience applause. Letterman acts surprised.]
> **McCain:** Hi, Letterman. . . . You think that stuff's pretty funny, don't you? Well, you look like a guy whose laptop would be seized by the authorities. You look like a guy who was caught smuggling reptiles in his pants. You look like a guy who the neighbors later say "He mostly kept to himself." You look like the night manager of a creepy hotel. And you look like the guy who enjoys getting into a hot tub and watching his swim trunks inflate.

The relationship between McCain and Letterman became fractious, however, when the Republican nominee canceled his September 24 guest appearance on short notice. The decision to cancel was made at the time he announced he would suspend his campaign and return to Washington to deal with the burgeoning economic crisis that burst into public view in mid-September. During his monologue and the segment that followed, Letterman made it very clear he was not happy with McCain's decision:

When you call up, and you call up at the last minute to cancel a show, ladies and gentlemen, that's starting to smell. I mean, this is not the John McCain I know. . . . It makes me believe something is going haywire with the campaign. . . . Someone [has] gotten to him and said, "You know what? Blow Letterman off. He's a lightweight." . . . This is not the way a tested hero behaves. Somebody is putting something in his Metamucil. . . . So now I wonder if he'll ever come back. . . . A hero, an honest to God hero, and an American hero. Maybe the only actual hero I know, I've met the man, and I know the guy, so I'm more than a little disappointed by this behavior. "We're suspending the campaign"? Are we suspending it because there's an economic crisis, or because the poll numbers are sliding?

Letterman's anger was taken seriously by the news media, and footage from the monologue was rebroadcast heavily on cable news, network news, and the Internet. Critics focused not only on McCain's decision to suspend his campaign but also on Letterman's forceful attack on McCain. However, the real importance of late night talk in the court of public opinion was illustrated by the fact that McCain agreed to appear on Letterman's show on October 16, 2008, three weeks after he canceled. Below is part of the exchange between the two after McCain sat down:

Letterman: Now, what exactly happened? [applause] I thought I was doing my part to save the economy, and then later I got to thinking, "Well, maybe I'm just not important enough."

McCain: Can I give you an answer?

Letterman: Please.

McCain: I screwed up. [applause]

Letterman: You called me an hour and a half [beforehand], and said, "We've got to get back to Washington," but you didn't go right back to Washington!

McCain: I screwed up. . . . What can I say? What can I say? It's been reviewed pretty well, what happened.

Letterman: Well, I'm willing to put this behind us.

McCain: Thank you. Thank you. Thank you very much. Thank you. Thank you.

Probably no other event from the 2008 campaign better illustrates the power of the late night talk show venue and the way political figures use guest appearances to improve their media images. Whether or not it was a case of political grandstanding, McCain canceled his appearance at a time when the US government was taking unprecedented actions to stave off a credit crisis that could easily have led to an economic depression. Nonetheless, the balance of power in the above exchange is unambiguous. The late night comedy host was in charge, and the war hero and presidential candidate was kowtowing to him in order to appeal to the voters in his audience.

The 2012 Election

Following a noticeable increase in the number of presidential candidate appearances on late night talk shows in election cycles from 2000 to 2008, a downturn occurred in 2012. We tracked fewer than half as many candidate appearances as there were four years earlier. The list of candidates was headed by President Obama's six appearances, one of them with First Lady Michelle Obama, who outstripped her husband with eight appearances of her own. The president's general election opponent Mitt Romney finished just behind, with five personal appearances, along with one by his wife and his five sons. Texas Senator Ron Paul also appeared five times, despite losing the Republican nomination fight.

The drop in appearances and the general lack of drama associated with them also reflects the fact that Obama had already made news as the first sitting president to go on a late night talk show. In effect, the late night circuit had been routinized as merely one more platform in his quest for reelection. On the Republican side, Romney briefly stirred up a mini-controversy, attracting news media criticism by refusing to appear on any of these shows throughout much of the fall because he believed he would be stepping into a hostile environment. Our joke data support his concerns: on the five late night talk shows on the broadcast networks, we counted 860 jokes about Romney during 2012, more than twice President Obama's total of 346 jokes.

Thus, like televised presidential debates, late night talk show appearances have evolved from closely watched, controversial, and highly consequential events to one more ticket every candidate needs to punch. These days you have to prove that you can survive an encounter with TV talk show hosts in order to convince the news media and the voters that you can stand up against America's competitors and enemies as chief of state. This observation would have seemed laughable to an earlier generation of presidential contenders, but today it is no laughing matter.

CONCLUSION

Once considered a stunt, the late night talk show guest appearance has become standard for presidential hopefuls. Bill Clinton resurrected his national political aspirations not once but twice by playing the saxophone on late night talk shows. And following in the footsteps of Richard Nixon on *Laugh-In,* candidates like Sarah Palin do cameo appearances on shows like *Saturday Night Live* to prove they can be good sports.

Both cameo appearances and sit-down interviews provide an opportunity for candidates to showcase their personalities in a casual setting that allows them to reach out to voters in a nonpartisan, policy-free manner. Swing voters, who tend to base their voting decisions on candidates' personal attributes rather than on partisanship or policy, are more apt to be influenced by a candidate's late night appearance. And as long as voters continue to look to a candidate's personal qualities for voting cues, candidates will attempt to exploit the late night venue to their benefit.

Candidates from both parties have responded to this opportunity by treating late night talk show appearances as one stop on their road to the White House. As is the case with most media appearances, however, the potential pitfalls of walking onto the late night stage must be weighed against the benefits. For example, correctly observing that he was the target of more late night barbs than was his opponent, Mitt Romney avoided an environment he judged to be hostile during much of the general election campaign.

While an appearance with Jay Leno or David Letterman may be less perilous than a sit-down interview on *Meet the Press*, efforts to be too funny or too self-deprecating can have significant consequences. And as John McCain learned in 2008, woe to the candidate who insults a talk show host with a late cancellation. Future candidates will be well advised to use caution when navigating the shoals of late night comedy.

NOTES

1. Joe McGinniss, *The Selling of the President* (New York: Simon and Schuster, 1969).

2. Ibid., 32.

3. Kliph Nesteroff, "The Comedy Writer That Helped Elect Richard M. Nixon," 2010, http://blog.wfmu.org/freeform/2010/09/richard-nixons-laugh-in.html.

4. Hal Erickson, *A Critical History of "Rowan and Martin's Laugh-In," 1968–1973* (New York: McFarland & Co., 2000); Laurence Maslon and Michael Kantor, *Make 'Em Laugh: The Funny Business of America* (New York: Hachette Book Group, 2008).

5. Ibid., 168.

6. Bill Clinton, *My Life* (New York: Knopf, 2004), 339.

7. Tom Shales, "The Numb and the Restless," *Washington Post,* July 21, 1988.

8. "Clinton the Big Topic," *Arkansas Democrat-Gazette,* July 22, 1988.

9. Ibid.

10. John Brummet, *Arkansas Democratic Gazette,* July 23, 1988.

11. Shales, "The Numb and the Restless."

12. Clinton, *My Life,* 342.

13. Associated Press, "On the Light Side," July 23, 1988.

14. Deborah Mathis, "Yes, There's Life After 'The Speech,'" *Arkansas Democrat-Gazette,* July 27, 1988.

15. Carolyn Callison, "Talkative Arkansas Governor Trades Quips with Johnny Carson," Associated Press, July 29, 1988.

16. Associated Press, "From Dog House to White House?" July 31, 1988.

17. Pew Research Center Biennial Media Consumption Survey, April 2008.

18. Lee Sigelman, "The Nonvoting Voter in Voting Research," *American Journal of Political Science* 26 (1982): 47–56.

19. Pew Research Center, "Cable and Internet Loom Large in Fragmented Political News Universe," January 11, 2004, http://www.people-press.org/2004/01/11/cable-and-internet-loom-large-in-fragmented-political-news-universe/.

20. Matthew A. Baum, "Talking the Vote: Why Presidential Candidates Hit the Talk Show Circuit," *American Journal of Political Science* 49 (2005): 213–234.

21. A. King, "Do Leaders' Personalities Really Matter?" In *Leaders' Personalities and the Outcomes of Democratic Elections,* ed. A. King (Oxford: Oxford University Press); Richard R. Lau and David P. Redlawsk, "Advantages and Disadvantages of Cognitive Heuristics in Political Decision Making," *American Journal of Political Science* 45 (2001): 951–971.

22. David Niven, S. Robert Lichter, and Daniel Amundson, "Our First Cartoon President: Bill Clinton and the Politics of Late-Night Comedy," in *Laughing Matters: Humor and American Politics in the Media Age,* eds. Jody C Baumgartner and Jonathan S. Morris (New York: Routledge, 2008).

23. Marty Rosen, "Prez Wanna-bes Try Late-Night TV," *New York Daily News,* March 2, 2000.

24. Ibid.

25. Ibid.

26. Ibid.

27. Ibid.

28. "Gore Jokes Around with Leno," *Contra Costa Times,* September 20, 2000.

29. Dana Perino, "Unlike Obama, Bush Thought Late-Night Shows Not 'A Place Where the President Should Be,'" *Mediaite.com,* http://www.mediaite.com/tv/dana-perino-unlike-obama-bush-thought-late-night-shows-not-a-place-where-the-president-should-be/.

30. Robert Jablon, "Howard Dean Makes Leno Show Appearance," Associated Press, October 1, 2003.

31. Associated Press, "Kerry Rides Motorcycle onto Leno's 'Tonight Show' Stage," November 12, 2003.

32. "Dean Plays Union Card in White House Race," *London Times,* November 13, 2003.

33. Patrick Gavin, "Leno Talks 'The Tonight Show's Political Humor," *Politico,* April 20, 2012, http://www.politico.com/blogs/media/2012/04/leno-talks-the-tonight-shows-political-humor-121140.html.

Chapter 8

Political Humor:
Prospect and Retrospect

Since the beginning of late night talk, politics and politicians have been the targets of punch lines. Different hosts of different shows in different eras have included various amounts of political content in their shows, but such content has been a consistent thread running through these programs. In general, jokes about politicians have focused on old tropes and deep-seated cultural images of government.

PUNCH LINES AND POPULISM

It is little wonder that a receptive audience exists for jokes that send up politicians. A suspicion of politics and politicians is deeply ingrained in American culture. After all, the United States was born of a revolution against political authority. In order to get the Constitution approved, the founding fathers had to add a Bill of Rights that specifies the limits of government power. Today these feelings continue to be expressed in such diverse ways as term limits for holders of public office; provisions for initiatives, referenda, and recalls in many states; and a professional civil service that replaced the "spoils system" in which politicians handed out government jobs and benefits to supporters.

So there has been a ready audience for jokes that portray politicians as incompetent, overpaid, sleazy, and corrupt since the days of Will Rogers, Mark Twain, and beyond. But the most frequently quoted jokes of these earlier humorists were often bipartisan. They attacked the whole political class, as in Rogers's gibe: "The more you observe politics, the more you've got to admit that each party is worse than the other." Also, earlier generations of humorists made liberal use of "evergreens"—jokes that don't grow stale over time. The lines we have quoted from Rogers and Twain are as funny in the twenty-first century as they were in the twentieth and nineteenth centuries, because they were not aimed at individual politicians who were forgotten long ago.

On late night talk shows, political jokes don't have to maintain a shelf life. On the contrary, the more topical they are, the better, since diverse national audiences are most likely to be at least somewhat familiar with people and events that are in the news. So the formula for comedians is to turn the daily news into nightly jokes. Toward this end, regular newsmakers, whether political leaders or entertainment celebrities, develop their own comic profiles. If the down-home George W. Bush mangles a sentence while giving a speech, it's going to end up in a comedy routine. If the cerebral Barack Obama does so, it won't, because it doesn't fit a preexisting comic stereotype.

Thus, the medium of television in general—and the nightly monologue format in particular—lends itself to jokes that focus on the personal foibles of particular politicians. Jokes about a politician's appearance, gaffes, and misbehavior all become fodder for punch lines. These topics, too, build off older tropes, so that verbal slips and misstatements are seen as indications of intellectual limits, while misbehavior speaks to a lack of character or to general venality. Such jokes can be biting and even cruel, so long as they are not seen as expressions of personal pique or partisanship, which could become ratings poison.

Since the hosts of late night shows appear several times a week, they can repeat and embellish their jibes with slight variations to build indelible images in the public's mind. Such jokes tend to be succinct and pointed, giving them potentially greater impact than a topical news discussion. Few people have any direct personal knowledge of their president, let alone their own congressman or -woman, so that void is easily filled by jokes.

Conventional wisdom once held that reacting to such barbs only gave the jokesters credence and a larger audience. By the 1980s, however, political operatives were beginning to keep an eye on late night comedy. Republican consultant Lee Atwater remarked that he regularly monitored the audience response to Johnny Carson's jokes on *The Tonight Show* to see how politicians played in Peoria.[1] In 1988, Atwater would put this knowledge to use as manager of George H. W. Bush's successful presidential campaign.

While Atwater's interest was based on practical concerns, the evidence we have reviewed suggests that audiences can and do respond to politicians partly in terms of their one-dimensional comedy caricatures. For example, if there are enough jokes about "old Bob Dole" or "old John McCain" on the campaign trail, voters will be primed to think of them at least partly in terms of their age. So politicians may have good reason to worry about any consistent image that comedians begin to sketch of them.

It was near the end of Johnny Carson's career before politicians would find a way to harness late night shows for their own purposes. By and large, sitting politicians and candidates for public office avoided the late night shows. Occasionally, retired politicians would consent to an interview, especially when plugging a new book or project—but not active politicians. This reluctance was driven by concerns that such appearances would reduce their gravitas, not to mention fears of appearing wooden and humorless.

As we learned, Bill Clinton broke this taboo by appearing first on *The Tonight Show* and then, as a presidential candidate, on *The Arsenio Hall Show*. In both cases, he responded to critical news coverage by doing an end run around journalists to find a more congenial venue. Clinton's foray into late night and his subsequent victory at the polls suggested that the public was not put off by a presidential candidate appearing on an unusual platform. This also reinforced the campaign's narrative that Clinton was a new kind of politician prepared to lead in a new age of mediated politics.

The year Clinton took office was marked by another major transition—from Johnny Carson to Jay Leno as host of *The Tonight Show*. This transition produced a marked increase in the political content of the show, as Leno expanded the length of the monologues and increased the number of jokes about politics and politicians. The increase in political material did not change the basic framework of Leno's stand-up routine; it just increased the number of politicians and events that could be referenced. From that point on, political humor became a regular part of late night talk show monologues. To the end of his tenure, Leno featured more political material than any other late night host on broadcast network television.

The increase in political material was accelerated by a change in the news media's willingness to peek behind the curtain that had long kept politicians' private lives in the shadows. Once journalists began to report on the sex lives of public officials, this juicy material became fair game for joke writers. Thus, over the past quarter century, a constant stream of philandering politicians has added a salacious veneer to late night political humor. And in some ways, the new material on sexual improprieties harkens back to older themes presenting politicians as self-serving, privileged reprobates who disregard law, morality, and social convention.

Of course, late night comics cannot create an image for a politician from whole cloth. In whatever form they take, these shows serve as selective echo chambers for the events of the day. They do not amplify events that can't be turned into a laugh line. But foibles, failures, scandals, and personal idiosyncrasies are all fair game that can make comedic tropes durable and difficult to change.

Moreover, late night comedians put politicians in double jeopardy. The day's bad news is echoed by that night's jokes. And we found that a surge of both bad news and late night jokes independently predicted a drop in the favorability ratings of presidential candidates. Both scholars and pundits have expressed concerns that voters have become cynical about politics, due to a rising tide of negativity in the tone of campaign news and the negative ads run by candidates and ideologically aligned groups. Our findings suggest that late night humorists have become another contributor to this process.

The political impact of late night humor is also a testament to the rise of "soft news" or "infotainment" in the American media system. These terms refer to media venues that impart information about politics and policies as a by-product of material that is primarily intended to entertain audiences. On television, for example, the lines were once clearly drawn between news programming, which dealt with serious issues of public concern, and entertainment programming, which provided audiences with an escape from serious matters. Gradually these lines became blurred, as tabloid-style news, dueling pundits, and fluffy newsmagazine shows pushed news in the direction of entertainment. The change is clearly shown by the evolving role of the late night talk shows from variety formats showcasing entertainers to shows that regularly include political humor and political discussion in the mix.

THE EMPIRE STRIKES BACK

Once late night talk became known as a source of political information, politicians discovered that they could secure valuable airtime and expect relatively mild questioning as guests on these shows. Despite Bill Clinton's earlier forays into the world of late night talk, however, it wasn't until 2000 that candidates began to treat these shows as a necessary stop on the campaign trail. During the general election that year, Al Gore, George W. Bush, Joe Lieberman, and Ralph Nader all did major interviews on late night shows.

All of these candidates largely followed the Clinton model, using the appearance to make a few jokes at their own expense and display their human side to voters who knew them only from thirty-second TV ads and ten-second sound-bites. Beyond introducing viewers to the men who wanted to be president, these appearances offered them a major platform to discuss some of their ideas or the reasons they should be elected. In fact, our research showed that both Bush and Gore enjoyed more airtime during their separate appearances on *The Late Show with David Letterman* than they did on the network evening newscasts for the entire month during which they made their late night appearances.

An important factor in the process of making late night talk shows a place for serious political discussion was the terrorist attacks on

September 11, 2001. The shows all went off the air for a few days after the attacks as the networks, hosts, and writers attempted to find the right way to go back to telling jokes after such a tragedy. The hosts marked their returns with lengthy monologues expressing grief, sympathy, and resilience in an effort to boost the national morale.

In the weeks following the attacks, there was a notable shift in the type of guests appearing on the shows. To be sure, actors, musicians, and popular authors still appeared on the shows, but sprinkled in more frequently were politicians like Senator Hillary Clinton, New York Mayor Rudy Giuliani, and Senator John McCain. The guest lists eventually reverted to their pre-9/11 mix, but this brief period opened the door wider for political guests. The post-9/11 period proved that discussions with politicians were not devastating to ratings, and that many of these individuals could successfully discuss issues and events with the hosts and create good television.

The clearest sign of the importance of these shows was the choice of prospective candidates to forgo announcing their intention to run for office in a traditional press conference in favor of making the announcement on network late night talk shows and even on Comedy Central. For example, Arnold Schwarzenegger announced his 2003 run for California governor on *The Tonight Show,* John McCain announced his 2008 presidential run on *Late Night with David Letterman,* and John Edwards announced his 2004 candidacy on *The Daily Show,* prompting Jon Stewart to remind him that "we're a fake [news] show."

It used to be that presidential candidates focused their initial attention on the early primary and caucus states. Increasingly, late night television has become another "primary" test for each candidate to pass. Notably, Tennessee Senator Fred Thompson actually declined an opportunity to participate in a Republican primary debate in 2008 so that he could officially announce his candidacy on Jay Leno's program the same night.

More recently Barack Obama has trumped his predecessors by becoming the first sitting president to appear on the late night talk shows. In fact, Obama has become something of a talk show president, at various times chatting with Jay Leno, David Letterman, Jon Stewart,

Oprah Winfrey, Barbara Walters, and others. First Lady Michelle Obama has also used late night appearances to promote her campaign against childhood obesity. It appears that "campaigning by talk show" may in fact be morphing into "governing by talk show."

Thus, soft news cuts both ways. The infotainment venue of late night talk brings new problems for politicians but also new opportunities. Their appearances have increased and become more important as audiences have grown more fragmented. Few news or public affairs programs can match the size of the audiences that tune in to the major network comedians. For a candidate to have the opportunity to address millions of viewers without the constraints of the news media is a huge opportunity. Although journalists may badger a candidate about the latest gaffe or kerfuffle on the campaign trail, the late night shows offer them an opportunity to joke about the problem and then move on to discuss issues that are part of their campaign message. And in today's media environment, a good appearance can be seen countless times on YouTube and the show's own website.

SATIRE AND PARODY ON TV

The satirical and parodic programs on Comedy Central represent an exception to many generalizations about late night humor that are based on broadcast network talk shows. Playwright George S. Kaufman once remarked, "Satire is what closes on Saturday night," and satirical programs have been few and far between on American television. The boldest have historically been short-lived, while those with longevity have softened their satirical edge to gain larger audiences. That changed when Jon Stewart took over *The Daily Show* in 1999. Stewart's rebooting of the program into the realm of political satire probably owed something to the increase in political content across late night and the continued good ratings for shows that included more topical material.

The Daily Show and its spin-off *The Colbert Report* have never avoided political jokes, political guests, or policy issues. As their popularity and critical acclaim have risen, so has the caliber of their guests. For example, during a two-week period in September 2006,

The Daily Show aired interviews with sitting Pakistan President Pervez Musharraf, former President Bill Clinton, former New Jersey Governor Jim McGreevey, and former Senate Majority Leader Trent Lott.

The fact that *The Daily Show* uses real news footage in fake newscasts and is topical in its focus has proven controversial. The controversies have grown more serious as research continues to suggest that substantial numbers of people are getting at least some of their political information from *The Daily Show*. This has led conservative groups and bloggers to complain about political bias and call for more balance in the show's content.

Stewart has insisted that "there is not a designed ideological agenda on my part to affect partisan change."[2] In response to being labeled a Democrat, he told Larry King that he was "more socialist or independent."[3] In any event, his audience is unlikely to complain. A 2012 Pew Research Center survey found that Colbert's and Stewart's shows attracted the second- and third-most-liberal audiences among twenty-four news sources, behind only MSNBC's *The Rachel Maddow Show*.[4]

Stewart and his writers clearly see their mission as exposing hypocrisy and deflating pomposity to create successful comedy. By commenting on the often absurd efforts of politicians to reframe issues in partisan ways, Stewart and Colbert pull back the curtain on political rhetoric. If they target Republicans more than Democrats, well, nobody ever said satire had to be fair and balanced. Exposing hypocrites is certainly the traditional role of satire, but in many respects *The Daily Show* and *The Colbert Report* go beyond that role to playing referee in political debates. And in recent years, both men have edged closer to engaging in real-world politics. Nonetheless, with apologies to George S. Kaufman, satire is what runs on Monday through Thursday nights every week on Comedy Central.

FAKE NEWS AND REAL POLITICS

In the last few years late night humorists have started to move in the direction of political activism, an area where they had previously feared to tread. It began in frivolous fashion. In 2006, Conan O'Brien noticed his physical resemblance to Tarja Halonen, who was running for reelection as president of Finland. With tongue in cheek, O'Brien turned this into a cause and urged Finns to vote for Halonen.

Such an endorsement would have been unimportant were it not for the fact that O'Brien's show was telecast in Finland five nights a week during this period. He went so far as to take his show to Finland during the campaign for a week of telecasts. Halonen won the election amid some controversy among Finns about the role of American media in their domestic politics. Whatever effect O'Brien had on the Finnish electorate, this marked the first time that a late night host had so overtly endorsed any political candidate.

Not surprisingly, the most overt forays into American politics came from Comedy Central's dynamic duo. In 2010, Jon Stewart and Stephen Colbert hosted a "Rally to Restore Sanity and/or Fear" that drew over two hundred thousand people to the National Mall in Washington, DC. The rally was billed as a call for reasonableness and an effort to mobilize the forces of moderation against extremism and partisanship. Although Stewart denied it, the rally was widely portrayed as a riposte to two recently held rallies led by polarizing figures on the political right and left, respectively: Glenn Beck's "Restoring Honor" rally and Al Sharpton's "Reclaim the Dream" rally.

Stephen Colbert has been the more willing to involve himself directly in politics. In 2010, he testified before a House subcommittee on the topic of migrant workers. After speaking in a humorous vein, he broke character to deliver a direct plea for better treatment of migrant workers. Three years earlier, in 2007, he had ventured directly into electoral politics, announcing his candidacy for president on his show, but only as a "favorite son" in his home state of South Carolina. A self-described Democrat, he tried to run in both the Republican and Democratic primaries. However, he was deterred by the $35,000 fee required to file in the Republican primary. Then the state Democratic Party refused to allow his name on the ballot, on the unassailable grounds that he wasn't a serious candidate.

Colbert tried again in the 2012 campaign. First he set up his own super-PAC, the ColbertPAC, which had the purpose of mocking recent changes in campaign finance reform. Then a poll found that he was supported by 5 percent of the electorate in the upcoming South Carolina primary. In response, Colbert announced that he was in the "exploratory phase" of his candidacy. He turned over his super-PAC to Jon Stewart to comply with government regulations prohibiting candidates from having their own PACs. Within a few days, however, he withdrew and (in character as a "right-winger") asked his audience to vote for Herman Cain, who had withdrawn from the presidential race following allegations of sexual harassment but was still on the ballot in South Carolina.

Although he has never run for office, Jon Stewart uses his show to lobby for legislation that he sees as being in the public interest. For example, in 2010 he devoted an entire show to the 9/11 First Responders Bill, which was being held up in the Senate by a Republican filibuster. The bill provided benefits for firemen, policemen, and others who had rushed to aid the victims of the terrorist strike at Ground Zero and later developed health problems, such as cancer and respiratory diseases, presumably from exposure to the thick clouds of building materials raised by the collapse of the World Trade Center buildings. The White House credited Stewart for raising public awareness of the bill, which eventually won passage.[5]

Similarly, in January 2013, Stewart used his first show after the holiday break to blast House Republicans for voting against a bill that would have supplied billions of dollars of aid to areas hit by Hurricane Sandy. During the show he shamed Republican legislators who voted against the original legislation and urged people to press Congress to pass an aid bill. Addressing these legislators on his show, he said: "This is just a simple, down-the-middle, black-and-white, cut-and-dry, warm cup of what would Jesus or any other human being that isn't an asshole would do, and you blew it. You blew it."[6] Once again, the legislation eventually passed. While shaming politicians and calling out hypocrites are commonplace on the show, such instances of taking an activist role on specific legislation suggest that this fake news show has a real editorial edge.

In April 2013, David Letterman followed suit with his "Stooge of the Night" campaign. In this case Letterman used his show to single out senators who had voted against a failed measure to expand background checks on gun control. The clips not only showed the senators voicing opposition for various reasons but also included graphics indicating how much money they had received from pro-gun groups. This was an overtly political segment from a host who is not usually so politically oriented. It is unlikely that Letterman's "Stooge" segment had any impact on the gun control debate, but it does suggest that we may see more such occurrences in the future.

Thus, in the past few years late night comedians have begun to test the waters of real-world politics. Stephen Colbert's forays into the presidential races of 2008 and 2012 seemed to be whimsical efforts to lighten the mood on the campaign trail. However, Colbert, Stewart, and Letterman have all injected themselves into political debates on issues they appear to feel strongly about. Given the ideological match between their own views and those of their audience, Comedy Central hosts will probably pay no penalty in reduced ratings for continuing in this vein. But this is traditionally an area that hosts of broadcast network shows, with their more politically diverse audiences, have avoided in the past. Letterman's position on background checks for gun sales is shared by a large majority of the American public, so his outspokenness may have been an exception to the rule. Nonetheless, a decade ago it would have been difficult to predict that the coming years would witness late night comedians forming PACs, running for president, making impassioned pleas before congressional committees, and using their influence to pressure legislators to change their votes.

CONCLUSION

It has been nearly a half century since Richard Nixon had his "Sock it to me" moment on *Laugh-In* and forty years since Chevy Chase forever altered President Ford's public image on *Saturday Night Live,* but it took a while for politics to establish a regular presence on late night television talk shows. Our study covers the golden era of late night political humor, which began in 1992. That year marked the transition from Johnny Carson to Jay Leno as host of *The Tonight Show* and the first appearance of a presidential candidate on a late night show.

More than twenty years later, Leno has handed *The Tonight Show* reins over to Jimmy Fallon, Stephen Colbert has been tapped to replace David Letterman, and the landscape of late night humor has changed in many ways. The late night comedy field is larger and more diverse, the format has expanded to include shows specializing in satire and parody, and some of the monologues have moved from PG- to R-rated content. The material is also far more accessible—and potentially more influential—today. Twenty years ago, if you fell asleep during a monologue, you missed it for good. Today you can catch it the next day (or the next week or month) via DVR, YouTube, Hulu, or the welter of websites that have sprung up to catalogue the jokes. Late night humor has indeed become entrenched as a force in American politics—sending up politicians and sometimes laughing them off the public stage, providing a (relatively) friendly platform for presidents and presidential candidates to appeal to voters, and transmitting a sometimes jaundiced view of politics to viewers who may come for escapist entertainment but leave as better-informed citizens.

The picture isn't entirely rosy. Nobody would call comedy routines the ideal way to communicate substantive and nuanced information about our democratic system. The relentlessly negative portrayal of politicians may contribute to the public's cynicism toward the political process. And whatever their intentions, the comedians aren't entirely equal-opportunity offenders. They find more laughs among Republican presidential candidates than among their Democratic opponents. There is also a small but growing tendency for late night hosts to become involved in partisan politics. Whether this is a problem depends on how you feel about parlaying media celebrity into political influence. Today there is only one (acknowledged) comedian in Congress—Minnesota Senator and *Saturday Night Live* alumnus Al Franken—and the Republic has so far survived.

Some things never change—Americans love to laugh at politicians. It's part of our populist DNA. Today, late night television offers more ways for us to indulge that desire than there were a generation ago.

But the joke may be on the audience. What we laugh at affects what we think about politicians and how we think about politics, whether we know it or not.

NOTES

1. S. Robert Lichter and Daniel Amundson, "Heeere's Politics," *Public Opinion* (1988): 45–46.

2. "Numbers Don't Lie: *Daily Show*'s Stewart Hammers Right Nearly 4 Times More," *Newsbusters*, July 18, 2011, http://newsbusters.org/blogs/erin-r-brown/2011 /07/18/numbers-dont-lie-daily-shows-stewart-hammers-right-nearly-4-times -more.

3. "CNN Transcript: *Larry King Live:* Jon Stewart Looks Back at Election 2000," *Larry King Live,* December 15, 2000 (retrieved March 25, 2007).

4. Quoted in "Demographics and Political Views of News Audiences," *People Press,* September 27, 2012, http://www.people-press.org/2012/09/27 /section-4-demographics-and-political-views-of-news-audiences/.

5. Lucy Madison, "White House Lauds Jon Stewart for Pushing Passage of 9/11 Health Bill," *CBS News,* December 21, 2010.

6. Meredith Blake, "Jon Stewart Lashes Out at House Republicans over Hurricane Sandy Aid," *Los Angeles Times,* January 8, 2013.

Bibliography

Alba, Ben. *Inventing Late Night: Steve Allen and the Original* Tonight *Show.* Amherst, NY: Prometheus Books, 2005.

Annis, Albert D. "The Relative Effectiveness of Cartoons and Editorials as Propaganda Media." *Psychological Bulletin* 36 (1939): 628.

Associated Press. "On the Light Side," July 23, 1988.

———. "From Dog House to White House?" July 31, 1988.

———. "Kerry Rides Motorcycle onto Leno's 'Tonight Show' Stage," November 12, 2003. http://usatoday30.usatoday.com/news/politicselections/nation/2003-11-12-kerry-leno_x.htm.

———. "Politicians Found Late-Night an Asset in 2008," December 29, 2008. http://www.cmpa.com/news/12_29_2008.pdf.

———. "A History of Political Sex Scandals." *Washington Post,* April 7, 2011. http://www.washingtonpost.com/wp-srv/special/politics/sex-scandal-timeline/index.html (accessed May 17, 2012).

Baek, Young Min, and Wojcieszak Magdalena. "Don't Expect Too Much! Learning from Late-Night Comedy and Knowledge Item Difficulty." *Communication Research* 36 (2009): 783–809.

Barilleaux, Ryan, and Jody Baumgartner. "Victims of Rogues: The Impeachment of Presidents Bill Clinton and Boris Yeltsin in Comparative Perspective." *White House Studies* 4 (2004): 281–299.

Baum, Matthew. *Soft News Goes to War: Public Opinion and American Foreign Policy in the New Media Age.* Princeton, NJ: Princeton University Press, 2003.

———. "Soft News and Political Knowledge: Evidence of Absence or Absence of Evidence?" *Political Communication* 20 (2003): 173–190.

———. "Talking the Vote: Why Presidential Candidates Hit the Talk Show Circuit." *American Journal of Political Science* 49 (2005): 213–234.

Baum, Matthew, and Angela Jamison. "The Oprah Effect: How Soft News Helps Inattentive Citizens Vote Consistently." *Journal of Politics* 68 (2006): 946–959.

Baumgartner, Jody. *The American Vice Presidency Reconsidered.* Westport, CT: Praeger, 2006.

——. "Humor on the Next Frontier: Youth, Online Political Humor, and the JibJab Effect." *Social Science Computer Review* 29 (2007): 319–338.

——. "Editorial Cartoons 2.0: The Effects of Digital Political Satire on Presidential Candidate Evaluations." *Presidential Studies Quarterly* 38 (2008): 735–758.

——. "No Laughing Matter? Young Adults and the 'Spillover Effect' of Candidate-Centered Political Humor." *HUMOR: International Journal of Humor Research* (forthcoming).

Baumgartner, Jody, and Peter L. Francia. *Conventional Wisdom and American Elections: Exploding Myths, Exploring Misconceptions,* 2nd ed. Lanham, MD: Rowman & Littlefield, 2010.

Baumgartner, Jody, and Jonathan Morris. "The 'Daily Show Effect': Candidate Evaluations, Efficacy, and the American Youth." *American Political Research* 34 (2006): 341–367.

——. "One 'Nation' Under Stephen? The Effects of *The Colbert Report* on American Youth." *Journal of Broadcasting and Electronic Media* 52 (2008): 622–643.

——. "Stoned Slackers or Super-Citizens? 'Daily Show' Viewing and Political Engagement of Young Adults." In *The Stewart/Colbert Effect: Essays on the Real Impact of Fake News,* edited by Amarnath Amarasingam. Jefferson, NC: McFarland & Co., 2011.

——. "Research Note: The 2008 Presidential Primaries and Differential Effects of 'The Daily Show' and 'The Colbert Report' on Young Adults." *Midsouth Political Science Review* 12 (2011): 87–102.

Baumgartner, Jody, Jonathan Morris, and Natasha Walth. "The Fey Effect: Young Adults, Political Humor, and Perceptions of Sarah Palin in the 2008 Presidential Election Campaign." *Public Opinion Quarterly* 76 (2012): 95–104.

Baym, Geoffrey. "'The Daily Show': Discursive Integration and the Reinvention of Political Journalism." *Political Communication* 22 (2005): 259–276.

——. "Serious Comedy: Exploring the Boundaries of Political Discourse." In *Laughing Matters: Humor and American Politics in the Media Age,* edited by Jonathan S. Morris and Jody Baumgartner. New York: Routledge, 2008.

——. "Stephen Colbert's Parody of the Postmodern." In *Satire TV: Politics and Comedy in the Post-Network Era,* edited by Jonathan Gray, Jeffrey P. Jones, and Ethan Thompson. New York: New York University Press, 2009.

Benton, Gregor. "The Origins of the Political Joke." In *Humor in Society: Resistance and Control,* edited by Chris Powell and George E. C. Paton. New York: St. Martin's, 1998.

"Bernard Madoff." *Biography.com.* http://www.biography.com/people/bernard-madoff-466366 (accessed May 1, 2012).

Blake, Meredith. "Jon Stewart Lashes out at House Republicans over Hurricane Sandy Aid." *Los Angeles Times,* January 8, 2013.

Bloustein, Jessica. "Political Punch Lines." *Newsweek* (Web Exclusive), September 11, 2008. http://www.newsweek.com/id/158301.

Brewer, Paul, and Xiaoxia Cao. "Candidate Appearances on Soft News Shows and Public Knowledge About Primary Campaigns." *The Journal of Broadcasting and Electronic Media* 50 (2006): 18–30.

Brewer, Paul R., and Emily Marquardt. "Mock News and Democracy: Analyzing *The Daily Show*." *Atlantic Journal of Communication* 15 (2007): 249–267.

Brummet, John. *Arkansas Democratic Gazette,* July 23, 1988.

Callison, Carolyn. "Talkative Arkansas Governor Trades Quips with Johnny Carson." Associated Press, July 29, 1988.

Cao, Xiaoxia. "Political Comedy Shows and Knowledge About Primary Campaigns: The Moderating Effects of Age and Education." *Mass Communication & Society* 11 (2008): 43–61.

———. "Hearing It from Jon Stewart: The Impact of *The Daily Show* on Public Attentiveness to Politics." *International Journal of Public Opinion Research* 22 (2010): 22–46.

Cao, Xiaoxia, and Paul Brewer. "Political Comedy Shows and Public Participation in Politics." *International Journal of Public Opinion Research* 22 (2008): 90–99.

Carr, David. "Comic's PAC Is More Than a Gag." *New York Times.* Last modified August 21, 2011. http://www.nytimes.com/2011/08/22/business/media/stephen-colberts-pac-is-more-than-a-gag.html?

Carter, Bill. *The Late Shift: Letterman, Leno, and the Network Battle for the Night.* New York: Hyperion, 1994.

———. *The War for Late Night: When Leno Went Early and Television Went Crazy.* New York: Viking, 2010.

Ceaser, James, and Andrew Busch. *Upside Down and Inside Out: The 1992 Elections and American Politics.* Lanham, MD: Rowman & Littlefield, 1993.

———. *Losing to Win: The 1996 Elections and American Politics.* Lanham, MD: Rowman & Littlefield, 1997.

———. *The Perfect Tie: The True Story of the 2000 Presidential Election.* Lanham, MD: Rowman & Littlefield, 2001.

———. *Red over Blue: The 2004 Elections and American Politics.* Lanham, MD: Rowman & Littlefield, 2005.

Ceaser, James, Andrew Busch, and John Pitney, Jr. *Epic Journey: The 2008 Elections and American Politics.* Lanham, MD: Rowman & Littlefield, 2009.

Center for Media and Public Affairs. "The Comedy Campaign: The Role of Late-Night TV Shows in Campaign '08." *Media Monitor* 22 (Winter 2008).

Cihasky, Carrie A. "Who's Laughing Now? Late Night Comedy's Influence on Perceptions of Bush and Gore in 2000." Paper presented at the annual meeting of the Midwest Political Science Association, Chicago, April 21, 2006.

Clawson, Rosalee A., and Eric N. Waltenburg. *Legacy and Legitimacy: Black Americans and the Supreme Court.* Philadelphia: Temple University Press, 2008.

Clinton, Bill. *My Life.* New York: Knopf, 2004.

"Clinton the Big Topic." *Arkansas Democrat-Gazette,* July 22, 1988.

"CNN Transcript: *Larry King Live:* Jon Stewart Looks Back at Election 2000." *Larry King Live,* December 15, 2000 (retrieved March 25, 2007).

Compton, Josh. "Political Punditry in Punchlines: Late Night Comics' Take on the 2004 Presidential Debates." In *Laughing Matters: Humor and American Politics in the Media Age,* edited by Jody C Baumgartner and Jonathan S. Morris. New York: Routledge, 2008.

"Congress and the Public." *Gallup.* http://www.gallup.com/poll/1600/congress -public.aspx (accessed May 7, 2012).

"Conventional Humor: When TV Turns Politics into a Laughing Matter." *New York Times,* July 18, 1992.

Cooper, Christopher, and Mandi Bailey. "Entertainment Media and Political Knowledge: Do People Get Any Truth out of Truthiness?" In *Homer Simpson Goes to Washington: American Politics Through Popular Culture,* edited by Joseph J. Foy. Lexington: University Press of Kentucky, 2008.

Coulson, Seana, and Robert F. Williams. "Hemispheric Asymmetries and Joke Comprehension." *Neuropsychologia* 43 (2005): 128–141.

Dalton, Russell J., and Steven A. Weldon. "Public Images of Political Parties: A Necessary Evil?" *West European Politics* 28 (2005): 931–951.

Danjoux, Ilan. "Reconsidering the Decline of the Editorial Cartoon." *PS: Political Science and Politics* 40 (2007): 245–248.

Davies, Christie. "Humour and Protest: Jokes Under Communism." *International Review of Social History* 52 (2007): 291–305.

Davis, Richard, and Diana Owen. *New Media and American Politics.* New York: Oxford University Press, 1998.

Day, Amber. *Satire and Dissent: Interventions in Contemporary Political Debate.* Bloomington: Indiana University Press, 2011.

"Dean Plays Union Card in White House Race." *London Times,* November 13, 2003.

"Demographics and Political Views of News Audiences." *People Press,* September 27, 2012. http://www.people-press.org/2012/09/27/section-4-demographics -and-political-views-of-news-audiences/.

Dudden, Arthur P. "The Record of Political Humor." *American Quarterly* 37, no. 1 (1985): 50–70.

"Eliot Spitzer." *Biography.com.* http://www.biography.com/people/eliot-spitzer -279076 (accessed April 24, 2012).

Elliott, Robert C. *The Power of Satire: Magic, Ritual, Art.* Princeton, NJ: Princeton University Press, 1960.

Erickson, Hal. *A Critical History of "Rowan and Martin's Laugh-In," 1968–1973*. New York: McFarland & Co., 2000.

Farhi, Paul. "Since Dick Cheney Shot Him, Harry Whittington's Aim Has Been to Move On." *Washington Post,* October 14, 2010.

Farnsworth, Stephen, and S. Robert Lichter. *The Nightly News Nightmare: Media Coverage of Presidential Elections, 1988–2008,* 3rd ed. Lanham, MD: Rowman & Littlefield, 2010.

Feldman, Lauren, and Dannagal G. Young. "Late-Night Comedy as a Gateway to Traditional News: An Analysis of Time Trends in News Attention Among Late-Night Comedy Viewers During the 2004 Presidential Primaries." *Political Communication* 25 (2008): 401–422.

Ferrante, Joan. *The Political Vision of the Divine Comedy.* Princeton, NJ: Princeton University Press, 1993.

Fitzgerald, Toni. "Seriously, Jon Stewart as Anchorman." *Media Life,* April 3, 2009. http://www.medialifemagazine.com/artman2/publish/Dayparts_update_51/Seriously_Jon_Stewart_as_anchorman.asp.

Ford, Gerald. *A Time to Heal: The Autobiography of Gerald R. Ford.* New York: Harper & Row/Reader's Digest, 1979.

Fox, Julia R. "Wise Fools: Jon Stewart and Stephen Colbert as Modern-Day Jesters in the American Court." In *The Stewart/Colbert Effect: Essays on the Real Impacts of Fake News,* edited by Amarnath Amarasingam. Jefferson, NC: McFarland & Co., 2011.

Fox, Julia, Glory Colon, and Volcan Sahin. "No Joke: A Comparison of Substance in *The Daily Show with Jon Stewart* and Broadcast Network Television Coverage of the 2004 Presidential Election Campaign." *Journal of Broadcasting and Electronic Media* 51 (2007): 213–227.

Froomkin, Dan. "Time Line." *Washingtonpost.com,* December 3, 1998. http://www.washingtonpost.com/wp-srv/politics/special/pjones/timeline.htm.

"Gary Condit." *Biography.com.* http://www.biography.com/people/gary-condit-9542435 (accessed April 24, 2012).

Gavin, Patrick. "Leno Talks 'The Tonight Show's Political Humor." *Politico.* http://www.politico.com/blogs/media/2012/04/leno-talks-the-tonight-shows-political-humor-121140.html (April 20, 2012).

Giglio, Ernest. *Here's Looking at You: Hollywood, Film & Politics,* 3rd ed. New York: Lang, 2010.

Goel, Vinod, and Raymond J. Dolan. "The Functional Anatomy of Humor: Segregating Cognitive and Affective Components." *Nature Neuroscience* 4 (2001): 237–238.

"Gore Jokes Around with Leno." *Contra Costa Times,* September 20, 2000.

Hatfield, Mark. *Vice Presidents of the United States, 1789–1993.* Washington, DC: US Government Printing Office, 1997.

Herzog, Rudolph. *Dead Funny: Humor in Hitler's Germany*. Brooklyn, NY: Melville House, 2011.

Hibbing, John, and Elizabeth Theiss-Morse. *Congress as Public Enemy: Public Attitudes Toward American Political Institutions*. Cambridge: Cambridge University Press, 1995.

Highet, Gilbert. *The Anatomy of Satire*. Princeton, NJ: Princeton University Press, 1962.

Hill, Doug, and Jeff Weingrad. *Saturday Night: A Backstage History of* Saturday Night Live. New York: William Morrow & Co., 1989.

Hoffman, Lindsay, and Tiffany Thomson. "The Effect of Television Viewing on Adolescents' Civic Participation: Political Efficacy as a Mediating Mechanism." *Journal of Broadcasting & Electronic Media* 53 (2009): 3–21.

Hollander, Barry A. "The New News and the 1992 Presidential Campaign: Perceived Versus Actual Political Knowledge." *Journalism and Mass Communication Quarterly* 72 (1995): 786–798.

———. "Late-Night Learning: Do Entertainment Programs Increase Political Campaign Knowledge for Young Viewers?" *Journal of Broadcasting & Electronic Media* 49 (2005): 402–415.

Holt, Jason. *The Daily Show and Philosophy: Moments of Zen in the Art of Fake News*. Malden, MA: Wiley-Blackwell, 2007.

Hutcheon, Linda. *A Theory of Parody: The Teachings of Twentieth-Century Art Forms*. London: Methuen, 1985.

Huxley, Aldous. *Brave New World*. New York: HarperPerennial Modern Classics, 2006.

Jablon, Robert. "Howard Dean Makes Leno Show Appearance." Associated Press, October 1, 2003.

James, Randy. "Straying Governor Mark Sanford." *Time.com*, June 25, 2009. http://www.time.com/time/nation/article/0,8599,1907022,00.html (accessed April 24, 2012).

Jamieson, Kathleen Hall, and Joseph N. Cappella. *Echo Chamber: Rush Limbaugh and the Conservative Media Establishment*. New York: Oxford University Press, 2010.

Jamieson, Kathleen Hall, and Paul Waldman. *The Press Effect: Politicians, Journalists, and the Stories That Shape the Political World*. New York: Oxford University Press, 2002.

Jones, Jeffrey P. "With All Due Respect: Satirizing Presidents from *Saturday Night Live* to *Li'l Bush*." In *Satire TV: Politics and Comedy in the Post-Network Era*, edited by Jonathan Gray, Jeffrey P. Jones, and Ethan Thompson. New York: New York University Press, 2009.

———. *Entertaining Politics: Satiric Television and Political Engagement*. Lanham, MD: Rowman & Littlefield, 2010.

Katz, Mark. "Mirth of a Nation: How Bill Clinton Learned to Tell Jokes on Himself—and Get the Last Laugh." *The Washington Monthly,* January/February 2004. http://www.washingtonmonthly.com/features/2004/0401.katz.html.

Kim, Young Mie, and John Vishak. "Just Laugh! You Don't Need to Remember: The Effects of Entertainment Media on Political Information Acquisition and Information Processing in Political Judgment." *Journal of Communication* 58 (2008): 338–360.

King, A. "Do Leaders' Personalities Really Matter?" In *Leaders' Personalities and the Outcomes of Democratic Elections,* edited by A. King. Oxford: Oxford University Press.

Klein, Joe. *The Natural: The Misunderstood Presidency of Bill Clinton.* New York: Broadway Books, 2002.

Kolbert, Elizabeth. "The 1992 Campaign: Media; Whistle-Stops à la 1992: Arsenio, Larry and Phil." *New York Times.* Last modified June 5, 1992. http://www.nytimes.com/1992/06/05/us/the-1992-campaign-media-whistle-stops-a-la-1992-arsenio-larry-and-phil.html.

Kranish, Michael. "With Antiwar Role, High Visibility." *Boston.com.* Last modified June 17, 2003. http://www.boston.com/globe/nation/packages/kerry/061703.shtml.

Kurtz, Howard. "Trial of the Century Now Joke of the Day." *Washington Post,* January 26, 1999.

———. "The Campaign of a Comedian: Jon Stewart's Fake Journalism Enjoys Real Political Impact." *Washington Post,* October 23, 2004.

Kurtz, Howard, Michael Dobbs, and James V. Grimaldi. "In Rush to Air, CBS Quashed Memo Worries." *Washington Post,* September 19, 2004.

Kurtzman, Daniel. "About.com" (no date). http://politicalhumor.about.com/od/funnyquotes/a/johnnycarson.htm (accessed June 10, 2012).

Kwak, Nojin, Lauren Guggenheim, Xiaoru Wang, and Brad Jones. "Feel Like Learning? An Analysis of Political Implications of Late Night Talk Shows in the 2004 Presidential Election." Paper presented at the annual meeting of the Association for Education in Journalism and Mass Communication (Communication Theory and Methodology Division), San Antonio, TX, August 2005.

LaFave, Lawrence. "Humor Judgments as a Function of Reference Groups and Identification Classes." *The Psychology of Humor: Theoretical Perspectives and Empirical Issues,* edited by Jeffrey H. Goldstein and Paul E. McGhee. New York: Academic Press, 1972.

LaFave, Lawrence, Jay Haddad, and Nancy Marshall. "Humor Judgments as a Function of Identification Classes." *Sociology and Social Research* 58 (1974): 184–194.

Lake, Anthony. "Confronting Backlash States." *Foreign Affairs* 73 (March/April 1994): 45–55.

LaMarre, Heather, Kristen Landreviller, and Michael Beam. "The Irony of Satire: Political Ideology and the Motivation to See What You Want to See in *The Colbert Report*." *The International Journal of Press/Politics* 14 (2009): 212–231.

Lau Richard R., and David P. Redlawsk. "Advantages and Disadvantages of Cognitive Heuristics in Political Decision Making." *American Journal of Political Science* 45 (2001): 951–971.

Leamer, Laurence. *King of the Night: The Life of Johnny Carson.* New York: William Morrow & Co., 1989.

Lee, Yih Hwai, and Elison Ai Ching Lim. "What's Funny and What's Not." *Journal of Advertising* 37 (2008): 71–84.

Lester, Paul Martin. *Visual Communication: Images with Messages,* 4th ed. Belmont, CA: Thomson Wadsworth, 2005.

Lichter, S. Robert, and Daniel Amundson. "Heeere's Politics." *Public Opinion* (1988): 45–46.

Lichter, S. R., L. Lichter, and S. Rothman. "Hollywood and America—The Odd Couple." *Public Opinion* 6, no. 1 (1983): 54–58.

Lordan, Edward J. *Politics, Ink: How Cartoonists Skewer America's Politicians, from King George III to George Dubya.* Lanham, MD: Rowman & Littlefield, 2005.

Madison, Lucy. "White House Lauds Jon Stewart for Pushing Passage of 9/11 Health Bill." *CBS News,* December 21, 2010.

"Martha Stewart." *Biography.com.* http://www.biography.com/people/martha -stewart-9542234 (accessed May 1, 2012).

Maslon, Laurence, and Michael Kantor. *Make 'Em Laugh: The Funny Business of America.* New York: Hachette Book Group, 2008.

Mathis, Deborah. "Yes, There's Life After 'The Speech.'" *Arkansas Democrat-Gazette,* July 27, 1988.

McBeth, Mark K., and Randy S. Clemons. "Is Fake News the Real News? The Significance of Stewart and Colbert for Democratic Discourse, Politics, and Policy." In *The Stewart/Colbert Effect: Essays on the Real Impacts of Fake News,* edited by Amarnath Amarasingam. Jefferson, NC: McFarland & Co., 2011.

McDonald, Kathy A. "Mainstream Media Remains in on Joke." *Daily Variety,* January 22, 2009.

McGinniss, Joe. *The Selling of the President.* New York: Simon and Schuster, 1969.

Mears, Walter. "The Political and Robbed Walt Gets Personal." Associated Press, July 27, 1996.

Media Monitor. "The Comedy Campaign: The Role of Late-Night TV Shows in Campaign 2008." *Media Monitor* 22, no. 3 (2008). http://www.cmpa.com/pdf /08winter.pdf.

Melton, R. H., and Susan Schmidt. "For Clinton, Whitewater Woes Continue." *Washington Post,* May 30, 1996.

Mickle, Paul. "1992: Gaffe with an 'e' at the End." *Capitalcentury.com.* http://www.capitalcentury.com/1992.html (accessed May 12, 2012).

Mills, David. "Sister Souljah's Call to Arms." *Washington Post,* May 13, 1992.

Morales, Lymari. "Distrust in U.S. Media Edges Up to Record High." *Gallup,* September 29, 2010. http://www.gallup.com/poll/143267/distrust-media-edges -record-high.aspx (accessed May 12, 2012).

Morreale, Joanne. "Jon Stewart and *The Daily Show:* I Thought You Were Going to Be Funny!" In *Satire TV: Politics and Comedy in the Post-Network Era,* edited by Jonathan Gray, Jeffrey P. Jones, and Ethan Thompson. New York: New York University Press, 2009.

Morris, Irwin. *Votes, Money, and the Clinton Impeachment.* Boulder, CO: Westview Press, 2002.

Morris, Jonathan. "'The Daily Show' and Audience Attitude Change During the 2004 Party Conventions." *Political Behavior* 31 (2009): 79–102.

Moy, Patricia, Michael Xenos, and Verena Hess. "Communication and Citizenship: Mapping the Political Effects of Infotainment." *Mass Communication & Society* 8 (2005): 111–131.

——. "Priming Effects of Late-Night Comedy." *International Journal of Public Opinion Research* 18 (2005): 198–210.

——. "The Political Effects of Late Night Comedy and Talk Shows." In *Laughing Matters: Humor and American Politics in the Media Age,* edited by Jody C Baumgartner and Jonathan S. Morris. New York: Routledge, 2008.

Murphy, Patti, and David Stout. "Idaho Senator Says He Regrets Guilty Plea in Restroom Incident." *New York Times,* August 29, 2007. http://www.nytimes .com/2007/08/29/washington/29craig.html?_r=1&oref=slogin (accessed September 1, 2007).

Myers, Dee Dee. "New Technology and the 1992 Clinton Presidential Campaign." *The American Behavioral Scientist* 37, no. 2 (1993): 181–184.

Nabi, Robin, Emily Moyer-Gusé, and Sahara Byrne. "All Joking Aside: A Serious Investigation into the Persuasive Effect of Funny Social Issue Messages." *Communication Monographs* 74 (2007): 29–54.

Nesteroff, Kliph. "The Comedy Writer That Helped Elect Richard M. Nixon." *Freeform.* 2010. http://blog.wfmu.org/freeform/2010/09/richard-nixons-laugh -in.html.

Niven, David, S. Robert Lichter, and Daniel Amundson. "The Political Content of Late Night Comedy." *Harvard International Journal of Press/Politics* 8 (2003): 118–133.

——. "Our First Cartoon President: Bill Clinton and the Politics of Late Night Comedy." In *Laughing Matters: Humor and American Politics in the Media Age,* edited by Jody C Baumgartner and Jonathan S. Morris. New York: Routledge, 2008.

Noonan, Peggy. *What I Saw at the Revolution: A Political Life in the Reagan Era.* New York: Random House, 2003.

"Numbers Don't Lie: *Daily Show*'s Stewart Hammers Right Nearly 4 Times More." *Newsbusters,* July 18, 2011. http://newsbusters.org/blogs/erin-r-brown /2011/07/18/numbers-dont-lie-daily-shows-stewart-hammers-right-nearly-4 -times-more.

Olson, Alison Gilbert. "Political Humor, Deference, and the American Revolution." *Early American Studies* 3 (2005): 363–382.

Oring, Elliott. "Risky Business: Political Jokes Under Repressive Regimes." *Western Folklore* 63 (2004): 209–236.

Orwell, George. *Animal Farm.* Fairfield, IA: 1st World Library, 2004.

Paine, Albert Bigelow. *Th. Nast: His Period and His Pictures.* New York: Harper, 1904.

Parkin, Michael. "Taking Late Night Comedy Seriously: How Candidate Appearances on Late Night Television Can Engage Viewers." *Political Research Quarterly* 63 (2010): 3–15.

Patterson, Thomas E. *Out of Order.* New York: Knopf, 1993.

———. "Doing Well and Doing Good: How Soft News and Critical Journalism Are Shrinking the News Audience and Weakening Democracy—and What News Outlets Can Do About It." John F. Kennedy School of Government, Harvard University, 2000. http://www.hks.harvard.edu/presspol/publications /reports/soft_news_and_critical_journalism_2000.pdf.

Perino, Dana. "Unlike Obama, Bush Thought Late-Night Shows Not 'A Place Where the President Should Be.'" *Mediaite.com.* http://www.mediaite.com /tv/dana-perino-unlike-obama-bush-thought-late-night-shows-not-a-place -where-the-president-should-be/.

Perry, Will. *No Cheers from the Alumni: The Wolverines: A Story of Michigan Football.* Huntsville, AL: The Strode Publishers, 1974.

Peterson, Russell L. *Strange Bedfellows: How Late-Night Comedy Turns Democracy into a Joke.* New Brunswick, NJ: Rutgers University Press, 2008.

Pew Research Center. "The Invisible Primary—Invisible No Longer." 2007. http:// www.journalism.org/node/8187.

———. "Winning the Media Campaign: How the Press Reported the 2008 General Election." 2008. http://www.journalism.org/node/13307.

———. "Cable and Internet Loom Large in Fragmented Political News Universe."

———. "Key News Audiences Now Blend Online and Traditional Sources," August 17, 2008. http://www.people-press.org/2008/08/17/key-news-audiences -now-blend-online-and-traditional-sources.

———. "Press Widely Criticized, but Trusted More Than Other Information Sources." Media Attitudes Release.pdf, September 22, 2011. http://www.people -press.org/files/legacy-pdf/9-22-2011 (accessed May 12, 2012).

———. "Supreme Court Favorability Reaches New Low." http://www.people
-press.org/files/legacy-pdf/5-1-12. Supreme Court Release.pdf (accessed May
12, 2012).

Pew Research Center Biennial Media Consumption Survey, April 2008.

Pew Research Center for the People. Retrieved from the iPOLL Databank, The
Roper Center for Public Opinion Research, University of Connecticut, April
2008. http://www.ropercenter.uconn.edu/data_access/ipoll/ipoll.html (accessed May 14, 2013).

———. Retrieved from the iPOLL Databank, The Roper Center for Public Opinion Research, University of Connecticut, May 2012. http://www.ropercenter
.uconn.edu/data_access/ipoll/ipoll.html (accessed May 14, 2013).

Pfau, Michael, Jaeho Cho, and Kirsten Chong. "Communication Forms in U.S.
Presidential Campaigns: Influences on Candidate Perceptions and the Democratic Process." *Harvard International Journal of Press/Politics* 6 (2001):
88–105.

Pfau, Michael, Brian Houston, and Shane Semmler. "Presidential Election Campaigns and American Democracy: The Relationship Between Communication Use and Normative Outcomes." *American Behavioral Scientist* 49 (2006):
113–134.

———. *Mediating the Vote: The Changing Media Landscape in U.S. Presidential
Campaigns.* Lanham, MD: Rowman & Littlefield, 2007.

Popkin, Samuel. *The Reasoning Voter: Communication and Persuasion in Presidential Campaigns,* 2nd ed. Chicago: University of Chicago Press, 1994.

Prichard, James. "Ford Showed Athletic Prowess at Michigan." *Boston Globe,* December 27, 2006. http://www.boston.com/news/education/higher/articles/2006
/12/27/ford_was_among_most_athletic_presidents/ (accessed March 9, 2012).

Prindle, D., and J. Endersby. "Hollywood Liberalism." *Social Science Quarterly*
74, no. 1 (1993): 136–149.

Prior, Marcus. "Any Good News in Soft News? The Impact of Soft News Preferences on Political Knowledge." *Political Communication* 20 (2003): 149–171.

———. "Political Communication." *American Journal of Political Science* 20
(2003): 149–171.

———. "News vs. Entertainment: How Increasing Media Choices Widen Gaps in
Political Knowledge and Turnout." *American Journal of Political Science* 49
(2005): 577–592.

Rieck, Donald. "Late-Nite Talk Shows Were Road to White House." Center for
Media and Public Affairs, December 29, 2008. http://www.cmpa.com/media
_room_12_29_08.html.

Roche, Walter. "Ex-Page Tells of Foley Liaison." *Los Angeles Times,* October 8,
2006. http://articles.latimes.com/2006/oct/08/nation/na-page8 (accessed May
22, 2012).

"Rod R. Blagojevich." *New York Times,* December 7, 2011. http://topics.nytimes
.com/top/reference/timestopics/people/b/rod_r_blagojevich/index.html.

Romano, Andrew. "How Dumb Are We?" *Newsweek,* March 20, 2011. http://
www.thedailybeast.com/newsweek/2011/03/20/how-dumb-are-we.html.

Rose, Alexander. "When Politics Is a Laughing Matter." *Policy Review* (2001):
59–71.

Rosen, Marty. "Prez Wanna-bes Try Late-Night TV." *New York Daily News,*
March 2, 2000.

Rosenstiel, Tom, and Amy Mitchell. "Journalism, Satire or Just Laughs? *The Daily
Show with Jon Stewart.*" Project for Excellence in Journalism, May 8, 2008.
http://www.journalism.org/files/Daily%20Show%20PDF_3.pdf.

Rothberg, Donald M. "Clinton's Day of Triumph Jarred by Aide's Resignation."
Associated Press, August 29, 1996.

Rutenberg, Jim. "TV's Pundits Pronounce Judgment: It's Over." *New York Times,*
May 8, 2008.

Sabato, Larry, Mark Stencel, and S. Robert Lichter. *Peepshow: Media and Politics
in an Age of Scandal.* Lanham, MD: Rowman & Littlefield, 2000.

Sarver, Danielle L. "No Laughing Matter: Late Night Television Talk Shows'
Coverage of the 2004 Democratic Presidential Primary." Paper presented at
the annual meeting of the American Political Science Association, Chicago,
September 2004.

Scherer, Michael. "The Truthiness Hurts." *Salon.com.* Last modified May 1, 2006.
http://www.salon.com/2006/05/01/colbert_10/.

Schutz, Charles E. *Political Humor: From Aristophanes to Sam Ervin.* Cranbury,
NJ: Associated University Press, 1977.

Sella, Martha. "The Stiff Guy vs. the Dumb Guy." *New York Times,* September 24,
2000. http://nytimes.com/2000/09/24/magazine/the-stiff-guy-vs-the-dumb
-guy.html?src=pm&pagewanted=1.

Shales, Tom. "The Numb and the Restless." *Washington Post,* July 21, 1988.

Shapiro, Ben. *Primetime Propaganda: The True Hollywood Story of How the Left
Took Over Your TV.* New York: Broadside Books, 2012.

Shenon, Philip, and David Johnston. "A Defender of Bush's Power, Gonzales
Resigns." *New York Times,* August 28, 2007. http://www.nytimes.com/2007
/08/28/washington/28resign.html?ref=albertorgonzales (accessed May 22, 2012).

Sigelman, Lee. "The Nonvoting Voter in Voting Research." *American Journal of
Political Science* 26 (1982): 47–56.

Sink, Justin. "Colbert Creates Shell Corporation to Lampoon Karl Rove's
Groups." *The Hill.* Last modified September 30, 2011. http://thehill.com/video
/in-the-news/184755-colbert-creates-shell-corporation-to-lampoon-rove
-money-laundering.

Speier, Hans. "Wit and Politics: An Essay on Laughter and Power." *American
Journal of Sociology* 103 (1998): 1352–1401.

Stein, Mary Beth. "The Politics of Humor: The Berlin Wall in Jokes and Graffiti." *Western Folklore* 48 (1989): 85–108.

Stimson, James A. *Public Opinion in America: Moods, Cycles, and Swings.* Boulder, CO: Westview Press, 1991.

Stranglin, Douglas. "Colbert Seriously Jokes to Congress About Migrant Agricultural Work." *USA Today.* Last modified September 24, 2010. http://content .usatoday.com/communities/ondeadline/post/2010/09/stephen-colbert-testifies -to-congress-today-on-immigration/1#.T-2u-7WAHSU.

Suls, Jerry M. "A Two-Stage Model for the Appreciation of Jokes and Cartoons: An Information-Processing Analysis." In *The Psychology of Humor: Theoretical Perspectives and Empirical Issues,* edited by Jeffrey H. Goldstein and Paul E. McGhee. New York: Academic Press, 1972.

Swift, Jonathan. A Modest Proposal *and Other Satirical Works.* Mineola, NY: Dover, 1996.

———. *Gulliver's Travels,* rev. ed. New York: Penguin, 2003.

Tally, Steve. *Bland Ambition: From Adams to Quayle—The Cranks, Criminals, Tax Cheats, and Golfers Who Made It to Vice President.* San Diego, CA: Harcourt Brace Jovanovich, 1992.

Taylor, Ronald A. "Clinton Raps Sister Souljah's Remarks." *Washington Times,* June 14, 1992.

Thompson, Nicholas. "The Tom DeLay Scandals: A Scorecard." *Slate,* April 7, 2005. http://www.slate.com/articles/news_and_politics/the_gist/2005/04 /the_tom_delay_scandals.single.html (accessed May 23, 2012).

Timberg, Bernard. *Television Talk: A History of the TV Talk Show.* Austin: University of Texas Press, 2002.

"Transcript: Vice President Gore on CNN's 'Late Edition.'" *CNN,* March 9, 1999.

Trier, James. "*The Daily Show with Jon Stewart.*" *Journal of Adolescent & Adult Literacy* 51, no. 5 (2008): 424–427.

Twain, Mark. "Foster's Case." *New York Tribune,* March 10, 1873.

———. *What Is Man?* San Diego, CA: The Book Tree, 1906.

"Two-Thirds of Americans Can't Name Any U.S. Supreme Court Justices." *PR Newswire,* June 1, 2012. http://www.prnewswire.com/news-releases/two -thirds-of-americans-cant-name-any-us-supreme-court-justices-says-new -findlawcom-survey-95298909.html (accessed May 12, 2013).

Van Biema, David, and Viveca Novak. "Clinton Crisis: Sparking the Scandal." *Time,* February 2, 1998. http://www.time.com/time/magazine/article /0,9171,987743,00.html.

Van Heertum, Richard. "Irony and the News: Speaking Cool to American Youth." In *The Stewart/Colbert Effect: Essays on the Real Impacts of Fake News,* edited by Amarnath Amarasingam. Jefferson, NC: McFarland & Co., 2011.

Vickers, Michael J. *Pericles on Stage: Political Comedy in Aristophanes' Early Plays.* Austin: University of Texas Press, 1997.

Vogel, Kenneth P. "S.C. Dems Reject Colbert Candidacy." *Politico,* November 1, 2007. http://www.politico.com/news/stories/1107/6674.html.

Voltaire. *Candide.* Translated by François-Marie Arouet. Mineola, NY: Dover, 1991.

Voth, Ben. "*Saturday Night Live* and Presidential Elections." In *Laughing Matters: Humor and American Politics in the Media Age,* edited by Jonathan S. Morris and Jody C Baumgartner. New York: Routledge, 2008.

Warner, Jamie. "Political Culture Jamming: The Dissident Humor of *The Daily Show with Jon Stewart.*" *Popular Communication* 5, no. 1 (2007): 17–36.

Warrick, Joby, and Walter Pincus. "Bush Inflated Threat from Iraq's Banned Weapons, Report Says." *Washington Post,* June 6, 2008. http://www.washington post.com/wp-dyn/content/article/2008/06/05/AR2008060501523.html (accessed May 22, 2012).

Washington, H. A., ed. *The Writings of Thomas Jefferson.* New York: H. W. Derby, 1861.

Weise, Richard E. "Partisan Perceptions of Political Humor." *Humor* 9 (1996): 199–207.

White, Mark. "Vicissitudes: 1992 and the Road to the White House." In *The Presidency of Bill Clinton: The Legacy of a New Domestic and Foreign Policy,* edited by Mark White. New York: Palgrave, 2012.

Wiener, Tim. "21 White House Workers Got Extra Drug Test, Official Says." *Austin-American Statesman,* July 16, 1996.

Williams, Bruce A., and Michael X. Delli Carpini. "Real Ethical Concerns and Fake News: *The Daily Show* and the Challenge of the New Media Environment." In *The Stewart/Colbert Effect: Essays on the Real Impacts of Fake News,* edited by Amarnath Amarasingam. Jefferson, NC: McFarland & Co., 2011.

Wyer, Robert S., Jr., and James E. Collins II. "A Theory of Humor Elicitation." *Psychological Review* 99 (1992): 663–688.

Xenos, Michael, and Amy Becker. "Moments of Zen: Effects of *The Daily Show* on Information Seeking and Political Learning." *Political Communication* 26 (2009): 317–332.

Xenos, Michael, Patricia Moy, and Amy Becker. "Making Sense of 'The Daily Show': Understanding the Role of Partisan Heuristics in Political Comedy Effects." In *The Stewart/Colbert Effect: Essays on the Real Impacts of Fake News,* edited by Amarnath Amarasingam. Jefferson, NC: McFarland & Co., 2011.

Young, Dannagal. "Late-Night Comedy and the Salience of the Candidates' Caricatured Traits in the 2000 Election." *Mass Communication and Society* 9, no. 3 (2006): 339–366.

———. "*Daily Show* Viewers Knowledgeable About Presidential Campaign." Last modified September 21, 2004. http://www.naes04.org (accessed May 1, 2012).

Young, Dannagal, and Russell Tisinger. "Dispelling Late-Night Myths: News Consumption Among Late-Night Comedy Viewers and the Predictors of Exposure to Various Late-Night Shows." *Press/Politics* 11 (2006): 113–134.

Young, Dannagal Goldthwaite. "*The Daily Show* as the New Journalism: In Their Own Words." In *Laughing Matters: Humor and American Politics in the Media Age,* edited by Jody C Baumgartner and Jonathan S. Morris. New York: Routledge, 2008.

Young, Dannagal Goldthwaite, and Sarah E. Esralew. "Jon Stewart as Heretic? Surely You Jest: Political Participation and Discussion Among Viewers of Late-Night Comedy Programming." In *The Stewart/Colbert Effect: Essays on the Real Impacts of Fake News,* edited by Amarnath Amarasingam. Jefferson, NC: McFarland & Co., 2011.

Zaller, John. *The Nature and Origins of Mass Opinion.* Cambridge: Cambridge University Press, 1992.

Zillmann, Dolf, Brien R. Williams, Jenning Bryant, Kathleen R. Boynton, and Michelle A. Wolf. "Acquisition of Information from Educational Television Programs as a Function of Differently Paced Humorous Inserts." *Journal of Educational Psychology* 72 (1980): 170–180.

Index